YOU BELONG TO THE
BRIDEGROOM

YOU BELONG TO THE
BRIDEGROOM

The bride belongs to the bridegroom. The friend who attends the bridegroom waits and listens for him, and is full of joy when he hears the bridegroom's voice. That joy is mine, and it is now complete. —*John 3:29*

ALIENE THOMPSON

nourish™
BIBLE STUDY SERIES

You Belong to the Bridegroom
Copyright © 2010, 2011, 2012, 2017, 2019, 2020 by Aliene Thompson

Published by Nourish Resources
1105 Classic Road Apex, NC 27539

ISBN 978-0-9822557-7-3

Printed in the United States of America

info@treasuredministries.com
www.TreasuredMinistries.com

To Holly White

CONTENTS

ACKNOWLEDGMENTS 9

HOW TO USE THE NOURISH BIBLE STUDY SERIES 11

Chapter 1: HE SPEAKS 13

Chapter 2: THE PROPOSAL 39

Chapter 3: IN HIS PRESENCE 59

Chapter 4: FREEDOM 75

Chapter 5: SEEDS OF SECURITY 95

Chapter 6: ROCK OF AGES 115

Chapter 7: THE DANCE 135

Chapter 8: HER HEART 155

Chapter 9: MY FATHER'S HOUSE 181

Chapter 10: NO HOLDING BACK 203

Chapter 11: QUIET STRENGTH 221

Chapter 12: HIS PASSION 243

SOURCE NOTES 265

Additional resources to enhance your study, including a corresponding video series and facilitator's guide, can be found online.
Visit www.nourishbiblestudyseries.com

ACKNOWLEDGMENTS

To my family…

My son Justin found a piece of red sea glass on the beach last summer, three weeks after a hurricane hit the North Carolina shores. If you have read *You Belong to the Bridegroom*, you know why sea glass has a special place in my heart. In this study, a woman shares her story to show that, just as broken pieces of sea glass can be vessels of beauty, God takes the broken things of our lives and makes them beautiful.

I love this imagery and have become a collector of sea glass treasures tossed on our North Carolina shores. Storms often dredge such treasures from the depths and cast them to the shore. Each piece of sea glass is a treasure, but red sea glass is the rarest treasure of all.

Not so long ago, I walked through a storm of hurricane proportions. I wanted to quit Treasured Ministries. I didn't want to write one more word. But because of my family, who loved me despite my imperfections and pointed me to God's perfection, I was able to get back up again and move on.

I found my greatest treasure in my family. The unconditional love I share with my husband, Jim, and my two boys, Josh and Justin, is my rarest treasure. Three beautiful pieces of spectacular red sea glass.

Through their compassion, I learned more about what real love is—it is giving with no motive attached. This love compels me to continue the work God has given me through Treasured Ministries. With their support, I found the courage to write again. They didn't see my past problems—they saw this potential: Jesus takes the broken things in our lives and makes them beautiful.

HOW TO USE THE
NOURISH™ BIBLE STUDY SERIES

1 WATCH THE INTRODUCTION VIDEO TO BEGIN.

The introduction video is designed to give you inspiration and a foundation for your journey ahead. Video session notes pages are provided to give you a way to journal while you watch.

2 READ CHAPTER ONE AND THEN WATCH THE CORRESPONDING VIDEO FOR THE CHAPTER.

Following chapter one, you will watch video session one. Continue to repeat this process with the remaining chapters of the Nourish Bible Study Series and discover truth for the life you were created to live.

3 EXPERIENCE THE LIFE-CHANGING EFFECTS OF GOD'S WORD.

You can gain the courage, confidence, direction, and freedom to become all God created you to be. And God's words—not the words you hear from others, but God's words—are the keys to unlocking this door. Uncover your full potential to live out your purpose as you make room for the Holy Spirit to speak to your heart and discover God's timeless truth for real issues women face today.

NOTE: An option to consider for a lighter load

Looking for a lighter load for weekly study? One solution that works well for many women is to simply divide each chapter in half and complete just three days of study each week instead of all six. This way, each chapter will take two weeks to complete. That's fine—there's no deadline. Use this method if it helps you create the margin necessary to get the most out of your study without sacrificing any content.

Additional resources to enhance your study, including a corresponding video series and facilitator's guide, can be found online.
Visit www.nourishbiblestudyseries.com

VIDEO SESSION NOTES

Introduction Session
YOU BELONG TO THE BRIDEGROOM
John 3:25-30

Videos located online at www.nourishbiblestudyseries.com

Chapter 1
HE SPEAKS

DAY 1

"The bride belongs to the bridegroom. The friend who attends the bridegroom waits and listens for him, and is full of joy when he hears the bridegroom's voice. That joy is mine, and it is now complete." —*John 3:29*

She was confident and stunning. With lace covering her shoulders and an heirloom tiara precisely positioned in her hair, Kate Middleton reflected a natural beauty on her wedding day. Elegance cascaded effortlessly as she advanced down the lengthy aisle of awe-inspiring Westminster Abbey on April 29, 2011. With her father by her side, every step along the royal red carpet brought her closer to being joined to Prince William in holy matrimony.

The royal wedding was not simply a grand affair—it was a global event. Ladies wearing fashionable hats in many hues and men, royalty and well-to-do, in their finest, witnessed history as a young lady became a princess. Besides those present, eyes from around the world connected through television and the Internet to be a part—if only remotely—of a stirring historic wedding.

Relaxing on a comfy couch before the flatscreen, I was one of the billions who set aside time to watch this spectacular occasion. I know fairy tales aren't real; still, I enjoyed lingering in a land of queens, kings, and castles where it's easy to imagine that fairy tales, as the song lyrics insist, can come true. Lost in the wonder and fanfare of the moment, I found myself forgetting that beyond this enchanting extravagance, marriage is a solemn and spiritual occasion designed by the Creator himself.

The Bishop of London, Dr. Richard Chartres, who officiated that day, reminded me of this. As he stood at the podium, his deep voice filled the hall with a warmth that beckoned my attention and shifted my focus to Jesus, my heavenly Bridegroom. Like a full moon that provides the brightest light in a star-filled sky, his carefully expressed homily highlighted this simple truth: only Christ can complete our lives and give us the security we need so we can give to others.

> As the reality of God has faded from so many lives in the West, there has been a corresponding inflation of expectations that personal relations alone will supply meaning and happiness in life. This is to load our partner with too great a burden. We are all incomplete: We all need the love that is secure, rather than oppressive; we need mutual forgiveness to thrive.[1]

Remarkable truth. As his words rolled around in my head for a moment, the glamour of this Cinderella day seemed to fade into the background. I realized that even a prince with the world at his fingertips could not provide his bride with enough security. Even a prince who bestows his bride with the title of princess cannot give her enough significance to satisfy.

Even a deeply devoted husband cannot provide his wife with all the love and acceptance she needs.

Everlasting joy, security, and true rest for our souls come not from belonging to a person or holding a certain position or gaining worldly possessions—but by belonging to a Savior.

Welcome to This Journey

Welcome to *You Belong to the Bridegroom: A Bible Study on the Gospel According to Mark*. Join me on a journey to finding our security in Christ. Together we will search the Scriptures with the goal of seeing Jesus as our heavenly husband. We will learn that we belong in the secure arms of his presence.

My prayer is that, like a beautiful bride advancing step-by-step toward her groom on her wedding day, you too will move closer to finding your security in Christ as you journey through the Gospel of Mark.

We Are the Bride of Christ

When I began to write this study, seeing Jesus as my heavenly husband seemed a little outside the box. I knew the Lord had impressed this theme on my heart for the study, but none of my Sunday school teachers had ever taught it. I was all right with embracing God as my heavenly Father, but Jesus as my heavenly husband? That was an uncomfortable stretch.

But then, *many* biblical concepts are uncomfortable at first, because God's ways are not our ways. And seeing Jesus as our Bridegroom is definitely God's idea. The Bible frequently compares believers' relationship with Christ to the marriage relationship (Isaiah 62:5; Jeremiah 2:2; Hosea 3:1; Luke 5:34; Ephesians 5:25). One reason for that, I believe, is to illustrate his desire for a deep relationship with us—a relationship so intimate and secure that we trust him completely and follow him, fully assured of his love.

In Jesus' day, the marriage process was different among the Jews than it is today. During the engagement (or betrothal), a man would leave his father's house and travel to his prospective bride's house to make a covenant with her. A price, or *mohar*, to be paid by the groom to the bride's father was negotiated. As a symbol of their covenant relationship, the bride and groom shared a glass of wine. After the marriage covenant was established, the groom would leave his bride, return to his father's house, and prepare a place for them to live after the wedding. Although the bride expected her groom to come back, she did not know the exact time of his return. When he did come back, their wedding feast and celebration took place.

The body of believers, collectively and individually, is the bride of Christ. As in the Jewish marriage process of Jesus' day, a covenant is formed: Jesus laid down his life so we can have all the blessings of a new covenant relationship with God. The marriage covenant of Bible days was commemorated by sharing a glass of wine. God's covenant with us is commemorated through Communion.

As a groom prepares a new home for his bride, Jesus went back to his Father to prepare a place for all who have entered a covenant relationship with him by trusting him as Lord and Savior. Days before the resurrection, Jesus gathered his disciples and gave them these words of reassurance that clearly imply his role as bridegroom and ours as bride:

> "Do not let your hearts be troubled. Trust in God; trust also in me. In my Father's house are many rooms; if it were not so, I would have told you. I am going there to prepare a place for you. And if I go and prepare a place for you, I will come back and take you to be with me that you also may be where I am. You know the way to the place where I am going." (John 14:1–4)

Trusting Our Bridegroom

Doubt, shame, worry, anxiety, insecurity, the need to control—these are symptoms of a woman afraid to trust her husband. They are also burdens that Jesus, as our heavenly husband, does not expect us to bear. Living with them neither solves our problems nor meets our needs; rather, it wears us down emotionally and physically. This is not God's plan for us.

How do these verses use marriage to illustrate God's desire for you to trust him completely, assured of his unconditional, amazing love?

Isaiah 62:5 _____

Jeremiah 2:2 _____

John 3:28–30 _____

Ephesians 5:25–30 _____

Revelation 19:6–9 _____

Like a bride waiting for her groom to return to claim her after preparing their home, the church is now waiting for Jesus to come back and take us to a place he has prepared for us in glory. As a corporate body and as individual believers, we are to wait with hopeful expectation for our groom. We don't know when he is coming, but we know he is. When he arrives, we will be swept up as his bride into a celebration, a wedding feast in heaven. But for now, he is asking us to trust him, to be faithful, and to find our security in him alone.

Jesus is worthy of that trust. His provision is not simply for the future, for everlasting life in heaven; his name already brings salvation and healing to our souls. Our salvation—our security in Jesus—begins with abundant life here on earth (John 10:10). He loves us unconditionally and wants the best for us.

Let this first day of this study be the first day of a whole new level of trusting Jesus, one that we can experience together. We belong to the Bridegroom—the only one who can complete our lives and give us the security we need so that we can freely give to others.

We are his treasure.

DAY 2

"When this had dawned on him, he went to the house of Mary the mother of John, also called Mark, where many people had gathered and were praying." —*Acts 12:12*

Imagine what it would have been like to hear the Holy Spirit urging you to write something that had never been written before: the first account of the life of Jesus. That had to happen to someone, and the man it happened to was John Mark, commonly known as Mark. It was Mark who penned the Gospel we are studying.

John Mark (John is his Hebrew name, and Mark is his Roman name), under the divine inspiration of the Holy Spirit, captured the miracles, the majesty, the message, and the meekness of our Bridegroom, Jesus Christ. There is a feeling of urgency in John Mark's Gospel, perhaps because of his desire to introduce Jesus—the only one who can rescue, restore, and redeem.

And an introduction it surely was, since in the early days of the church, the Gospel of Mark was the only written source for learning about Jesus. Scholars estimate that this early Gospel was written around AD 60.

Throughout this study, the Gospel of Mark will be our main source as we seek to know Jesus in a more intimate way as our Bridegroom—although when appropriate we will delve into the other three Gospels as well for more detail.

I love the simplicity of Mark's Gospel. Mark's writings are matter-of-fact and action-packed. Jesus' disciple Peter was Mark's mentor. Peter's personality was bold and abrupt at times, and Mark's edgy writing resembles his mentor's style. Mark's writing moves along almost like our world of fast-paced text messages and news sound bites. In my busy world, the simplicity and directness of Mark brings a refreshing focus. Mark gets straight to the point. The first verse summarizes the gospel in a nutshell: "The beginning of the gospel about Jesus Christ, the Son of God" (Mark 1:1). Jesus is the Christ, Mark tells us, the Messiah, the one who came to bring salvation. He is the Son of God.

The primary audience Mark expected for his Gospel was the Romans, who valued what a person accomplished. So Mark wrote more about the *actions* of Jesus than about his teachings. As we read Mark's account of those actions, we will see our heavenly husband's strength and his desire to serve. His strength is sufficient to allow our weary souls to rest from our desperate self-reliance. The desire of his heart to serve his bride can give us the confidence to lay down our will and surrender to his.

The Influence of Women

Mark's mother must have known she was a beloved bride of Christ. From Acts 12:11–14, what do you learn about Mark's mother?

_____

_____

_____

_____

Mary, Mark's mother, was a wealthy woman who opened her home so that people could gather and pray. That may not sound so revolutionary to those of us who live in societies where opening our homes to Christian activities such as Bible studies is legal and has no negative consequences. But Mary offered her home despite the persecution faced by the early church. Interestingly, some scholars believe that the room in Mary's home where the church gathered was the same upper room Jesus used for the Last Supper, and also the room where Pentecost occurred.[2]

Scripture tells us nothing about Mark's father, but it does tell us that Peter thought of Mark like a son. Where was John Mark's father? Was Mary a single mom? Was she a widow? Did she work to support her family? The Bible doesn't tell us.

Whatever Mary's domestic situation, as she freely opened the doors of their home to be a place of prayer, John Mark was no doubt watching and absorbing what it meant for a person to be completely sold out to Christ. His mother's devotion to Christ was contagious. She influenced Mark, and Mark influenced countless others with his gospel of love and hope through an awesome Savior. That influence continues even today.

John Mark reminds us that we can influence those in our care simply by the way we choose to live our lives. A stay-at-home mom, a working mom, a single mom, a married mom, a mom with three little youngsters at her heels. A mom with teenagers testing her faith, a mom with grown children who have left the nest. A foster mom, or simply someone who is "like a mother" to someone. No matter which of these describe you, don't ever underestimate your influence on those around you. Like Mary's, your service to Jesus is contagious.

As women fully committed to following Christ, our actions can affect generations to come. By your becoming the woman God created and redeemed you to be, not only your life but also the lives of those you influence may affect the world for centuries—as Mark's has.

Second Chances

John Mark also reminds us that our God is a God of second chances. Mark traveled with Paul and Barnabas on their first missionary journey, but for whatever reason he decided to desert them and return home (Acts 13:13; 15:37–38). When preparing for their second missionary journey, Paul didn't want to take John Mark along—he considered him a quitter.

Barnabas disagreed. But Paul was so firm about keeping Mark off the team that Paul and Barnabas had "such a sharp disagreement that they parted company" (Acts 15:39). Paul chose a different helper, Silas, and went one way, while Barnabas and Mark went another.

I wonder what happened between Barnabas and Mark on that mission trip. Did Barnabas take John Mark under his wing and restore his steadfastness in serving the Lord? Whatever happened, Mark must have matured, and Paul's confidence in Mark's faithfulness must have been restored, because Mark afterward served alongside Paul. Years later Paul said, "Get Mark and bring him with you, because he is helpful to me in my ministry" (2 Timothy 4:11; Philemon 24). What a legacy! Not only was Mark helpful to the apostle Paul, but his influence continues to the present day through the Gospel he wrote.

Let Mark's life remind you as you walk through the Gospel of Mark that your life matters.

God designed each of us to bring value to this world and to make a difference as we walk in the direction of our God-given purpose. However, when we measure ourselves by the world's standards, by the mistakes we have made, and by what others think, we can never fully uncover the truth of who we are in the eyes of our Creator. *We are treasured.* God created us to be nourished by him and his Word. But just as there is a God who loves us, there is also an enemy of our soul who would love nothing more than to use the brokenness of this world to convince us God does *not* love us and we are *not* valuable.

When God created the world, he did not rest until he had created a woman, because she was a necessary part of his plan. Still today, women are a part of his great story. But when a woman does not know she is treasured by God, when instead she is confused by other sources of information, she cannot live out her purpose. When that happens, our world suffers. We all lose—because every woman is created to bring value to this world.

Jesus provided a solution. He made a way for us to reconnect to the true Source of Life, so that our hearts could be nourished and we would be able to love and give to others the way God designed us to do. He provided forgiveness and eternal life through faith and grace. He also provided a new way of living—*by faith in him and his words*.

When Jesus spoke to women in the Scriptures, his words were empowering and life changing. Jesus is still speaking to women today with empowering and life-changing words, primarily through the Bible. When we accept Jesus as the source for our value and direction for our lives, we will be empowered to become all he redeemed and created us to be.

Like Mark, you are here for a purpose beyond yourself. Whatever mistakes you've made in your past, whatever your weaknesses or disgraces have been, take the hand of your Bridegroom and let him lead you in the direction of your purpose.

DAY 3

"The [Holy] Spirit and the bride (the church, the true Christians) say, Come! And let him who is listening say, Come! And let everyone come who is thirsty [who is painfully conscious of his need of those things by which the soul is refreshed, supported, and strengthened]; and whoever [earnestly] desires to do it, let him come, take, appropriate, and drink the water of Life without cost." —*Revelation 22:17 AMPC*

Searching in All the Wrong Places

True security is found in the arms of Jesus. Not in ourselves. Not in other people. Not in money or success. Only in Jesus. Are you anxious, weary, or frustrated? Where or in whom are you placing your trust?

And have you, as I did for many years, allowed the voices that surround you, and even your own voice in moments of weakness, to define you with words that do not reflect your true identity? Did you not know for sure who you were in the world, because you had—again, as I did for many years—allowed others to write your story? When this was true of me, it left my heart drowning in a pool of insecurity. How about you?

Instead of reaching out to Jesus, I believed my rescue depended on me. I was a people pleaser to the core. Although I never articulated it, I settled on a formula that I thought would help me find happiness, worth, and identity: *I will work hard to succeed because that will prove I am valuable. I have to be the best. I can never fail. I must please others. If I am not perfect, I am not good.* I became a self-reliant, driven perfectionist.

I needed affirmation from people, and achieving success got that affirmation for me. The world applauds success. Success became my drug of choice—almost a weapon. I was an approval addict who could not say no. I developed unhealthy, codependent relationships. While on the outside I looked like a confident teenager with titles and accolades, inside I was terrified. In my struggle to be perfect, failure was unacceptable. I was alone in my heart. That is a very scary place to be.

But of course that didn't work. Success is certainly not bad. Setting goals is not bad. Getting encouragement from people is not bad. But when these things are your source, you are living on shaky ground. Finally I dropped to my knees in prayer, crying out to Jesus for help.

Jesus threw me a lifeline and pulled me to shore by introducing me to his Word. My fear and worry faded as I experienced a new determination taking shape in the depths of my soul: *Jesus, I want to know you in a new way. I don't want to be afraid to trust you anymore. I want to rest in the security of your love.*

When I understood that my true value and the purpose for which I was created can only come from Jesus himself, I gained courage, confidence, direction, and the freedom to become all God created me to be.

You too can find this same freedom by reaching out to Jesus as you journey through the Gospel of Mark. Let his words define you. Get to know him intimately through his Word. It's only through living the truth of God's Word that we can experience all it means to belong to Jesus Christ as his bride, that we can trust him completely, and that we can live the life we were created and redeemed to live.

Jesus said that if we seek him, we will find him. Let's seek Jesus with an open heart that dares to believe that our Bridegroom is all we'll ever need. We belong in his strong and secure arms.

Here's a challenge: As you explore Mark, try to see Jesus with fresh eyes. Let go of the Jesus you've learned from others, from the world. Look instead at the Jesus of the Bible as the source for living water to quench your soul's thirst. My prayer is that you will see not only how remarkable Jesus is and how much he loves you—but that you will also see that your only true security is in him.

And that challenge brings us to a wonderful story: the Samaritan woman at the well. Although it's found outside the Gospel of Mark, this story is a wonderful depiction of the foundational aim of our study. These Scriptures capture the Bridegroom's character—and his desire for women to trust him with their whole heart. In this first week of our study together, we'll ponder this passage from several angles to uncover timeless treasures to hide in our hearts. It was after this Samaritan woman saw Jesus with fresh eyes that she realized her earthly relationships could never satisfy her thirst. Then Jesus touched her heart and changed her life forever.

The history of the Samaritan people began about 721 years before Jesus was born. The Assyrians captured the northern ten tribes of Israel. To colonize this area, the king of Assyria deported the Israelites and brought in influential Assyrians. But after interpreting lion attacks as punishment from God, the king of Assyria sent Israelite priests back to northern Israel to teach the new Assyrian colonists how to appease the God of Israel. These colonists learned from the priests, but they mixed and mingled their own Assyrian culture and religion with what they learned. They "worshiped the LORD, but they also served their own gods in accordance with the customs of the nations from which they had been brought" (2 Kings 17:33). Naturally, this mixed religion caused intense friction and hatred between Jews and Samaritans, and that friction continued during the time Jesus was here on earth.

One day a Jewish Savior settled beside a well, waiting for a Samaritan woman whose soul was thirsty. She would quickly discover this man was not just another man in her life. He was her Savior. History was about to change!

The Woman at the Well

Read John 4:1–30. From verses 16–18, what evidence do you see that the Samaritan woman was stuck in a destructive cycle of depending on relationships for security but not finding any that satisfied her soul?

_____

_____

_____

Where do you find your heart most prone to wander apart from Christ—toward people, possessions, or positions? How has this left you thirsty?

_____

_____

_____

From verses 4:10–14, John 7:38–39, and Revelation 22:17, what are some differences between living water and well water?

_____

_____

_____

How does the picture of living water encourage you to seek Jesus, rather than the world's resources, to meet the needs in your thirsty soul?

_____

_____

_____

When I think about the Samaritan religion, with its mix of Judaism and the pagan beliefs of the Samaritans' Assyrian past, I can't help but take a good look at my own relationship with God. I have realized all too recently that I can go to church, teach the Bible, sing as many worship songs as my little voice can handle, and yet still hang on to other, lesser gods that do not have the ability to satisfy my soul. Our hearts were designed to worship something or someone—and sometimes, like the Samaritans, in our eagerness to fulfill that design, we choose the wrong objects for our worship. There's only one right choice: Giving our hearts fully to Jesus is true worship—and freedom (John 4:23; Galatians 5:1).

Jesus wants to be your Messiah and your Savior. Are you still looking elsewhere and seeking a rescue that will never fully satisfy? If you choose to be a halfhearted Christ follower, you may have a "religion"—but true belief in Christ is much more than religion, and until you find that relationship, you will never find the joy that springs from the living water flowing within all who believe.

As the story in John chapter 4 develops, we discover that the woman of Samaria was caught in a destructive cycle of seeking rescue through relationships—bad ones. And each new relationship left her empty and thirsty.

Earthly relationships give us meaning and help us grow. After our relationship with God, I believe that relationships with people are our next priority. However, they cannot give us everlasting security. Relationships, like water, are vital in life, but they cannot be our gods. God designed us to live in community, to love and give to others—not to lean on them for what only God can give us. Jesus conveyed this truth to the woman at the well by describing himself as living water, explaining that her most essential needs could be satisfied only in his arms. His resources are limitless and given in abundance with love. From the safety and richness of a relationship with him, we can truly give to others out of the overflow of our hearts. When our security and provision rest in Christ, we are free to say no to unhealthy relationships.

Once she had grasped this truth, the Samaritan woman seemed to forget about the water she had come for; she threw down her jug. Now she knew about an unending source of living water. Similarly, I encourage you to enter the journey of this study with high expectation of something new and better. Throw down your "water jug" and drink the living water only Jesus can give. You no longer have to run from person to person, from possession to possession, from position to position to seek security. You no longer have to depend on yourself. Your Bridegroom loves you unconditionally and wants to meet your needs.

In the fairy tales, it's usually a prince who waits at the end of the aisle. But this is no fairy tale, and in truth, it's the King of Kings and Lord of Lords who is waiting to take your hand. He is pursuing you.

Are you thirsty? All the glory and splendor of this world cannot compare with the living water that flows from Jesus and satisfies the thirsty soul. Are you ready to find confidence that cannot be shaken? It's time to advance down the aisle to embrace the reality of belonging to the Bridegroom.

Turn around, beautiful bride of Christ. "I who speak to you am he" (John 4:26).

DAY 4

"So, my dear brothers and sisters, be strong and immovable.
Always work enthusiastically for the Lord, for you know that nothing
you do for the Lord is ever useless." —*1 Corinthians 15:58 NLT*

For Just One

Jesus went to great lengths to reach the Samaritan woman. He crossed all cultural boundaries and social norms to journey to the well at Samaria, where he sat waiting to speak with just one woman. He was weary from his long trip, but she was worth his journey (John 4:4–8).

Great lengths just for one. I just love this about Jesus—don't you?

> "Suppose a woman has ten silver coins and loses **one.** Won't she light a lamp and sweep the entire house and search carefully until she finds it? And when she finds it, she will call in her friends and neighbors and say, 'Rejoice with me because I have found my lost coin.' In the same way, there is joy in the presence of God's angels when even **one** sinner repents." (Luke 15:8–10 NLT, *emphasis mine*).

Sometimes when we make great efforts but reach only one, we may become weary and question whether we are really making a difference. Was this meager result worth so much time and energy?

The world would say success is found only in great numbers. However, Jesus found fulfillment in just being faithful to do his Father's will (John 4:34). Sometimes this meant going to great lengths for just one.

Do you feel defeated because you don't see the results you expected? Take heart today by considering *his* heart. Jesus went to great lengths for just one. And now he calls you and me to do the same. *As long as we are following Jesus and putting our faith into action, we are making a difference, whether or not we can see that difference.*

> Have you ever felt nudged by God to take a step, just one step, that seemed small, but it made a huge difference in the life of one person? How did this make you feel? What does success look like in God's eyes?

"So, my dear brothers and sisters, be strong and immovable. Always work enthusiastically for the Lord, for you know that nothing you do for the Lord is ever useless."
(1 Corinthians 15:58 NLT)

Nothing you do for the Lord is useless, brave heart. Nothing!

Our Grace Journey

One step taken following Jesus creates more impact than knowing it all and trying to do it all. During this study of the book of Mark, we want to not only connect with Jesus and listen to his voice—we also want to share Jesus with others. How? By applying his truth to our lives and taking steps to follow him. As we nourish our hearts with truth and put that truth into action, we will make a difference in the lives of others in the way God intended.

On that grace journey, what's your next step? You may not know until it's time to take it. As you complete each step, Jesus will give you the next one—in his time. Your steps form a pathway for you to live as God intended. You don't have to figure out the plan—just follow. There is no such thing as a small step taken in faith. Each step, small or large, creates impact.

It's all about abiding in Christ, listening to the promptings of the Holy Spirit, following them, trusting in his strength, and receiving joy (Galatians 3:2–5; John 15:1–11). His wisdom and love for you are completely pure, so you can trust the leading of the Holy Spirit (James 3:17; John 10:10–12, 27).

> What do you learn about following Jesus and making a difference in the following verses?
>
> Galatians 3:25 _____
>
> John 15:1–11 _____
>
> 1 Corinthians 15:58 _____
>
> Romans 8:1–17 _____
>
> Matthew 11:28–30 _____

Jesus came to give us abundant life. We find true freedom and joy when we listen to and follow his voice. John 15:9–12 tells us our obedience flows out of trusting God's love for us.

Jesus laid down his life for you. There could be no greater gift. You don't have to figure out life on your own—Jesus invites you simply to listen and follow him.

Let's imagine for a moment that we can hear God talking to us about the journey of grace that he has called all of us to:

Walk with me, brave heart. Learn the "unforced rhythms of grace" (Matthew 11:29 MSG). Walk by faith by moving to the promptings of my Holy Spirit. Experience in abundance my presence today. My presence is not something to reach for through your goodness but something to receive through your faith in Christ.

This morning is full of wonder. Catch the wind of the Holy Spirit in your sails. Throw down the rudder of my Word and go against the current of the culture that surrounds you. I want to live through you. Yes—you! I died for you; now live for me and find the life you have been looking for.

I love you too much to share all the details about where I want to take you. *If you knew everything, you might be tempted to rely on your own strength, and I am taking you to places where only **my** strength and power will sustain you. If you knew everything about your future, you might just pull your heart back into the harbor, where life is safe and there are no waves.*

Instead, I am calling your heart into deep waters to live as I intended—calling your heart for my glory. It's a costly choice that requires courage, but it leads to the life you were created and redeemed to live.

The adventure of abundant life is found not in your safe harbor but in the center of my will. *It is there that you will find the deepest joy, no matter what storms may surface.*

You are my treasure. Walk with me, brave heart.

Learn the unforced rhythms of grace, moving to the promptings of the Holy Spirit—and find the life you've been looking for.

DAY 5

"O Lord, you have searched me and you know me. You know when I sit and when I rise; you perceive my thoughts from afar. You discern my going out and my lying down; you are familiar with all my ways. Before a word is on my tongue you know it completely, O LORD." —*Psalm 139:1–4*

Can you imagine the shock on the Samaritan woman's face when Jesus revealed to her some of the most intimate details of her life? He knew all about her—everything—and wanted to point her to the true, everlasting security that only he could bring. Jesus saw a life filled with one broken relationship after another, a life spent chasing a dream that offered a mere mirage of security to her thirsty soul.

In those days, a "good" Israelite would rather die than associate with a Samaritan, much less a woman. Jesus was traveling from Judea in the south to Galilee in the north. The most direct route was to pass directly through Samaria, but the Jews' disdain for Samaritans was so great that a "good" Jew would go out of his way to travel around Samaria instead.

But not Jesus. The Bible says Jesus "had to go through Samaria" (John 4:4). Why? There were other routes, though longer. But he had to go through Samaria because he had life-changing truths to speak to the weary woman running in endless pursuit of so-called saviors. He intended to capture the heart of a woman who would in turn change her entire hometown by pointing them to him. He had to get there to save her heart for eternity.

Listening to Jesus

Let's read a little further into the story of the woman at the well in Samaria. Review John 4:1–30, and then read verses 31–42.

When Jesus spoke, the Samaritan woman listened to his voice. How would this story have turned out differently if the woman in Samaria had listened to someone other than Jesus? For example, what if she had listened to what the disciples might have told her, or her forefathers' beliefs, or the world's opinions, or her personal patterns with relationships?

According to John 8:31–32 and 17:17, what is truth, and why was it important for Jesus to share the truth with the Samaritan woman?

How does this story inspire you to seek Jesus and listen to him for truth?

Jesus knew everything about the woman at the well, and he reached out to her despite her flaws (John 4:29). Jesus spoke the exact words she needed to hear. He gave her the truth—not to condemn her, but rather because he knew the truth would set her free.

Many voices were swirling around the woman, but she chose to listen to Jesus.

The voices of the culture around her said Jews and Samaritans did not associate with each another. This was true—but it was not God's truth! If she had listened to those voices, she would have never heard Jesus' life-changing words.

Her forefathers gave her a religion based on untruths. If she had continued listening to them instead of Jesus, she wouldn't have learned about true worship.

Jesus' disciples were shocked that he was talking to the woman. If she had listened to their opinions about women, perhaps she would not have felt worthy to testify to the town of Samaria.

Perhaps her years of failed marriages and relationships with men had tarnished her reputation with the local townspeople. If she had continued listening to others' opinions about her instead of listening to Jesus' words of love and salvation, she would have continued in a life of anxiety and failure.

But the Samaritan woman didn't listen to any of those voices; she sought the voice of Jesus instead. As a result, her life was transformed and she confidently shared Jesus with others. Jesus used her testimony to change an entire town.

I don't imagine that it was easy for the woman to change the beliefs she had held for a lifetime and communicate that change to skeptical townspeople. It was no job for a woman who had lost faith in herself. But I believe the Samaritan woman's confidence was in the One who knew all about her. The One who saw her heart and loved her anyway. The One who understood her—and spoke to the needs in her soul.

Just as Jesus knew all about the Samaritan woman, he knows all about you. Jesus says he even knows how many hairs are on your head (Matthew 10:30). He is fully involved with your life, and the desire of his heart is to lead you into his perfect plan. Jesus knows you intimately and completely and loves you unconditionally. He desires to speak to you personally and teach you the truth through his Word.

Jesus longs to spend time with you. He will go to great lengths to find you, as he did with the Samaritan woman, because he has so much to say to you (Luke 15:4–7). He put it this way: "The sheep that are My own hear and are listening to My voice; and I know them, and they follow Me" (John 10:27 AMPC).

Living Water

Wouldn't you be amazed if you met someone who was able to tell you everything you had ever done? The Samaritan woman was (John 4:29). And you *will* be astounded by how personally the Lord will speak to you through his Word. Jesus spoke plainly and powerfully to the Samaritan woman because he had a life purpose for her—just as he has a life purpose for you.

Discovering that God wanted to speak to me through his Word changed my life. John the Baptist remarked that he was full of joy when he heard the Bridegroom's voice (John 3:29). As you hear his still, small voice speaking clearly to your heart, you will also discover the freedom and the *treasure* of following Christ.

Jesus introduced himself to the Samaritan woman as the source for living water, and he is still the source today. He wants to speak directly to you, his bride, just as he spoke to her. She wasn't perfect—far from it. But she was thirsty. Are you thirsty? Then allow the Word to wash over your soul like living water as Jesus speaks to you (John 1:1).

The Samaritan woman gained enough confidence from her conversation with Jesus to influence her entire village. By resting in our Bridegroom's presence and spending time with him, we can gain that same confidence, enabling us to influence the lives of those around us. Resting in Jesus' great love for us provides us with the resources we need to give to others and inspires us to follow him and share his goodness. Like the Samaritan woman, we will bear fruit for his glory.

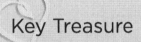

Key Treasure

Are you thirsty? Then allow the Word to wash over your soul like living water as Jesus speaks to you (John 1:1).

DAY 6

"People do not live by bread alone, but by every word that comes
from the mouth of God." —*Matthew 4:4 NLT*

Jesus taught us in Matthew 4:4 that his revealed words are daily food, essential for nourishing our souls. Spending personal time with God to hear his word for you is not merely a goal to aspire to but also a necessary element for the health of your soul.

Ready to nourish your soul?

The Nourish™ Bible Study Method is a key that helps unlock truth for the life you were created to live by giving you a proven, effective, three-step approach to Bible study that connects you with Jesus. When I developed this method, I had this goal in mind:

> for every woman to be able to look at every God-inspired word in the Bible and see his truth shine through to light her path—a path that always starts with Jesus.

Starting in chapter two, you will begin to use the Nourish Method for the first three days of each chapter by applying one step of the Nourish Method each day to a weekly Nourish Scripture.

So, for today, I'd like to equip you for your journey by teaching you the Nourish Bible Study Method step by step.

What should you do if you are already familiar with the Nourish Bible Study Method? Simply skip this day of study, or continue reading to review and discover how the method is incorporated into each chapter of the Nourish Bible Study Series.

Nourish™—A Three-Step Bible Study Method to Connect with Jesus

So, let's get started!

Jesus carved out time in his day to break bread with others. Whether in an intimate setting with his disciples, a wedding celebration at Cana, a seaside fish dinner cooked over a fire with friends, or miraculously feeding thousands with five loaves and two fishes, Jesus paused to eat food with those he loved.

Think of your time with Jesus as gathering around a family dinner table he has prepared for you with much love and care.

Reveal, *Respond*, and *Renew* are the three steps of the Nourish Bible Study Method. Think of each step in the Nourish Bible Study Method as an ingredient in a recipe for a nourishing meal. Each ingredient is important and plays a role. Each ingredient interacts with the others. Combined, they enable you to find and understand life-giving truths in the Word that you had never seen before and nourish your soul for your journey in life.

Here are the three steps that Nourish™ will lead you through:

- **DAY 1:** *Reveal.* Connect with Jesus by studying the Scriptures and allowing the Holy Spirit to reveal truth in the Scriptures.
- **DAY 2:** *Respond.* Apply the truth using our IMPACT questions so that your life can impact the lives of those around you.
- **DAY 3:** *Renew.* Let the truth you've just learned from God's word renew your mind. Allow God to anchor his Word in your heart. Putting this life-changing discipline into your daily routine, using our practical method, will change the way you think and live.

Reveal. Respond. Renew. Starting next week, for the first three days of each chapter, you will take one Nourish step each day to help you take a break from the hustle and gather around the table with Jesus through the study of his Word.

Let's take a closer look at each of those three steps.

The *Reveal* Step

Connect with Jesus and Allow Him to Reveal Truth

There is something special about sharing a meal with others—it is more than just eating food. It is about coming together to be with one another. Gathering at the table to break bread brings pause and a place to connect.

As you carve out time to dive into Bible study and pull your chair up to the table, don't come just to read. Come to connect with Jesus by relying on the Holy Spirit to reveal his word to you.

Switching Up Your Goal: Why Are You Studying the Bible?

What if you switched your goal from completing your study to connecting with Jesus? What if you let go of the aspiration to understand it all or do it all? What if you saw the Bible as a way to connect with your Creator instead of a way to learn a list of rules to follow? This is what the *Reveal* Step is all about.

So often, we make the mistake of coming to our table with Jesus to cross it off our to-do list rather than just to listen and let him lead and teach us. You see, God knows the nourishment need and when we need it.

Discovering the difference between diligently studying the Scriptures for information and allowing the Holy Spirit to reveal truth through those Scriptures is life-changing—because Jesus is life-changing.

The goal of the *Reveal* Step is not to study the Scriptures solely to gain information. It is to connect with Jesus through the Bible and allow the Holy Spirit to nourish us with life-giving truth.

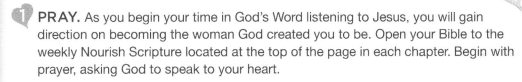

How to put the *Reveal* Step into practice during DAY 1.

1 **PRAY.** As you begin your time in God's Word listening to Jesus, you will gain direction on becoming the woman God created you to be. Open your Bible to the weekly Nourish Scripture located at the top of the page in each chapter. Begin with prayer, asking God to speak to your heart.

2 **JOURNAL.** Prayerfully read and reflect on the weekly Nourish Scripture. Phrases, verses, or words will catch your attention because the Holy Spirit is highlighting truth for you—mark them. Journal any thoughts you may have in the space provided for you on Day 1. Taking pen to paper will help you to process the truth God is revealing just for you.

3 **DISCOVER.** Some days, you will simply mark up the day's passage in your Bible and journal. Other days, the Lord will prompt you to learn more about a certain word or verse or to investigate background information on the Nourish Scripture by using outside resources. Let him be your guide. For a list of some of my favorite outside resources and ways I use them as I study the Bible, download a FREE printable PDF at www.TreasuredMinistries.com/BibleStudyResources.

The *Respond* Step

Respond to Jesus by Applying the Truth to Your Life

When God initiates the process by revealing truth and we respond to that truth, it impacts our lives and the lives around us. Holy Spirit revelation requires application for activation.

How do you study the Word in a way that *activates* the greatest *impact* in your life? You do this by *asking the right questions.*

This approach provides the focus that will help you refine the truth further and apply it more directly and profoundly to your life. That was the purpose we had in mind when we created our six IMPACT questions for this step.

How to put the *Respond* Step into practice during DAY 2.

Return to the weekly Nourish Scripture and ask yourself the six IMPACT questions found below. What happens if some days, you can't seem to come up with an answer to all six questions? Simple—don't worry about it. If after thinking about it for a few moments, no answer to a question occurs to you, then move on to the next one.

IMPACT™

IMAGE OF GOD TO TRUST? An attribute of God, Jesus, or the Holy Spirit to trust.

MESSAGE TO SHARE? A word of encouragement, truth, or prayer to share.

PROMISE TO TREASURE? A promise in the Bible to believe.

ACTION TO TAKE? A specific step God is calling you to take.

CORE IDENTITY IN CHRIST TO AFFIRM? A truth about how God sees you to affirm.

TRANSGRESSION TO CONFESS? A sin to acknowledge for help, healing, and restoration through Christ.

Now that you know the IMPACT™ acronym, you know what to look for when you are studying a passage. Review the table on the next page to dive more deeply into each question so you can see why each one is important in your journey to apply the truth to your life.

IMPACT™	
IMAGE OF GOD TO TRUST?	It is important that we begin here, since what we believe about God directly affects our thoughts and actions. Attributes of God, Jesus, or the Holy Spirit can be stated directly or implied by actions in the Bible. It is eye-opening when we allow the Bible to define God's image instead of allowing our circumstances to shape how we perceive God.
MESSAGE TO SHARE?	A message to share is a word of encouragement, truth, wisdom, or prayer from the Nourish Scripture that you feel led to give to another. It is also perhaps a message God simply wants to share with you. God's truth refreshes your soul, and when you share this with others, you will find yourself refreshed also.
PROMISE TO TREASURE?	A promise to believe is a promise in the Bible to stand on by faith. Imagine the difference it would make in your life and the lives around you if you moved from knowing God's promises to believing them. God is ever faithful to his Word—always.
ACTION TO TAKE?	During your time in God's Word, if he prompted you to take an action step, follow through and take that step as soon as you can. Faith and action walk hand in hand. This step is all about abiding in Christ, listening to the promptings of the Holy Spirit, following them, trusting in his strength, and receiving joy (Galatians 3:2–5; John 15:1–11). Each step, small or large, creates impact.

CORE IDENTITY IN CHRIST TO AFFIRM?	For this step, write "In Christ I am" statements that line up with the truth in God's Word. Finding your core identity in Christ is not about frantically striving to be someone, but about surrendering to God by allowing his Word to define who you are and the purpose for which you were created. This is a precious treasure to guard by faith against outside influences (what others say, our circumstances, our actions, our past, our feelings, how others treat us, worldly standards) so that you can truly give to others by embracing all God has created you to be.
	
	Below are some examples.
	  I am God's child (John 1:12).
	  I am completely forgiven (Romans 3:21–22).
	  I am very valuable to God (Matthew 10:31).
	  I am confident in asking God for wisdom (Jeremiah 33:2–3).
	  I belong to the body of Christ (Mark 3:33–35).

TRANSGRESSION TO CONFESS?	The Holy Spirit highlights transgressions—not to condemn you, but to free you to become all God created you to be. Instead of bringing God your good behaviors (self-righteousness) or justifying, hiding, or trying to change on your own, bring your sin to God through confession. Here you will find the grace, healing, and transformation that only Christ can bring.

The *Renew* Step

Renew Your Mind to Anchor the Truth in Your Heart

Have you ever left out a vital ingredient by mistake because that particular ingredient was just a small amount, but its omission had adverse effects? I think we've all been there.

Just like a dismayed contestant on the Food Network show *Chopped* who forgets a small basket ingredient because it was hiding under a dish towel, we can be disappointed with the results of our time in God's Word because we have missed a vital ingredient to weave into the fabric of our lives: *biblical meditation*.

For years, although I was deep in Bible study, I shied away from biblical meditation and missed out on a vital ingredient for soul nourishment.

> *How could just five minutes a day focusing on one verse heal me?*
> *Isn't that a New Age thing?*

I heard a lot about the importance of Bible study but nothing about biblical mediation.

Here's What Happened When I Added the Five-Minute Ingredient

When I began to put God's prescription of renewing my mind into practice by starting my quiet time meditating on God's Word for just five minutes, the results were incredible.

The shift in my life personally was so profound that I decided to renovate the Nourish Method to devote one entire step to this spiritual discipline.

God does not neglect to tell us about this vital ingredient. Over and over again in the Bible, God tells his people to remember, reflect on, and renew their minds with his Word, his promises, his goodness. In fact, *meditate* is mentioned over 20 times in the Bible. This is for a good reason.

What you think determines how you live. What you practice in your thinking determines what grows in your life.

Just like a boat tied to its anchor, God wants our thoughts to remain steady on his truths for our lives. God alone is our anchor of truth. As an anchor exists to secure a vessel so it ceases to wander, God's Word secures our minds and hearts to him no matter what currents or waves we may face during the day.

How to put the *Renew* Step into practice during DAY 3.

An Anchor of Truth can be one word, truth, or verse that the Holy Spirit emphasizes to you during your time in God's Word—from your Nourish Scripture or any passage in the Bible.

1 **SEEK GOD TO FIND YOUR ANCHOR.** Prayerfully review the weekly Nourish Scripture and the journal entries you made during the first two days. Ask God to identify for you the one anchor of truth he wants you to take away from the weekly Nourish Scripture.

2 **RECORD YOUR ANCHOR.** Write your Anchor of Truth in the space provided on your Nourish Notes on Day 3 and on your Anchor of Truth Card. Tuck this card into your Bible or workbook just like a bookmark, so that you can be grounded in your truth daily. (Anchor of Truth cards available at www.TreasuredMinistries.com/shop.)

3 **RENEW YOUR MIND WITH YOUR ANCHOR.** Start your daily quiet time by meditating on your Anchor of Truth. Utilizing your Anchor of Truth Card as a bookmark makes this daily habit easy! Quiet your thoughts. Focus on the truth. Read the truth. Pray the truth. Continue to reflect on your Anchor of Truth daily until the next week, when God reveals another truth to you in the course of your study.

You're invited

The table is set, and Jesus is ready to dine with you! He has truth to nourish your soul. Carve out time to open his Word and feed your soul with the Bread of Life.

Nourish. A Bible Study Method for Life. *Reveal* > *Respond* > *Renew*.

You matter.
     You're invited.
          Come gather at his table!

nourish™
BIBLE STUDY METHOD

VIDEO SESSION NOTES

Session 1

HE SPEAKS

John 4:4–43

Videos located online at www.nourishbiblestudyseries.com

Chapter 2
THE PROPOSAL

DAY 1

Nourish Scripture: Mark 1:1–20

 ① PRAY.

Begin your time with God in prayer.

② TAKE THE *REVEAL* STEP OF THE NOURISH™ BIBLE STUDY METHOD.

Connect with Jesus by studying the Weekly Nourish Scripture and allowing the Holy Spirit to reveal truth in those verses. Prayerfully read over and reflect on the passage. Mark any phrases, verses, or words that catch your attention. Journal and learn as the Lord leads you.

DAY 2

Nourish Scripture: Mark 1:1–20

1 PRAY.

Begin your time with God in prayer.

2 TAKE THE *RESPOND* STEP OF THE NOURISH™ BIBLE STUDY METHOD.

Respond to activate truth in your life. The acronym **IMPACT**™ provides questions to help you apply the truth from your weekly Nourish Scripture. **Sometimes you may not have answers for all six questions.**

IMAGE OF GOD TO TRUST? An attribute of God, Jesus, or the Holy Spirit to trust.

MESSAGE TO SHARE? A word of encouragement, truth, or prayer to share.

PROMISE TO TREASURE? A promise in the Bible to believe.

ACTION TO TAKE? A specific step God is calling you to take.

CORE IDENTITY IN CHRIST TO AFFIRM? A truth about how God sees you to affirm.

TRANSGRESSION TO CONFESS? A sin to acknowledge for help, healing, and restoration through Christ.

DAY 3

Nourish Scripture: Mark 1:1–20

 PRAY.

Begin your time with God in prayer.

 TAKE THE *RENEW* STEP OF THE NOURISH™ BIBLE STUDY METHOD.

Like an anchor that secures its vessel, biblical meditation secures truth to transform your life. Take five minutes to *renew* your mind by focusing on one word, verse, or truth that the Holy Spirit revealed through the Bible during your week of study. Record your truth below and on your Anchor of Truth card.* Quiet your thoughts. Focus on the truth. Read the truth. Pray the truth.

UTILIZE YOUR *ANCHOR OF TRUTH* CARD AS A BOOKMARK TO CULTIVATE A DAILY PRACTICE OF BIBLICAL MEDITATION.

Place your Anchor of Truth Card* in your Bible study workbook to bookmark tomorrow's day of study. Let your Anchor of Truth bookmark remind you to pause and renew your mind on God's Word. Repeat this process daily, continuing to reflect on your Anchor of Truth to start your quiet time until the next week, when God reveals another truth to you.

*Anchor of Truth Cards are available at www.TreasuredMinistries.com/shop

DAY 4

"I delight greatly in the LORD; my soul rejoices in my God. For he has clothed me with garments of salvation and arrayed me in a robe of righteousness, as a bridegroom adorns his head like a priest, and as a bride adorns herself with her jewels." —*Isaiah 61:10*

His proposal was her rescue.

She was beautiful on the outside. Those who looked at her outward appearance naturally assumed that her life was all together. Many even envied her. She seemed to carry success so easily. But the Bridegroom saw her heart. He knew she was dying on the inside.

Her fragile heart was breaking under the incredible weight of a cloak she wore. It hung heavy on her because it was a garment of shame reflecting the gray thought life that echoed endlessly in the hollow chambers of her heart. I'm not good enough, I'm not good enough, I'm not good enough. Haunted by her inadequacies and past mistakes, she faced each day bearing the weight of the cloak. A forced smile masqueraded her feelings, but like a stubborn shadow, her shame was ever present.

She tried religion, but it offered no relief from the pain. The rules of religion only brought more condemnation because she couldn't measure up, and she sank deeper into despair.

One morning the Bridegroom came to break the silent shame in her life and bring her the good news. He called this good news the gospel.

"I have a proposal for you. Shame is not the garment I am asking you to wear. Give me your shame, take my hand by faith, and rest under the cover of my righteousness. I want to cover you with a garment of salvation. Repent and believe the good news."

She was stunned. There before her was a new garment of such beauty. As she gazed at the beautifully built tapestry, it seemed to dance with the splendor of a new glory. Just seeing it began reviving something in her soul.

She reached toward the cloak but then suddenly pulled back. Feelings of inadequacy told her she could not receive the gracious gift. She wrestled with the words resounding in her mind ... I'm not good enough, I'm not good enough.

Jesus knew her thoughts—as he always had. Walking beside her for a lifetime, he had seen every mistake she made and loved her all the same. Others had hurt her. She shouldered unnecessary shame by assuming their cruelty was somehow her fault. He had watched as she had attempted to rescue herself with her success and titles, with her hard work and determination, but they were never enough. All the numbing escapes she ran to could only bring temporary relief—he longed to give her true and lasting rest.

He came to rescue her with a divine exchange.

The Bridegroom's heart beat with compassion for her, and a wide smile brimmed his face. "You don't have to be good enough. In fact, you could never be good enough. I did not say you have to be perfect. I said to repent and believe this good news ..."

> *"For God so loved the world that he gave his one and only Son, that whoever believes in him shall not perish but have eternal life. For God did not send his Son into the world to condemn the world, but to save the world through him." (John 3:16–17)*

He held out the new garment, a robe loomed from his perfection and sacrifice and asked her to give him her robe of shame. Blinking back her tears of unbelief, she was weary from trying to do life on her own. Whosoever believes. She let him take her shame and reached out for his righteousness. Covering herself with his righteousness, she knew she was forgiven—not because of anything she had done, but because of the price her Bridegroom had paid on the cross. He made her new as she took his hand by faith and accepted his proposal. Now when God looked at her, all he saw was Jesus' robe of righteousness.

She wore his garment daily. She had never felt more beautiful.

> *"I delight greatly in the LORD; my soul rejoices in my God. For he has clothed me with garments of salvation and arrayed me in a robe of righteousness, as a bridegroom adorns his head like a priest, and as a bride adorns herself with her jewels." (Isaiah 61:10)*

Jesus Provided a Garment of Righteousness for His Chosen People

God has had a plan since before the beginning of time. He knew mankind would fall, and he didn't want anyone to wear the garment of sin and shame.

When John the Baptist began calling people to repentance and baptizing them, some were ready to turn from their sin. People from the entire Judean countryside and Jerusalem flocked to John to be baptized in the Jordan River. The dusty roads of sin had left them dirty, and this was a place of new beginnings. I can only imagine the tears of joy as men and women freely confessed hurts and hidden secrets that had been pinned so deeply in their hearts. *Could this be the Savior the prophet Isaiah spoke of so long ago?*

But John was not that Savior. He offered a baptism of repentance for the forgiveness of sins to prepare the people for the only one through whom salvation can come: Jesus, the Messiah. While John's baptism was liberating, it was not enough to cover their sins. By humbling themselves through confession and baptism, they were declaring their need for a Savior.

But not all the people were ready to humble themselves and admit their need. The religious leaders were the most stubborn. They wouldn't admit their sins to themselves or anyone else. They walked in pride and did not believe they needed a Savior. They would depend on themselves and keeping the Law.

But the ones who persisted in this stand failed to get right with God. Why? Because they were trying to attain righteousness themselves instead of trusting in God. John, on the other hand, exclaimed he was not fit to untie Jesus' sandals (Mark 1:7; John 1:29–34). He found freedom by recognizing his need for Jesus. If John the Baptist, who was "great in the sight of the Lord," needed Jesus, why do we try to find freedom any other way (Luke 1:15)?

People Haven't Changed

We haven't changed all that much since the time of John the Baptist. We have all sinned. Some of us recognize our shortcomings and turn to Jesus for forgiveness and help. Others of us, like the Pharisees, stubbornly refuse to recognize our need for a Savior.

To sin literally means to miss the mark. We fail to obey God's commands and so miss God's best in our lives. Shame is one of the negative side effects of sin. Shame places glasses over our eyes, clouding our view of God's goodness. Shame keeps us from God. Instead of turning to the one who wants to help us, we turn away. We strive to feel better by doing more or being better. We long to gain the approval of other people. We look to earthly escapes to cope with shame but only find temporary relief. But these methods cannot take away the shame in our lives. The solution to sin and shame can be found only in a Savior—Jesus Christ.

Before you decide to close the covers of this Bible study because I am bringing up that taboo word *sin*—stick with me a bit. God knows you are not perfect. Your mistakes are not a surprise to him. That's why he gave us Jesus—so we could rest in his perfection. This is the good news—this is the gospel.

God's Plan

God is holy. Because of his holiness, there can be no sin in his presence. That presents a problem. He loves us and wants us to spend eternity with him, but we have all sinned. And so God provided the only possible solution: his Son, Jesus.

In his great love, the Creator of the universe sent his Son to die in our place. Jesus, the perfect Lamb of God, died on the cross to pay the price for our sin. All we have to do is accept his invitation for a divine exchange: our sin and shame for his garment of righteousness.

> "God showed how much he loved us by sending his one and only Son into the world so that we might have eternal life through him. This is real love—not that we loved God, but that he loved us and sent his Son as a sacrifice to take away our sins." (1 John 4:9–10 NLT)

For centuries, the Jewish priests had offered sacrificial lambs and other animals repeatedly to atone for the sins of the people. Then Jesus shed his blood on the cross so all sins—past, present, and future—could be forgiven. He was the Lamb sacrificed for us that we might live under grace (God's undeserved favor), not law. We are saved from our sins not because of anything we do or don't do, but because of what Jesus did.

> "When God our Savior revealed his kindness and love, he saved us, not because of the righteous things we had done, but because of his mercy. He washed away our sins, giving us a new birth and new life through the Holy Spirit." (Titus 3:4–5 NLT)

Only Jesus, the Lamb of God, can take away our sins (John 1:29). The gospel of Jesus Christ is not about making ourselves perfect for God—it is about receiving forgiveness for our sins by accepting Jesus as our Savior. Gospel means "good news," and this is very good news. When we humble ourselves and recognize our need for Christ, we receive all of Jesus' righteousness and the power of the Holy Spirit, molding us and making us more like our Savior (Mark 1:8).

When we recognize our sin and put our faith in Jesus as Lord and Savior, he forgives us and clothes us in his righteousness. From that point, when God looks at us, he sees not our sin, but Jesus' righteousness covering us.

> "I am overwhelmed with joy in the LORD my God! For he has dressed me with the clothing of salvation and draped me in a robe of righteousness. I am like a bridegroom dressed for his wedding or a bride with her jewels." (Isaiah 61:10 NLT)

Trust in Jesus

Read the following scripture aloud. Circle the words *believe* and *profess*.

> "If you declare with your mouth, 'Jesus is Lord,' and believe in your heart that God raised him from the dead, you will be saved. For it is with your heart that you believe and are justified, and it is with your mouth that you profess your faith and are saved. As Scripture says, 'Anyone who believes in him will never be put to shame.' For there is no difference between Jew and Gentile—the same Lord is Lord of all and richly blesses all who call on him, for, 'Everyone who calls on the name of the Lord will be saved.'" (Romans 10:9–13 NIV 2011)

Your trust belongs to the Bridegroom. Your belief in him makes you his bride. Your profession establishes your position in Christ. This was the message of John the Baptist as he passionately pointed people to Christ. This is the message of this study. This is his proposal. Don't look to yourself—or others or anything else. Look to Jesus and trust him completely.

> Isaiah 61 has been described as Jesus' job description because it paints the beautiful exchange that occurs through our faith in Christ (Luke 4:17–19). Read Isaiah 61 and list the things Jesus wants to exchange in your life. For example, he gives me freedom for my captivity (Isaiah 61:1). He gives me comfort for my mourning (Isaiah 61:2). He gives me a crown of beauty instead of ashes (Isaiah 61:3).
>
> _____
>
> _____
>
> _____
>
> Circle the exchange that is most meaningful to you in your life right now and journal why.
>
> _____
>
> _____
>
> _____

What Wardrobe Will You Choose?

Imagine two closets. The first is filled with garments of shame, despair, condemnation, pride, and hopelessness. The second closet is filled with garments from Jesus labeled forgiveness, beauty, everlasting joy, righteousness, splendor, salvation, praise, provision, comfort, peace, everlasting hope . . . and unconditional love.

Which wardrobe will you choose? The first closet is available if you want to trust in yourself and in the opinions of others. If you want to put your faith in things, or position, or popularity. The wardrobe in the second closet comes only through trusting Christ and making him Lord of your life.

Fix Your Eyes on Christ

If you choose Christ's way, will all your problems go away? No. Even Jesus had problems when he walked on earth. However, when you are clothed with the wardrobe he provides, you can weather any storm and thrive in any drought. He will give you peace through the storm. Joy in every circumstance. Strength for every task. And his unconditional love to see you through.

Some of you may need to learn more about your Bridegroom before you can make your choice. Learning about Jesus is exactly what this study is about. I have no doubt that when you see Jesus for who he really is, you will fall head over heels in love with him. His

proposal for salvation by grace is a standing invitation. You can review these thoughts by turning back to this chapter anytime as we move forward in this study.

Making a Commitment

Prepare yourself to be a bride by saying "I do" to all Jesus has done! The Bible says when we confess with our mouths and believe in our hearts that Jesus is Lord, we are saved from the penalty and power of sin. When we trust IN HIM we will never be put to shame (Romans 10:8–13). We become his bride.

For some, this may be your first time to take his hand. For others, like me, you may already be a bride but need to let go of unnecessary shame and condemnation by putting your trust back in Christ and not in your circumstances, yourself, or what others say. Let today be a day of rededication of putting your trust in Christ. Although God has forgiven you, you may need to forgive yourself. Holding on to past mistakes is a heavy garment. Forgive yourself by receiving God's forgiveness through Christ today.

Let's go to the mercy seat again in prayer and open our hearts to the Father's love. If you are ready, give him your garment of shame and take his garment of righteousness by faith. Choose forgiveness, choose freedom, choose life—choose Jesus. Please pray with me.

> *Father, thank you for sending Jesus to die in my place. I accept your proposal and take your hand by faith for a divine exchange. Your grace is so vast I cannot understand it, and so I come before you in simple trust to let go of my shame. I admit I cannot earn my salvation in my own ability. I acknowledge the power of sin is taken away only by your grace. I choose to believe you today and trust in the supernatural strength of the Holy Spirit. I choose to take my eyes off what others say about me, off myself, and off my circumstances. I choose to look only toward you. Thank you, Jesus, for taking all my shame. I lay it at your cross and take up your robe of righteousness. Thank you, Jesus, for taking all the penalty of my sins—past, present, and future. I lay them at the cross and by faith put on your garment of righteousness. I confess you are my Lord and Savior. I will run to you for help, and I can trust you because I am your bride. You paid it all for me, and I am prepared to give my life to you. AMEN!*

Key Treasure

When we recognize our sin and put our faith in Jesus as Lord and Savior, he forgives us and clothes us in his righteousness. From that point, when God looks at us, he sees not our sin, but Jesus' righteousness covering us.

DAY 5

"Trust in the LORD with all your heart and lean not on your own understanding;
in all your ways acknowledge him, and he will make your paths straight."
—*Proverbs 3:5–6*

"Where do I belong?" she asked her Bridegroom. Now that she was his bride through faith in him, what was next?

"Come and follow me," Jesus replied.

Jesus' Love Makes the Difference

During the time of Jesus' earthly ministry, women were usually considered second-class citizens. But Jesus didn't see them that way. He took every opportunity to reach out to women and empower them for a life of passion and purpose. The broken, the hurting, the poor, the prostitute, the homemaker, and the businesswoman—he loved them all. And because of his love, they could look at themselves differently.

I believe Jesus made them feel beautiful and secure—and the results were radical. Whether it was breaking an alabaster jar to anoint Jesus for burial (Matthew 26:6–13), supporting Jesus out of their own means (Luke 8:1–3), washing his feet with tender tears (Luke 7:36–50), or being the first chosen to share the news that he had risen (John 20:10–18), women became fully devoted followers of Christ because they came to realize that they mattered. They knew they belonged to someone. They held the hand of someone who had a strength beyond what they had ever experienced.

John the Baptist knew where he belonged—and where every follower of Christ belongs. Preparing the way for the Messiah, John was passionate about pointing people to Christ. He knew that in Jesus—and only in him—we can find truth, redemption, abundant life, healing for the ache in our souls, and our purpose.

"To this John replied, 'A man can receive only what is given him from heaven. You yourselves can testify that I said, "I am not the Christ but am sent ahead of him." The bride belongs to the bridegroom. The friend who attends the bridegroom waits and listens for him, and is full of joy when he hears the bridegroom's voice. That joy is mine, and it is now complete. He must become greater; I must become less.' " (John 3:27–30)

To whom does John say the bride belongs?

Yes, the bride belongs to the Bridegroom. The word *belong* comes from the Greek word echo. One of the definitions for echo is "to hold in your hand."[1] I cannot think of a better place to be than being held in the hands of Jesus. Jesus came to redeem his bride—to bring her to a place of security and significance so she could hold her head high and serve him with faith and confidence.

When Jesus preached the good news, he said simply to repent, believe, and follow (Mark 1:15–17). In our performance-driven world, it is difficult to believe the gospel can be that simple. We tend to make it more complex, but Jesus calls us to come to him just as we are and follow him.

After Jesus approached Peter and Andrew, what did he ask them to do? (v. 17)

Jesus wants us to follow him so closely that our lives intertwine with his, resting in the security of his love. What better way to live my life than having Jesus live it through me! Thank God, I can stop trying to figure it out. I love that Jesus never tells us to fix our problems or try to figure things out. He simply tells us to follow him.

I want to challenge you during this study to not simply "learn it"—but also to "live it." You belong to the Bridegroom and your life has purpose! Allow those IMPACT questions to inspire you to follow Jesus. If he prompts you with a step to take, drop those nets, take his hand, and follow him.

You may only receive one step at a time. As you complete each step, Jesus will give you the next one—in his time. Your steps form a pathway for you to accomplish your purpose. You don't have to figure the plan out—just follow. As you take each step by faith, you will find where you need to cast your nets to become a fisher of men. Like John the Baptist your purpose will lead you to point others to Christ.

Trusting Jesus Instead of Nets

Andrew, Simon, John, and James were all fishermen by profession. They fished not for sport but to make a living. Their nets represented their financial security. In those days, being a fisherman provided a comfortable income. Since James and John had hired help, they were most likely successful fishermen. Yet when they met Jesus, they let go of their nets to follow him. Not only did they leave their nets—they left family and everything familiar to them.

Sometimes to hold his hand we have to let go of something that is already in ours. Jesus is calling us to trust him with everything. Sometimes when we make the initial decision to follow him, we are reluctant to let go of our nets—the places we have looked for security—and trust only him. When we continue clinging to our nets, we cannot fully take hold of our life purpose.

Why would Jesus ask them to leave the security of their nets? What was he thinking when he asked them to leave the familiarity of their families? He didn't want them to go hungry, to be without family, or to give up success. In essence, I believe Jesus was saying, "You have been trusting your nets for security. Now I want you to trust in me. I have a greater purpose for you to fulfill."

The Bible says, "At once they left their nets and followed him" (Mark 1:18). I just love that—the "at once" factor! There was no delay.

When the Holy Spirit prompts me to take an action step, sometimes I start to reason and analyze the step he is asking me to take. Although I start with every intention of following through, delay sets in as I try to figure things out instead of simply following him. Procrastination pushes me away from my purpose. Caught up in the *what ifs*, I waffle in the waves instead of setting sail (James 1:6-8).

The Lord showed me that my need to figure everything out is my attempt to make sure I stay in control so I won't get hurt or face any negative circumstances. Staying in control is my "net." Although I am following the Holy Spirit, I also have a plan "B" of my own. Instead of resting in his plan, I worry. Can any other brides out there relate?

> Are you clinging to a net that is hindering you from accomplishing your life purpose? Describe.
>
> _____
>
> _____
>
> _____

Using your answer from the question above, fill in the blanks below and then read the completed sentence aloud. I have provided my sentence for you as an example.

Jesus said to Aliene, "Come and follow me." At once Aliene let go of trying to figure it all out and her need to control and followed Jesus to find and fulfill her purpose.

> *Jesus said to _____ (your name), "Come and follow me". At once _____ (your name) let go of _____ (your net) and sought to follow Jesus to find and fulfill her purpose.*

Those fishermen who belonged on the boats now belonged to Jesus. What was it about Jesus that captured their devotion so quickly? I believe it was the promise of something greater in exchange for the security of those nets: Jesus told them he would make them fishers of men. Jesus wanted to empower them for a life of passion and purpose far greater than they had known.

Sometimes we have to drop our nets so he can expand our ability to fill his nets. The disciples were not sure that day what their future would hold. But they knew, as we need to, that when the Lord asks us to lay something down, he has something greater in store.

The disciples would later experience a greater catch. Jesus provided in abundance for their security by supplying so many fish that their nets broke (John 21:11)! But this was not their greatest catch. Jesus allowed them to be fishers of thousands of men in those early days of the church (Acts 2:38–41). As you enter your walk with Jesus, you will discover he has great things in store for you too. He has a good plan and purpose for your life, but you can become all he designed you to be only if you are willing to trust him completely.

Learning to let go of our nets is a lifelong process. But the less we cling to them—and the more we cling to Jesus—the more we allow Jesus to do the amazing in our lives.

"Come to me and follow me," he said to her again. She let go of her agenda and took his hand and walked closely with him. She finally knew where she belonged. And as she looked back over her shoulder where once the thick shadow of shame had hovered, she saw one set of footprints. Her life was seamlessly intertwined with his— and she trusted him completely as he led her into his amazing plan for her life.

Key Treasure

Learning to let go of our nets is a lifelong process. But the less we cling to them—and the more we cling to Jesus—the more we allow Jesus to do the amazing in our lives.

DAY 6

"I remember the devotion of your youth, how as a bride you loved me
and followed me through the desert, through a land not sown." —*Jeremiah 2:2*

As she followed him, she found herself in an empty desert, and the drought caused confusion as her faith began to waver. Where are you, God? Why am I here? She could not consider why he would take her through barrenness. I thought it was beauty not barrenness for my ashes (Isaiah 61:3). Frantically she looked at her garments and was relieved to find the garment of salvation still gracing her back. If she was still his bride and he promised divine exchange, why would she find herself in this lonely desert place?

Finding Purpose in the Desert

Even after making the choice to follow Christ and trust in him, we will experience dry times. Times we don't feel his presence. Times when our prayers seem to go unanswered. But that doesn't mean he has left us. He never will! That doesn't mean we no longer belong to him. Nothing can ever separate us from his love.

It is in silence that I find myself seeking the Lord. The stillness causes my inner self to thirst for the living God. And often the silence and barrenness of my life bring me back to a place of trust and security in Christ's sufficiency. Sometimes the desert is designed to prepare us for our purpose. Often barrenness is the birthing ground for beauty as we draw closer to our Bridegroom.

Sometimes the silence comes in response to unfaithfulness to God—but not always. Even Jesus experienced a desert time here on earth. But as Mark's Gospel opens, Israel is in a dry place. Israel, God's chosen people, had run after other gods and found themselves exiled from their Promised Land. They had first been under the control of the Babylonian government. At the time Jesus was born, they were under Roman rule.

While the Israelites were under the control of the Babylonians, God sent many prophets to speak to them. Then God was silent for 400 years. *Where was their Lord? When would their Messiah come?*

Silence Broken

Then God broke the silence in a dramatic way. He sent Gabriel to Zechariah with the announcement that his barren wife Elizabeth would have a child who would prepare the way for the Lord. The pronouncement of Christ's birth to Mary and the angel's words to Joseph followed. Jesus was born, and in the years that followed, as our Lord prepared to begin his earthly ministry, John went before him in the spirit and power of Elijah to make the people ready and prepare them for Jesus, the Messiah.

The Birth of John the Baptist

John the Baptist is living proof that out of barrenness God can birth something beautiful. Read Luke 1:5–25. Step into Elizabeth's shoes and imagine her experience of going from being barren to giving birth to John the Baptist. What impressed you most about this story?

_____

_____

_____

Elizabeth was upright in the sight of the Lord and obeyed all his commandments and regulations (Luke 1:6), yet she was barren and well into her years. I wonder how many times she looked at other women having babies and blinked back the tears in her eyes. In those days, being barren was considered dishonorable. Did her shame come from comments made by other women, or was it from a feeling of failure (Luke 1:25)? I wonder if her prayers ever turned into cries to the Lord. _Where are you, God? I don't see you. I can't hear you. I am following you, Lord, with all my heart and I feel as if I have failed. Do you love me? Why are you silent to my pleas for a child?_

Silence in Your Life

What is barren in your life? What pleas have you placed before the Lord and have yet to hear from him? Where do you feel as if God is silent in your life?

_____

_____

_____

Silence does not mean God has stopped working. Even during those 400 years of silence experienced by Israel, God was at work. However, sometimes circumstances can make us _feel_ as if our hurts are hidden from God. But nothing could be further from the truth.

The truth was that God was working behind the scenes orchestrating his beautiful symphony so at just the right time his perfect plan could unfold in Elizabeth's life for his glory. Perhaps you can identify with Elizabeth. Perhaps you cannot see God working in your life even though you have committed to following him with your whole being. Take heart today knowing God loves you and is for you. He is working on your behalf even though you cannot see it right now. This is a time when you must choose to flex your faith muscle. Faith is believing in what you cannot see. Faith says I know that God has a good plan for my life even though he seems silent right now. Today I choose to believe he is working on my behalf.

God was getting ready to bring Jesus, his greatest gift, to the Israelites even after they had walked away from him to follow other gods. God will never leave you or forsake you—even if you have turned away (2 Timothy 2:13).

Allow those times of silence to lead you closer to him. Press into Jesus and find your sufficiency in him. Joy that comes from Jesus is constant because your Bridegroom is the same yesterday, today, and forever (Hebrews 13:8).

> Glance back at Mark 1:11–13. After Jesus was baptized, what did God affirm about him?
>
> _____
>
> _____
>
> _____
>
> After the Lord spoke those words of affirmation over his Son . . .
>
> Who led Jesus into the desert? _____
>
> When was he led there? _____
>
> What happened in the desert? _____

Do you feel as if you have failed because you chose to follow Christ but now find yourself in a desert or wandering in the wilderness? Are you questioning your call and wondering if you heard God correctly? Did you let go of a "net" and find yourself free-falling?

If you have chosen to follow Christ but now find yourself in a desert season, you have not failed! Remember it was the Holy Spirit who led Jesus into the desert even though God was well pleased with him. God has not deserted you. He is perhaps pulling you away to prepare you. Some lessons can be learned only by dwelling in the desert. Some kinds of wisdom can only be gleaned in a wilderness time. God is building your faith and dependence on him (James 1:2–4).

When we are in the desert and everything we thought was secure is falling apart around us, it can be frightening. During such times, the temptation to turn away from God can become strong.

Our faith must be in God's Word above all else. Jesus spoke scripture back to Satan when he was tempted in the desert (Matthew 4:4). I have heard it said the Word of God is our only offensive weapon in the armor of God (Ephesians 6:13–19). Use it! Write out scriptures on index cards and stick them in your Bible. Read them daily. When you react out of fear, doubt takes over and you are more prone to make unwise decisions.

I believe Elizabeth's barrenness operated like a dark cloud eclipsing Zechariah's belief in God's faithfulness. And so when he heard God's word for his situation, he reacted out of doubt instead of faith.

Zechariah said to the angel, "Do you expect me to believe this? I'm an old man and my wife is an old woman."

"But the angel said, 'I am Gabriel, the sentinel of God, sent especially to bring you this glad news. But because you won't believe me, you'll be unable to say a word until the day of your son's birth. Every word I've spoken to you will come true on time—God's time.'" (Luke 1:18–20 MSG)

Zechariah doubted, and Gabriel took away his ability to talk until after John was born. Perhaps the Lord was doing Zechariah a favor. Excessive doubt can sometimes make us so double-minded we are tossed about like a boat on the sea, and our faith slowly floats away (James 1:5–8). Complaining is simply verbalizing doubt in God. Our words affect those around us. Complaining spreads like a cancer to those around us, damaging their faith. Perhaps Zechariah's doubt would have caused waves in Elizabeth's faith, and the Lord knew that Mary, the mother of Jesus, would soon need Elizabeth's support. Sometimes it is better to be silent rather than speak words of doubt.

Cling to your faith by trusting and speaking God's word above all others. Even during times of silence, God is in control. His love for you never diminishes. Stay calm and steady by believing the truth that your Bridegroom is for you and will never leave you nor forsake you (Romans 8:31–32; Hebrews 13:5–6). Remember you wear the garment of salvation.

Jesus Is Our Foundation—Stay Focused on Him

Recently, I was walking in a dry desert and the barrenness had become almost unbearable. Angry with God, I could identify with Zechariah's lack of faith. I had never felt so insecure and condemned. Although I had been a Christian for many years, I had lost my joy and suffered under terrible shame, guilt, and condemnation. The burden of insecurity was so great I lost any confidence to make decisions and stood still in silent shame. Like Zechariah, although I had the truth in God's Word, I was believing other voices that had captured my attention.

In prayer, I reached out to God. Climbing into his lap like a frightened child, I clamored for answers as I prayed. *Why do I feel this way, Lord? If I am your child, why do I feel this shame? What happened to the joy and splendor in my life? Where are the peace and rest you promised me through divine exchange? Do you really expect me to believe you came to bring beauty from my ashes—look at my life!*

This is what I journaled as the Lord spoke to my heart:

My precious child, these are not the garments I am asking you to wear. Your garment of salvation, the garment of everlasting praise and joy, is still there, but you are covering it with garments formed by what others say about you, the expectation you place on yourself to be perfect and accusations from the enemy. They are smothering you, and there is no rest in your life. And so on the days when people give you a garment of praise, you wear it and feel good about yourself. But when scorn and slander come your way, you wear that garment and fall under unnecessary shame. Although I have forgiven you, you have trouble receiving this gift because you will not forgive yourself. This opens a door for the enemy to torment you with condemnation (2 Corinthians 2:10–11; Matthew 18:34; Romans 8:1).

Don't listen to the enemy, who is tempting you to believe you are not my child and I don't love you. Take off the garments formed by his lies by taking out my words of truth and speaking them. Take off the garments formed by what others say about you and what you think of yourself and put your trust in me again by believing and speaking my words about your situation.

Only Christ can heal and restore. Speak his Word. Isaiah 61 is a great passage to meditate on to move your mind from barrenness to belief. Trust in him again.

Beauty from the Silence

God heard Zechariah and Elizabeth's prayers. After years of barrenness, the birth of their son brought something beautiful. Jesus said of John, "Among those born of women there has not risen anyone greater than John the Baptist" (Matthew 11:11). Yes, John the Baptist was fearless and passionate about pointing others to trust in Christ's sufficiency. He led many Israelites back to God by leading them to Jesus.

In the wilderness, John pointed the Israelites through confession and baptism to their need for a Savior and prepared them for his presence. Allow your desert experiences to lead you to Jesus by trusting in your Bridegroom to bring something beautiful out of your barrenness.

Sometimes it is when God seems silent that we learn sufficiency in Christ alone. It's in the desert that we discover that he is the Treasure!

As she leaned on her Bridegroom in the desert, she learned that her joy stemmed from one source: Jesus. She opened her mouth to speak new words of faith. Instead of my shame I will receive a double portion, and instead of disgrace I will rejoice in my inheritance; and so I will inherit a double portion and everlasting joy will be mine (see Isaiah 61:7).

Key Treasure

Faith says, *I know that God has a good plan for my life even though he seems silent right now. Today I choose to believe he is working on my behalf.*

VIDEO SESSION NOTES

_____

_____

_____

_____

Session 2
THE PROPOSAL
Mark 1:1–20

_____

_____

_____

_____

_____

_____

_____

_____

_____

_____

_____

_____

Videos located online at www.nourishbiblestudyseries.com

Chapter 3
IN HIS PRESENCE

DAY 1

Nourish Scripture: Mark 1:21–45

PRAY.

Begin your time with God in prayer.

MEDITATE ON GOD'S WORD.

Using your Anchor of Truth Card* from last week's Nourish Notes, renew your mind on that truth. Quiet and focus your thoughts. Pray the truth. Say the truth. Meditate on God's truth.

TAKE THE *REVEAL* STEP OF THE NOURISH™ BIBLE STUDY METHOD.

Connect with Jesus by studying the Weekly Nourish Scripture and allowing the Holy Spirit to reveal truth in those verses. Prayerfully read over and reflect on the passage. Mark any phrases, verses, or words that catch your attention. Journal and learn as the Lord leads you.

---

*Anchor of Truth Cards are available at www.TreasuredMinistries.com/shop

DAY 2

Nourish Scripture: Mark 1:21–45

1 PRAY.

Begin your time with God in prayer.

2 MEDITATE ON GOD'S WORD.

Using your Anchor of Truth Card* from last week's Nourish Notes, renew your mind on that truth. Quiet and focus your thoughts. Pray the truth. Say the truth. Meditate on God's truth.

3 TAKE THE *RESPOND* STEP OF THE NOURISH™ BIBLE STUDY METHOD.

Respond to activate truth in your life. The acronym **IMPACT**™ provides questions to help you apply the truth from your weekly Nourish Scripture. **Sometimes you may not have answers for all six questions.**

IMAGE OF GOD TO TRUST? An attribute of God, Jesus, or the Holy Spirit to trust.

MESSAGE TO SHARE? A word of encouragement, truth, or prayer to share.

PROMISE TO TREASURE? A promise in the Bible to believe.

ACTION TO TAKE? A specific step God is calling you to take.

CORE IDENTITY IN CHRIST TO AFFIRM? A truth about how God sees you to affirm.

TRANSGRESSION TO CONFESS? A sin to acknowledge for help, healing, and restoration through Christ.

---

*Anchor of Truth Cards are available at www.TreasuredMinistries.com/shop

DAY 3

Nourish Scripture: Mark 1:21–45

1 PRAY.

Begin your time with God in prayer.

2 MEDITATE ON GOD'S WORD.

Using your Anchor of Truth Card* from last week's Nourish Notes, renew your mind on that truth. Quiet and focus your thoughts. Pray the truth. Say the truth. Meditate on God's truth.

3 TAKE THE *RENEW* STEP OF THE NOURISH™ BIBLE STUDY METHOD.

Like an anchor that secures its vessel, biblical meditation secures truth to transform your life. Take five minutes to *renew* your mind by focusing on one word, verse, or truth that the Holy Spirit revealed through the Bible during your week of study. Record your truth below and on your Anchor of Truth card.* Quiet your thoughts. Focus on the truth. Read the truth. Pray the truth.

My Anchor of Truth

4 UTILIZE YOUR *ANCHOR OF TRUTH* CARD AS A BOOKMARK TO CULTIVATE A DAILY PRACTICE OF BIBLICAL MEDITATION.

Place your Anchor of Truth Card* in your Bible study workbook to bookmark tomorrow's day of study. Let your Anchor of Truth bookmark remind you to pause and renew your mind on God's Word. Repeat this process daily, continuing to reflect on your Anchor of Truth to start your quiet time until the next week, when God reveals another truth to you.

*Anchor of Truth Cards are available at www.TreasuredMinistries.com/shop

DAY 4

"Arise, my darling, my beautiful one, and come with me." —*Song of Solomon 2:10*

The presence of Jesus was captivating. Many traveling rabbis came to teach in the synagogues, but this man's words carried power. Who was he? His teaching came with authority. His presence brought peace and order. His words pushed evil away, and the people were amazed. His power was paired with a compassion that moved him to heal the hurting and touch the untouchable. People followed Jesus everywhere. His teaching and touch captivated the hearts of those he would save.

Jesus is still captivating hearts today.

A Tender Invitation

"Arise, my darling, my beautiful one, and come with me" (Song of Solomon 2:10). Softly and tenderly, Jesus calls to his bride. He waits patiently. Love never demands attention. He invites us to return his embrace so he can lead us beside the still waters of his presence as the storms of life swirl to steal our peace.

Pausing from life's pressures to spend time with Jesus through prayer is a gift. We learn to trust as we learn more about the one who is trustworthy. Time with our Bridegroom is essential to the health of our souls. Knowing God, seeking him through his Word and prayer—pausing and pulling away to experience his presence is powerful.

The presence of Jesus freed the man controlled by evil spirits in the synagogue at Capernaum (Mark 1:23–26). His testimony must have been amazing to hear. I wonder how many Sabbaths he had sat in the synagogue hoping to be delivered from the demon's control. While going to the synagogue was a good thing, it was the power of Jesus' presence that set him free.

Only His Presence

Do you constantly struggle against some negative force? Anger? Worry? Depression? Insecurity? An addiction? The demon of an unforgiving spirit?

Jesus came to set us free from anything that seeks to control us. Attending church is a wonderful part of our Christian faith, but only Jesus can free us from the life-controlling issues we face. That day in Capernaum, Jesus silenced the evil and freed the man with his stern and passionate command to the demon: "Come out of him!" (Mark 1:25). Jesus is as passionate about bringing rest to your soul as he was to free this man. As you sit in his presence, he will set you free from negative forces so you can be guided by the Holy Spirit.

This summer I struggled with terrible unforgiveness. This evil force controlled my thoughts. As hard as I tried to "just forgive," those feelings of hurt simply controlled me. I knew in my mind I needed to forgive to be free from the bitterness in my soul. I tried to stop dwelling on the past, but my mind continued to wander and replay the hurt over and over again. A good friend reminded me that forgiveness is supernatural and I could not move forward until I asked Jesus to help me let go of the hurt. I took a long walk on the beach and talked to God about all the pain. Many tears fell on the sand that day. I cried out to Jesus saying, "I cannot do this on my own. Please help me!" At that moment, I felt a release in the depths of my soul. Much like the presence of Jesus had freed the man at Capernaum, the presence of Jesus, my Bridegroom, came to rescue me.

Finding Rest

Rest. Healing. Direction. Restoration. Transformation. We will never find any of these until we turn away from our busy schedules and come into the healing presence of Jesus.

Sometimes rescue is immediate—as it was for the man at Capernaum and many others in our text this week. Other times, it is a process. We must trust Jesus to transform us in his way and in his time (Philippians 1:6). When we abide in him, we bear fruit that matters (John 15:5). Jesus longs to be with his bride, and it is when we are in his presence that living water can wash over our weary souls, renew our minds, and direct our steps. The ability to lead fruitful lives comes from abiding in his presence.

> Life can overwhelm us, but peace and rest are never found in perfect circumstances—peace and rest are found in Jesus. According to Matthew 11:28, what are the results of coming to Jesus when you are overwhelmed?

_____

_____

_____

Jesus tells us that when we come to him, he will give us rest. Restoration does not come to us naturally—it is something God gives us as we spend time with Jesus. We can find temporary relief by doing relaxing things like vacationing, exercising, or watching TV—but only Jesus can give us true rest and restoration as we take his hand and abide in his presence.

Simon Peter's mother-in-law was resting in bed to relieve herself from her fever, but her complete restoration and strength to serve came from Jesus (Mark 1:29–31).

Isaiah 40:29–31 says this:

> "He gives strength to the weary and increases the power of the weak. Even youths grow tired and weary, and young men stumble and fall; but those who hope in the LORD will renew their strength. They will soar on wings like eagles; they will run and not grow weary, they will walk and not be faint."

Focusing on Jesus

I have found that beginning my prayers by remembering and focusing on Jesus and all that he is brings me into his presence. He is my mountain mover. Remembering his greatness and majesty brings up a trust from the depths of my soul as I realize I am his bride. He is my support and my peace. If I focus and depend on him, I will never be on my own.

Increase your faith as you use the first IMPACT acronym question in the Nourish Bible Study Method to define attributes of Jesus. As you reflect and record the attributes of Christ, your trust will increase in the only one who is trustworthy. In addition, the way you see your Bridegroom determines how you will relate to him. If you see him as the lover of your soul, you will consider your time with him a delight. If you see him as powerful and compassionate, you will trust in his strength as you see your problems in light of his grace. When you sit in the light of his presence, your problems will fade away with the hope that "If God is for us, who can be against us?" (Romans 8:31).

Renew your mind on the greatness of our Bridegroom during your prayer time. You might say, "Jesus, I love you because you are my healer, and you help me when I am weak. Thank you, Jesus, that I can rest in the strength of your arms."

Jesus said the greatest commandment is to love the Lord your God with all your heart, soul, and mind (Mark 12:30). This is the core of Christianity. Before we can love others, we have to fall in love with him.

A Thankful Heart

As you pray, keep an attitude of gratitude. Thank God by remembering all the good things he has done in your life. It's not that God needs our worship and praise. He knows that when life's pressures surround us, it's easy for us to become discouraged. Feeling out of control and frantic is a natural reaction to our fears. Giving thanks to the Lord for all things opens our eyes to the many blessings he surrounds us with daily.

> "Do not be anxious about anything, but in everything, by prayer and petition, with thanksgiving, present your requests to God. And the peace of God, which transcends all understanding, will guard your hearts and your minds in Christ Jesus."
>
> (Philippians 4:6–7)

Jesus touched Peter's mother-in-law and the leper when he healed them. Our Bridegroom touches our lives in many tangible ways. A good friend of mine ends her day by taking time before she falls asleep to review her day and remember how the Lord blessed it — in little and large ways. To close out our lesson for today, use the following blanks to record the ways Jesus has touched your life personally. Spend some time in his presence remembering who he is and thanking him for the ways he has personally touched your life this week.

_____

_____

_____

_____

Jesus never promises that our circumstances or the people around us will be perfect, but he does promise that when we come to him, he will give us rest. True rest is never found in people or things. True rest is found in knowing you belong to the Bridegroom. He has the authority and power to help you through any challenge you may face.

DAY 5

"Very early in the morning, while it was still dark, Jesus got up, left the house and went off to a solitary place, where he prayed." —*Mark 1:35*

I have found that while abiding sounds simple, my many to-dos and the worries of this world distract me from simple solitude with my Savior. My to-do list mentality seeps its way into my time with the Lord. My prayer list becomes a daily checklist—and Bible study a duty. In our fast-moving world, I find myself trying to keep up with a frantic pace of striving in my own strength. My frenzied pace prevents me from keeping in step with the Spirit. Ironically, it is because of my to-dos and the worries of this world that I need to spend time with Jesus every day. Just as our bodies need to breathe air, our spirits need to breathe God's presence. We need Jesus every day.

Our culture glorifies production and performance. Even my "vacations" are filled with endless lists of activity. I have bought into the lie from the enemy: if I am busy, I have value. Work, of course, is not a bad thing. Before the fall, God gave Adam and Eve a "role"—to tend the garden (Genesis 2:15). It's not that the Lord wants us to sit back and not fulfill our callings, but when we don't stop to rest in his presence through prayer, we are not relying on him. Then self-reliance can rear its ugly head!

Jesus says we can do nothing apart from him (John 15:5). Paul's words to the Galatians speak to my heart. "Are you so foolish? After beginning with the Spirit, are you now trying to attain your goal by human effort?" (Galatians 3:3).

Having a stuffed schedule does not make me more spiritual or special to God. Why am I tempted to tie my worth to my accomplishments instead of to who I am: a bride of Christ?

My responsibilities are real. It's not that I don't want to stop and enjoy what really matters— but if I stop, what will happen to all the balls I am juggling in the air?

Jesus Has Been There

Jesus knows what it is like to have many important responsibilities. He is not necessarily asking you to drop all those balls, but he does want you to come to him so he can help carry your load. He knows what it is like to have people pulling on you from all different sides. He knows what it is like to carry the weight of the world on your shoulders. He knows what it is like to be responsible for so many in your care. In this week's passage, he traveled, taught in the synagogue, drove demons from those oppressed, and healed the sick. Jesus was also responsible for training the disciples and for teaching and preaching

the Word while he was on the earth. People pressed in to meet Jesus. Sick people, broken people, and needy people wanting to find relief. Jesus knows what it feels like to be pulled in many different directions—with so many under his care, so many wanting him and needing him. Mark 1:33 records that "the whole town gathered at the door." I smiled as I read this passage, remembering that many of my quiet times in the morning are over as soon as my boys wake up and appear at my door, in need of their mama for something!

Jesus' Retreat

When he healed the leper, Jesus requested that the man keep the news of his healing quiet. The man ignored Jesus' request and bubbled over telling others about how Jesus had healed him. Can we blame him? Lepers were cast out of their community and even had to leave their families to stop the spread of the disease. This outcast could now return to the people he knew and loved. Once the news spread, Jesus tried to keep a low profile by staying outside of towns in "lonely places," and "yet the people still came to him from everywhere" (Mark 1:45).

Not only did Jesus live with people constantly coming to him for help, but the weight to save the world was on his shoulders. All the while he ministered, he knew a day was coming that would bring the cross. He had a right to worry and a right to want to run away—but Jesus chose to retreat into the presence of God. He never neglected time with his Father despite the needs swirling around him.

Mark 1:35 describes Jesus' retreat. Read the verse and cite as many details as you can.

_____

_____

_____

Your Retreat

Just as Jesus retreated to spend time in prayer, he wants you to retreat and spend time with him. Describe one way you will apply what you learned from Jesus' retreat to your life.

_____

_____

_____

The Lord is not asking you to neglect those in your care, but to give the best care to those you love you need to spend time in God's presence. Jesus never neglected his responsibilities, but he let go of them long enough to pray. Our time with God equips us to handle the mountains and valleys in our path.

Jesus was a servant to all but did not hesitate to take time to pull away. Simon Peter and his companions were looking for Jesus. When they finally found him, they exclaimed, "Everyone is looking for you!" (Mark 1:37). You may be thinking, *How can I take time out when so many people need me? How can I have any time of solitude in prayer when I have a million things to do today?* The reality is that because we have so much on our plates, we need the presence of Jesus in our lives.

Although people pressed Jesus from every side with real needs, guilt never grabbed him for taking time out to pray and rest in God's presence. The guilt we feel when we say "no" so we can spend time with our Bridegroom is not from God. Don't ever feel guilty for pulling away to be with Jesus. It is in his presence that we find the power and provision to carry on. American evangelist, pastor, and educator R. A. Torrey said, "We are too busy to pray, and so we are too busy to have power. We have a great deal of activity, but we accomplish little; many services but few conversions; much machinery but few results."[1]

Deliberate Steps

Solitude—quiet time with the Lord—does not just happen. We have to take practical and deliberate steps to carve out time to spend with him. Our Bridegroom is always there for us, but he will never force us to be with him. He invites us, rather than demanding our presence, because love is not about control, demand, or condemnation. Our Bridegroom has given us free choice because he loves us.

Jesus found a time of solitude on this occasion by getting up early to spend time with the Father in prayer. Finding a place and time free from distractions is a key to spending time with Jesus. You may be thinking, *OK, but solitude does not exist in my house.* Perhaps, like Jesus, you should get up early before your household awakes. This has worked for me. Certainly, the Lord's presence is with me throughout the day, and he invites me to pray to him at all times. However, I look forward to my date with my Bridegroom those few moments in the morning. Using those early morning hours is the best way for me to find solitude. It also helps set the tone for the remainder of the day and turns my thoughts toward him. As I come to Jesus to be filled with living water in the morning, I find that during the day I am less likely to look elsewhere to find fulfillment.

Firstfruits

Jesus gave the Lord the "firstfruits" of his day. In the wilderness, the Lord asked the Israelites to give him the firstfruits of their crops (Deuteronomy 26:10). When Israel gave their firstfruits to the Lord, they were essentially saying, *Everything we have belongs to the Lord. Every good and perfect gift comes from the Lord. We trust in God's provision to provide the rest of our crops.*

In today's world, time is a much more precious commodity than crops. Spending time with the Lord in the morning is like giving him the firstfruits of your day. When you give the Lord the firstfruits of your time, you are essentially trusting him with the rest of your day. Just as the Israelites' crops were multiplied when they gave the Lord their firstfruits, watch and see how the Lord will multiply your time during the day if you give those first minutes to him. Getting up early to allow for extra minutes to pray is well worth the sacrifice. Make that appointment with the Lord. Meeting Jesus in the early morning hours will bring beauty and peace throughout your day.

Corrie ten Boom belonged to her Bridegroom and made setting aside time in his presence a priority. Corrie was part of a family that allowed their home to be a hiding place for Jews in Holland during World War II. Her family was eventually caught by the Nazi police and taken to concentration camps. Corrie was the only surviving member of her family and realized that her life was a gift from God. At age 53, she embarked on a worldwide ministry testifying of God's love and proclaiming victory in Jesus to 60 countries over a span of 33 years. Corrie was a busy bride of Christ, but she never forgot the importance of making time to spend in the presence of the Lord. She said, "Don't pray when you feel like it. Have an appointment with the Lord and keep it. A man is powerful on his knees."[2]

God does not condemn you for not coming into his presence, but he is waiting. He invites you to spend time with him not just in those early hours of the morning but throughout the day. He wants to awaken your soul so you may sing. Getting to know your Bridegroom on a deeper level does not come by following a formula but simply flows from his presence.

Key Treasure

Getting to know your Bridegroom on a deeper level does not come by following a formula but simply flows from his presence.

DAY 6

"Do not conform any longer to the pattern of this world, but be transformed
by the renewing of your mind. Then you will be able to test and approve what
God's will is—his good, pleasing and perfect will." —*Romans 12:2*

Andy Stanley, pastor of North Point Community Church, understands the importance of focus. In his book *Next Generation Leader*, Andy notes that being busy does not necessarily mean being productive. Productive leaders are those who prioritize and plan their day focusing on God's unique direction for their lives. When we fill our days with duties that are not designed for us, we can become distracted and frustrated but not fruitful. We cannot do it all, and Jesus does not expect us to do it all![3]

Jesus called the weary to come to him and take his yoke or direction for their lives (Matthew 11:28–29). God has created each of us to be unique with different gifts and abilities for a yoke that is our own. Picking up someone else's yoke will seem heavy and difficult—essentially a waste of time. When your days are focused on God's priorities for your life, you will be able to do less but accomplish more.[4]

Spending time with the Lord gives us direction for our day and makes us more productive. To find our unique direction for our lives and for each day, we must stop and pray. Your Bridegroom will reveal to you where you belong. When your days are ordered in his plans for your life, you have the freedom to say "no" to distractions that can leave you overwhelmed and drawn away from your true course in life.

Finding Direction

After Jesus came out of his solitary time, he announced, "Let us go somewhere else—to the nearby villages—so I can preach there also. That is why I have come" (Mark 1:38). His vision of bringing the gospel remained the same, but his direction had changed. Spending time in prayer can result in learning the next step. Isaiah 50:4 prophesies this about Jesus: "The Sovereign LORD has given me an instructed tongue, to know the word that sustains the weary. He wakens me morning by morning, wakens my ear to listen like one being taught."

Your life's vision or calling may remain the same, but often the Lord wants to change your direction. Daily time with him is vital to keeping in step with the Spirit. When we find the time to fix our eyes on Jesus, he will keep us on his perfect course for our lives. The Bible tells us it is only after we renew our minds that we can "test and approve what God's will is—his good, pleasing and perfect will" (Romans 12:2). Keeping in step with the Spirit can save us from striving and taking extra steps that are not part of God's plan for our lives. When the Lord brings clear focus into our day, our priorities come into place with his perfect will, and we can let go of any responsibilities he is not asking us to bear (Matthew 11:28–29).

Simplicity and Focus

It was during a mission trip to Ecuador that Charlie White had a revelation about the importance of keeping our eyes on Jesus so that we may find his purpose in our lives. Days after he returned from his trip, his life tragically ended in a skateboarding accident.

I have included an excerpt from his last blog—just days before his death. We'll close our chapter this week with his words of wisdom. Let them settle in your soul and awaken your heart to find his purpose for your life.

He writes in his blog:

The trip to Ecuador was a wonderful revival for my soul and my mind. Away from all of our worldly distractions like phones, email, work, and chores at home I was able to focus on God and people. I saw beauty in people that I haven't seen before. When we get rid of distractions and work together for God and that's all you have to think about awesome things happen. It was a time for building relationships with God, the people of Ecuador, and our team. I can't say that Holly and I have ever experienced a week like this. It was a revival for our relationship as well. I saw so much new beauty in my wife. She showed God given strength, compassion for others, and an all trusting faith. She is my superhero.

I know that I am not there and I know that things are different here in our country but honestly I can see parts of my everyday life that are now suddenly filled with a supernatural beauty that didn't exist before Ecuador. Before the trip I was always on a mission to complete the task at hand and get to the next task. Now I see my tasks as being only part of the mission. The tasks are methods used by God to put us where He needs us so that we can be a part of something so much bigger and if we are only open to it we can experience some great moments. It's not about the work, it's about His work. Don't get me wrong I have not become lazy, I still work hard and do all I can to get the job done but I am more likely to pay attention to the people that have been placed around me because there is a reason that we have all been brought together in a particular moment in time even if I never know what it is. I want to be sure that I keep my eyes on Him and not miss His purpose even in the smallest things.[5]

Living with this eternal perspective will change the way you live. Living for his glory will alter your priorities. Pursuing your calling creates a passion and urgency because our time here is so short. And as you focus on watching for Jesus, your heart will be tied not to the things of this world but to your Bridegroom. Eyes fixed on heaven will bring hope as you battle through this fallen world.

The temptation to get involved in many "good things" can distract us from our calling. As we become sensitive to his leading, simplicity and focus come into our day. Our priorities fall into place, and we learn we can stop and take time for the meaningful relationships in our lives. Seek the Lord for simplicity and focus. Ask him to show you his will for your life. Know that adding anything else, however good it may be, to our plate can rob our joy and rob others of opportunities meant for them.

Jesus knows how much we can handle. Since our worth is not tied to what we do, we can rest in his sufficiency for our callings. As we come to him daily, he will lead us step by step.

Come Away with Jesus

"Arise, my darling, my beautiful one, and come with me" (Song of Solomon 2:10). Your Bridegroom invites you to come and know him in a deeper, more intimate way.

The Bible tells us that Jesus went to a solitary place to pray. Jesus retreated. Sometimes a change of scenery can be a good thing. Getting away to another location for a short time can do wonders. Pulling away from our normal scenery to spend time with the Lord can bring things into perspective.

Plan times of Sabbath to play and rest. You have your Creator's permission to do so. Make plans for a mini retreat—even if it is spending time at a local park on a Sunday afternoon. Pulling away each morning to come into the presence of Jesus through prayer is priceless—even if it's for ten minutes. Learn how healing and refreshing it can be.

Enjoy the splendor of being captivated by your Bridegroom.

VIDEO SESSION NOTES

Session 3
HIS PRESENCE
Mark 1:21-45

Videos located online at www.nourishbiblestudyseries.com

Chapter 4
FREEDOM

DAY 1

Nourish Scripture: Mark 2:1–3:35

① PRAY.

Begin your time with God in prayer.

② MEDITATE ON GOD'S WORD.

Using your Anchor of Truth Card* from last week's Nourish Notes, renew your mind on that truth. Quiet and focus your thoughts. Pray the truth. Say the truth. Meditate on God's truth.

③ TAKE THE *REVEAL* STEP OF THE NOURISH™ BIBLE STUDY METHOD.

Connect with Jesus by studying the Weekly Nourish Scripture and allowing the Holy Spirit to reveal truth in those verses. Prayerfully read over and reflect on the passage. Mark any phrases, verses, or words that catch your attention. Journal and learn as the Lord leads you.

---

*Anchor of Truth Cards are available at www.TreasuredMinistries.com/shop

DAY 2

Nourish Scripture: Mark 2:1–3:35

1 PRAY.
Begin your time with God in prayer.

2 MEDITATE ON GOD'S WORD.
Using your Anchor of Truth Card* from last week's Nourish Notes, renew your mind on that truth. Quiet and focus your thoughts. Pray the truth. Say the truth. Meditate on God's truth.

3 TAKE THE *RESPOND* STEP OF THE NOURISH™ BIBLE STUDY METHOD.
Respond to activate truth in your life. The acronym **IMPACT**™ provides questions to help you apply the truth from your weekly Nourish Scripture. **Sometimes you may not have answers for all six questions.**

IMAGE OF GOD TO TRUST? An attribute of God, Jesus, or the Holy Spirit to trust.

MESSAGE TO SHARE? A word of encouragement, truth, or prayer to share.

PROMISE TO TREASURE? A promise in the Bible to believe.

ACTION TO TAKE? A specific step God is calling you to take.

CORE IDENTITY IN CHRIST TO AFFIRM? A truth about how God sees you to affirm.

TRANSGRESSION TO CONFESS? A sin to acknowledge for help, healing, and restoration through Christ.

*Anchor of Truth Cards are available at www.TreasuredMinistries.com/shop

DAY 3

Nourish Scripture: Mark 2:1–3:35

 PRAY.

Begin your time with God in prayer.

MEDITATE ON GOD'S WORD.

Using your Anchor of Truth Card* from last week's Nourish Notes, renew your mind on that truth. Quiet and focus your thoughts. Pray the truth. Say the truth. Meditate on God's truth.

TAKE THE *RENEW* STEP OF THE NOURISH™ BIBLE STUDY METHOD.

Like an anchor that secures its vessel, biblical meditation secures truth to transform your life. Take five minutes to *renew* your mind by focusing on one word, verse, or truth that the Holy Spirit revealed through the Bible during your week of study. Record your truth below and on your Anchor of Truth card.* Quiet your thoughts. Focus on the truth. Read the truth. Pray the truth.

My Anchor of Truth

UTILIZE YOUR *ANCHOR OF TRUTH* CARD AS A BOOKMARK TO CULTIVATE A DAILY PRACTICE OF BIBLICAL MEDITATION.

Place your Anchor of Truth Card* in your Bible study workbook to bookmark tomorrow's day of study. Let your Anchor of Truth bookmark remind you to pause and renew your mind on God's Word. Repeat this process daily, continuing to reflect on your Anchor of Truth to start your quiet time until the next week, when God reveals another truth to you.

*Anchor of Truth Cards are available at www.TreasuredMinistries.com/shop

DAY 4

"Then you will know the truth, and the truth will set you free." —*John 8:32*

Jesus invited his bride to place her confidence in him and rest from her self-efforts, allowing the Holy Spirit to transform her heart from within. He brought her new wineskins to carry the new wine of the new covenant.

However, she clutched tightly to her old wineskins, afraid of change. *I must pour this new wine into my old wineskins,* she thought. *I will depend on Jesus, yes ... and on myself.* Her mix of self-efforts and faith in Jesus gave her a false sense of security. She thought she could control her world ... but she couldn't. Eventually her old wineskins burst, and her new wine spilled out.

Her life had not been easy. She had been wounded long before, but she had determined to survive—alone. *I must be strong to protect myself from pain,* she vowed, and that vow became her religion. She was so busy trying to be strong and shielding herself from grief that she didn't give to Jesus what he truly desired: her pain. Her burdens. Her weakness. Her needs.

What he truly wanted was a relationship with her.

> *My bride,*
>
> *Before you were born ... even before I created the world ... I loved you (Ephesians 1:4). Loving you was not something I felt I had to do out of obligation. No, it was my heart's desire to love you, and loving you brought me great joy (Ephesians 1:5) . In fact, I loved you so much that I gave my Son so you could be completely free to love me (Ephesians 1:6–8). Sin cannot and will never separate us. Nothing you have done or will ever do could take away my love for you ... therefore, you and I can have a relationship with no barriers (Ephesians 3:12). No pretending. Nothing between you and me. You cannot lose me. Not even death can separate us (Romans 8:38).*
>
> *Grace is a gift I give in abundance—it is the essence of who I am. Because authentic love never involves control, I will never force you to love me back. I am always here. All you have to do is come to me and receive my love (Matthew 6:33). But I will never force it on you ... because I love you.*

Jesus invited her to let go of her religion based on self-reliance and trust him in a relationship based on walking by faith. He reminded her not to deny herself his transforming power by trying to put the wine of the new covenant into old-covenant wineskins. "No one pours new wine into old wineskins. If he does, the wine will burst the skins, and both the wine and the wineskins will be ruined. No, he pours new wine into new wineskins" (Mark 2:22).

The old wineskins represent our efforts to be good enough to win God's favor. To work things out on our own. To earn our way by keeping the law. But the new wineskins represent the grace brought to us by Jesus.

True freedom and confidence to become the woman God created you to be are released through real love—God's *agape* unconditional love. God's perfect love casts out fear and invites us to walk by faith. God's love changes us and compels us to reach out to others with his love. She who is brave is free to live for him.

Religion is based on working for rewards. Working to make ourselves worthy. We can make a religion about anything: family, life, work. Religion turns our hearts to stone because it sets us up to feel superior to others.

Relationship is not about following rules; it's about a relationship with God the Father. He already loves us, and nothing we do can add to his love. None of us can live up to the standards set by the Law, but Jesus brought us a new way. Depending on him instead of ourselves. Counting on his grace and not our perfection.

Legacy of Legalism

Pharisees were like lawyers. They had great knowledge of the Scriptures, and the people looked to the Pharisees to interpret the laws. And the Pharisees did—but in doing so they turned God's law into a complex code by adding many other so-called laws. In their interpretation of the Sabbath, they lost the heart of the Law.

> Read Mark 2:23–3:6. How had the Pharisees lost the heart of the Sabbath law? How did their religion get in the way of the rest that comes from a relationship with Christ?

Sabbath law had been designed by God to encourage life and rest. Healing and restoration. Preserving life and thanking God for all he had done. God had designed Sabbath as a blessing for man. Sabbath laws, like all God's laws, were made *for us* (Mark 2:27).

The Pharisees tried to turn something God meant to bless people into a bondage. They added their own controlling rules to make sure the people did not break the Sabbath. Then, instead of being able to enjoy the day of rest as the Lord intended, the people had to work to keep the Pharisees' rules for the Sabbath.

In their efforts to enforce God's law, the Pharisees had made even more rules. They had turned ten commandments into hundreds of rigid rules that no one could follow. Their legalism heaped a load onto the shoulders of the people that no one could bear (Matthew 23:4).

The myriad of added rules confused the people, resulting in a sense of hopelessness. Because the old covenant causes us to try in our own strength to do what only God can do, the result is condemnation. When our hope is based on our own efforts to keep the Law perfectly, we find ourselves in a prison of striving to perform, to achieve—and the only possible end result is defeat.

The truth is, we no longer need to rely on our ability, or religious achievement, or anything else except him. He invites us to depend on him completely as we learn to walk by faith.

Jesus Brought New-Covenant Wineskins of Grace and Freedom

However godly they looked on the outside, the Pharisees and their religion did not impress Jesus. According to Mark 2:1–12, what impressed Jesus?

_____

_____

_____

Read Hebrews 4:1–12. What is true rest and how do we enter it?

_____

_____

_____

_____

Jesus is the Lord of Sabbath—because he is life. He is the true rest (Hebrews 4:1–10). Our salvation is not about what we can do for God. Our salvation is about what Jesus has done for us. Jesus is all about complete restoration (Mark 3:5).

There was Jesus, the true rest, right in front of the Pharisees, and they completely missed him, blinded by all the rules and religion they had created and by the coldness of their own hearts.

When, in the second chapter of Mark, the men lowered their paralytic friend through the ceiling to Jesus so the man could be healed, Jesus was impressed with their persistent faith—they proved they would do whatever it took to get their paralyzed friend to Jesus.

Walking by faith does not mean a lack of action or responsibility on our end. The men took action because of their faith in Jesus. Faith and action always walk hand in hand.

God uses his Word to impact our lives by changing our core beliefs about who he is, how he sees us, who we are in him, and what we have with our spiritual inheritance. Each day, all of us act by faith in something or someone. What we believe drives our actions and determines our steps. Beliefs always affect behavior.

As the Holy Spirit prompts us and we respond, we find ourselves moving away from self-sufficiency toward complete dependence on God. This movement toward him not only impacts our lives but also the lives around us. We take hold of God's purpose for our lives by being led by the Holy Spirit to become all he has created us to be. "I will put my Spirit in you and move you to follow my decrees." (Ezekiel 36:27). This is not a call to legalism or fixed formulas but an invitation to follow Jesus so that the greatest story—the gospel of Jesus Christ—can be told.

The men with the paralyzed friend sought Jesus across all boundaries because they believed their friend's healing depended on the Lord. They knew self-effort was pointless—they couldn't do anything about their friend's paralysis on their own. With a word, Jesus healed the man from his frozen state. With the authority only he had, he announced that the man's sins were forgiven. Jesus declared that the "Son of Man has authority on earth to forgive sins" (Mark 2:10).

When Jesus offered us new wineskins, he offered a way of life that didn't depend on keeping the Law or achieving perfection—it depended on faith in Jesus.

Unlike the friends of the paralytic man, who knew their hope was in Jesus and not themselves, the Pharisees continued to live in pride and self-righteousness. The joy and freedom from the new-covenant wine was right before their eyes, yet they missed the blessing. They refused to let go of their old wine. Luke's Gospel puts it this way: "No one after drinking old wine wants the new, for he says, 'The old is better'" (Luke 5:39).

The religious leaders didn't like the change Jesus brought. Change, even when it is positive, can be scary because we are letting go of what we can see for what we cannot understand. But that is just what walking by faith and not by sight means, and this is the life we were created and redeemed to live.

When faced with a battle, we can be tempted to go back to the legalism and self-reliance found in our old wineskins. We try to take back the reins of life, fighting our way through obstacles on our own. During past battles, we learned how to use those old coping mechanisms for survival—mechanisms like manipulation, control, self-reliance, seeking power from people, people pleasing, performance, anger, and unforgiveness.

But things have changed—now we belong to Jesus, the shepherd and overseer of our souls. He invites us to receive his power by standing in *his* mighty strength as we walk by faith (1 Peter 2:18–25).

This truth is at the heart of the Nourish Bible Study Method: connecting to Jesus and walking by faith in his words. One small step at a time!

Legalism tries to regulate behavior through determination and willpower. Self-reliance. Control. But when we place our faith instead in Jesus and rely on him, we are transformed through the power of the Holy Spirit. Only Jesus can change our hearts, setting us free to do what legalism can never accomplish for us: follow Jesus in simple obedience.

Satan Is a Defeated Foe

Who accuses you and tries to make you feel insecure in your faith? Revelation 12:10 tells us Satan can and does accuse us day and night. His tormenting tools include fear, shame, and condemnation. When you feel these emotions, remember that they are not coming from God. When you as a believer do not feel worthy to call yourself a child of God, you are believing the lies of Satan. But—in our Nourish Scripture this week, Jesus affirmed his power over the enemy (Mark 3:27). And we can claim and receive that power.

If you are living in legalism, Satan can wreak havoc in your life. Since you cannot keep the Law—or even self-imposed standards, for that matter—perfectly, Satan will accuse you of failure. But your righteousness does not depend on your own perfection. It rests on what Jesus has done for you.

Renewing our minds to our new-covenant position in Christ is never a one-and-done exercise—it's a lifelong journey.

Affirm Your Position in Christ

Christians have always tended to drift too easily into legalism and self-effort.

> Read Galatians 3:1–3. What are some ways we can tend to depend on our self-effort (old wineskins) instead of relying on the power of the Holy Spirit (new wineskins) to walk out our faith in Christ? How can we keep on the right track of walking by faith?
>
> _____
>
> _____
>
> _____
>
> _____

Early Christians in Galatia experienced struggles with this issue, which is why Paul wrote a beautiful letter to them to set things straight. Paul also wrote another letter to minister to the church in Ephesus. He began by reminding those believers of key beliefs about God and their inheritance in Christ. I am certain that, ten years earlier, when Paul founded and discipled this church for two years, he taught these same fundamental truths. **Paul started with belief, not behavior.** Renewing our minds is where we must start too. Renewing our minds is a lifelong process that brings transformation because our faith and action always walk hand in hand. Let's close today by remembering our spiritual blessings in Christ found in the book of Galatians.

You are free to receive all these blessings. Simply do so by faith.

IN CHRIST ...

I am rescued from this present evil age according to God's will (Galatians 1:4).

I am a servant of Christ, no longer trying to win the approval of people (v. 10).

I am set apart from birth and called by grace (v. 15).

I am completely justified by faith in Christ (2:16).

I am dead to the Law, and I now live for God (v. 19).

*I am crucified with Christ. I no longer live, but Christ lives in me.
The life I live in the body, I live by faith in the Son of God (v. 20).*

I am blessed as a child of Abraham (3:6–7).

*I am redeemed from the curse of the Law so that by faith I receive the promise
of the Spirit (vv. 13–14).*

*I am God's child and have full rights as his daughter (4:3–5).
I have received his Spirit in my heart (v. 6).*

I am an heir to God's glorious inheritance (v. 7).

*I am free to walk in the Spirit, be led by the Spirit, keep in step with the Spirit,
and sow in the Spirit. I have the fruit of the Spirit (5:22–23, 25).*

I belong to Christ (v. 24).

I am a new creation (6:15).

I am free to live by the Spirit and love others (5:6). AMEN!

4. FREEDOM:
DAY 5

DAY 5

"It is better to take refuge in the LORD than to trust in man." —*Psalm 118:8*

Although she was known as "the small woman," Gladys Aylward was anything but small in her faith and in the eyes of her Bridegroom. As a young woman in London in the early 1900s, she heard a message preached about dedicating your life to Jesus. Feeling the tug of God on her heart, she surrendered to her Bridegroom, and he called her to be a missionary in China. Although every missionary society turned her down, their rejection did not stop Gladys from following Jesus and fulfilling his role for her. Obedient to Jesus her Lord, she set out for China completely dependent on her Bridegroom to provide for her and direct her steps. After traveling through war zones in Russia and central Asia, Gladys made it to China. The Lord opened many doors for her to spread the gospel of Jesus Christ there, even in seemingly impossible situations. She won many hearts to Christ. She cared for hundreds of orphans and ministered to many women. She was known for being fearless. "One time, she went into a bloody prison riot all alone and stopped it cold, using nothing but her authority in Jesus."[1]

One of her roles in China involved serving the Chinese government in an official capacity as a foot inspector. It was tradition in that country to bind the feet of little girls so their feet would stay small. With their feet wrapped tightly for their entire lives, women were not able to run or walk freely but instead wobbled slowly. A new law had been passed forbidding such footbinding. As she went from house to house, not only was Gladys able to free the women's feet, which had been bound for years, but she was also able to share Jesus and set their hearts free with the gospel message.

Gladys knew she belonged to the Bridegroom, and she chose to honor his authority and follow him in whatever he asked, even when people said otherwise. Rejection by man did not change her direction. Surrendered to Jesus, she had the confidence to obey him. She knew she had Jesus' authority, and she found her freedom in following him.

An Important Choice for Every Bride

Every day, every minute, we have an important choice to make: What words will shape our lives?

> By faith we understand that the **worlds [during the successive ages] were framed (fashioned, put in order, and equipped for their intended purpose) by the word of God**, so that what we see was not made out of things which are visible. (Hebrews 11:3 AMPC, *emphasis mine*)

By faith, I understand that God framed the world with his words.

Which words do I allow to frame my life? To give order to my steps? To equip me for my intended purpose?

All words have the ability to shape and impact my life, but God's Word is the only source of truth. Truth to set me free. Truth to guide my steps. Truth to shape my authentic identity. Truth to guide me to my God-given purpose.

Women hear words all day long that don't reflect the truth. It's a moment-by-moment choice that will frame your world. Whom will you allow to write your story? Take the pen and place it in God's hand by surrendering to his words so he can shape your soul.

True freedom is stepping into your authentic, God-given identity and becoming the woman God created you to be despite words around you that might suggest otherwise.

The Freedom to Become You

True freedom is found in knowing you belong to Jesus and allowing him to be the Lord of your life. Freedom is precious—it was bought with the blood of your Bridegroom. Although Jesus has purchased your freedom, you will need to stand firm so that you don't surrender to another yoke. "It is for freedom that Christ has set us free. Stand firm, then, and do not let yourselves be burdened again by a yoke of slavery" (Galatians 5:1).

In Day 4 we discussed the yoke of depending on ourselves to fill that void when we are not depending fully on Jesus. Another yoke we can link ourselves to is people.

Don't get me wrong. We are called to be in community with one another. *But people are not here to give us life—they are here for us to love.* If we look to them for the kind of happiness, peace, and joy only God can give, we place a burden on them that they simply cannot bear. Placing our unrealistic demands on them will ultimately lead to bitterness and unforgiveness. Why? Because people are imperfect and cannot give us what only God can give. Indeed, this points us to a great reality: We cannot love others unconditionally until we see God as our ultimate source for life. We cannot give out what we don't have. God is love, and as we look to him, we can receive his love and give it out to others.

Jesus must be the final authority in our lives. Only Jesus can bring us into our authentic selves. Only Jesus can give us our purpose.

> What do these verses teach us about the dangers of giving man more authority than God in our lives?
>
> Jeremiah 17:5–8 _____

Galatians 1:10 _____

Proverbs 29:25 _____

Jesus wants you to follow him. If instead you try to live up to another person's standards, that's a type of slavery. Living according to another person's standards means you are living a lie. Plus, you're surrendering to an impossible master. When you follow Jesus instead of striving to be someone you are not in order to please other people, you are free. You are never truly free when you turn the keys of your happiness over to another person, because only the Lord can fill your emotional needs. No person can provide another person's happiness or acceptance. Until we seek to please Jesus above all others, we are never truly free.

God Has a Special and Unique Role for You

In our Nourish Scripture this week, Jesus calls the twelve disciples. When Jesus sent his disciples out, he gave them the roles of preaching and, with his authority, driving away evil (Mark 3:15). From tax collector to fisherman to political Zealot, these men were all different yet ordinary. Ordinary but called to extraordinary works when they accepted their authority from Christ to do what God had called them to do.

Just like Gladys and the disciples, you too have a unique role Jesus designed you to fill in this life to bring him glory, a role as unique as your fingerprint. God doesn't reserve special roles only for people in ministry or famous leaders. You—and every follower of Christ—have an important role to play. You are a royal priesthood before the Lord. You are a masterpiece created and fashioned for a role God has for you (Ephesians 2:8–10).

Jesus Stood Firm and Fulfilled His Role on Earth

Of all the roles given to mankind since time began, Jesus had the most important role to play. Without him, there would be no freedom and no new wineskins. Jesus didn't allow the Pharisees' accusations to control him—or to rile him. With every answer, he remained focused on his calling and sought to please God.

This week in our Nourish Scripture, we saw where he faced criticism and accusations with the truth of the Scriptures. He focused on pleasing God, not people. He healed multitudes and brought them his life-changing words. By doing so, he brought us new-covenant wine that would change the lives of every person throughout history, everyone living today, and everyone yet to be born.

The religious leaders weren't the only ones who tried to control Jesus and stop his ministry. His family also sought to "take charge of him."

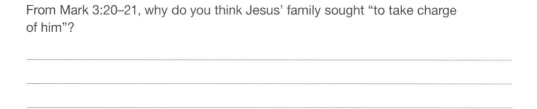

From Mark 3:20–21, why do you think Jesus' family sought "to take charge of him"?

_____

_____

_____

The Bible says they believed Jesus was "out of his mind." Perhaps his family had another motive for trying to stop him: love and protection. Perhaps they feared that if they didn't stop him, the Pharisees would kill him. Or could his brothers have been jealous, seeing this one they had grown up with gain such popularity?

Whatever the reason, knowing that our Lord himself experienced lack of support from his earthly family might comfort those of you whose families don't support your choice to follow the Lord. You're in great company. Before his resurrection, Jesus' brothers thought his calling was not genuine and tried to stop his ministry. But Jesus kept his focus on what his Father was calling him to do.

As the Lord opens impossible doors, allowing you to carry out your calling, don't be surprised if well-meaning loved ones try to stop you. When you know God has given you something to do, don't let others discourage or stop you. Don't depend on their encouragement. Depend totally on Jesus.

Today the enemy wants to stop you from being the person God has called you to be and accomplishing what God has called you to do. He would like nothing more than for you to hide your gift and not share it with others (Matthew 5:16). Every attack on your God-given identity can ultimately be traced back to the enemy of your soul (Ephesians 6:12). But always remember—greater is Jesus than the one who is in the world (1 John 4:4). So anchor your heart in your authentic identity and stand firm (Ephesians 6:11).

Christ lives through you as you abide in him and obey his commands. If you trust in Christ's strength, the enemy cannot prevent you from sharing Christ's love. Your heart for his glory.

Keep ... On ... Moving

You cannot control what others say, but you *can* control your response. You can blame no one else for the way you respond—it's *your* responsibility. Don't retaliate. Instead, forgive, and detach yourself from the harsh words by releasing them. Then determine to keep moving forward by anchoring your heart to the true source of your authentic identity—God's Word.

The things others say about us can create a storm in our lives, but Jesus will still that storm if we keep our eyes on him. You've decided to follow Jesus. You were redeemed to bear fruit. No turning back!

What is your God-given purpose? When you seek God's plan by approaching him through the Bible, the Holy Spirit will reveal God's words—his plan for you—to your heart. Whatever he reveals to you about your purpose, it will be something that brings value to this world and glorifies God. God is the author of your story. He is the only one who can write those words on your heart.

You are a treasure. God created you to shine by reflecting his glory as you turn your heart to his.

The words God whispers to your heart are holy, for they are his. Guard them. They are meant to guide your personal story so that the greatest story—the gospel of Jesus Christ—can be told by your life.

Don't ever trample on the holy ground of your God-given purpose by giving more weight to the words of other people than to God's. Stay close to God by meditating on the Bible so that his words are the loudest, so that they drown out words from others—and even from yourself—that would contradict God's Word or distract you from your God-given purpose. His words are a sacred trust. They are the framework for the holy ground where seeds of the gospel may be planted for others to see Christ. Don't argue with others or defend yourself. The great I AM is calling you, dear friend, and that is enough.

Whether discouragement came from protective friends and family or the Pharisees, Jesus stayed true to God's purpose. He surrendered to the will of the Father and stayed firm in his commitment. Even when he faced the cross, he obeyed the Father. Thus he fulfilled God's plan for himself by bringing us forgiveness, joy, and healing.

Stand firm in your freedom so that you, like Jesus, can be free to follow the lead of the Holy Spirit in your life. Jesus never allowed fear of man to control his decisions and his direction in life. Neither should you.

Key Treasure

Stand firm in your freedom so you can be free to follow the lead of the Holy Spirit in your life. Jesus never allowed fear of man to control his decisions and his direction in life. Neither should you.

DAY 6

"Blessed are the pure in heart, for they will see God." —*Matthew 5:8*

While many flocked to Jesus to find freedom from sickness and sin, the Pharisees viewed this so-called Savior with a skeptical eye. *Who does he think he is, saying he can forgive sins?* Jesus was encouraging the people to shift from depending on a religious system to trusting a Savior, and that didn't sit well with the Pharisees. You would think that with all the miracles taking place around them, they would be willing to consider that he might be who he said he was, that he might be able to free them from the Law. But they didn't want to be freed from the Law. Bound up in legalism, they missed Jesus.

Why Did They Miss the Truth?

What insight does Jesus give us in Mark 2:8, Mark 3:5, and Matthew 5:8 about why the religious leaders were unaware of the greatness that stood before them?

_____

_____

_____

_____

Jesus said, "Blessed are the pure in heart, for they will see God" (Matthew 5:8). When the religious leaders of Israel stood in the presence of Jesus, right there before their eyes stood their Savior—and yet because of their hard hearts, they remained stubborn, self-reliant, unbelieving, and unable to trust him. They could not see Jesus as their Messiah. Instead of rejoicing for those who had been healed, the Pharisees resisted the truth of the miracles because of their legalism. Their stubbornness made Jesus angry.

Legalism Can Lead to Being Judgmental and Self-Focused

I believe Jesus' frustration with the Pharisees arose because they refused to put their trust in him. They were missing God's greatest gift—his Son. I believe their bitter, judgmental, critical spirits prevented them from receiving the mercy and freedom Jesus came to bring. They were missing God's plan for their forgiveness. They were choosing legalism and missing God's grace. And as religious leaders, they influenced others to miss Jesus as well, people who were hurting and needed the Savior.

Read Mark 2:13–19. How would you describe:

Jesus' attitude toward himself and others? _____

_____

The Pharisees' attitude toward themselves, Jesus, and others? _____

_____

The "sinners'" attitude toward themselves, Jesus, and others? _____

_____

If we, like the Pharisees, trust in ourselves and our own abilities and perfection instead of depending on God's mercy, we become self-righteous and prideful. This blinds us. We will not be able to love or accept ourselves in that condition, because the Law demands perfection—and we are not perfect. Our thoughts will fill with self-hatred, frustration, and condemnation of ourselves and others.

Self-righteousness also keeps us from loving others. It breeds a conditional love based on what people do, not on who they are. When we demand perfection from ourselves, we tend to demand it from others. We become critical and judgmental.

When we depend on ourselves instead of God's mercy, we cannot give mercy to others. We cannot give to others what we don't have ourselves.

Legalism chokes out love in our lives. Self-righteousness breeds pride and turns our hearts to stone because it sets us up for being superior to others. People who believe their worth and value are based on what they do often have a need to pull other people down by labeling them. We are all on a journey, but in different places. We are not called to judge others. We simply are not qualified (Matthew 7:1–5).

Only when we give up trying to make it on our own and recognize our need for God's mercy in every area of our lives will we be able to accept and love ourselves—and others.

Receive God's mercy for your imperfections, and let that grace flow to others as well.

How Is Your Heart?

I can't throw stones at those religious authorities. This week's passage has caused me to pause and reflect on my heart condition. Are there parts of my life I am afraid to trust to Jesus because of what is in my heart? Have I missed miracles because of my stubbornness in continuing to rely on myself? Am I missing out on the freedom Christ died to give me because I am afraid to give him complete control of my life? Am I failing to give mercy to others because I have not received it for myself?

When our hearts are hard, we may be "ever seeing but never perceiving" (Mark 4:12). Proverbs 4:23 says, "Guard your heart, for it is the wellspring of life." Hypocrisy, pride, bitterness, and unforgiveness can lead to a hardened heart (Matthew 18:35; 23:28).

Search Your Heart

Take some time to search your heart, asking God to shine a light on any wrong there. If there is bitterness, pride, unbelief, and unforgiveness in your heart, they will blind you to the ways God is working in your life. Confess each hurt and sin one by one, and allow him to bring you the beauty of Jesus. As you walk by faith, you may not understand the Lord's direction in your life, but you can trust that his path is best.

As Jesus walked through Palestine, he offered those in his path an invitation to follow him—an invitation that brought freedom. Freedom from condemnation, freedom from sin, freedom from legalism. Freedom to follow our Good Shepherd into abundant living (John 10:10). Freedom to follow a Shepherd who would lay down his life to bring us forgiveness, transformation, and joy.

Guard your heart so you can follow his guidance at every turn and experience his freedom.

Jesus said, "It is not the healthy who need a doctor, but the sick. I have not come to call the righteous, but sinners to repentance" (Luke 5:31–32). Jesus came with the medicine of mercy and sought sinners because only he could make them well. His purpose was to bring not only forgiveness but also transformation through repentance. Only Jesus has the authority to forgive sins, and only he can heal us from our sins and transform our lives.

Don't condemn yourself for the sins you struggle with—take them to Jesus, our Great Physician, and ask him to transform you through the power of the Holy Spirit. He will heal you and set you free. The presence of Jesus brings joy to his bride (Mark 2:19). If you make a mistake, receive his mercy so you can move on, change directions, and grow in the Lord. When we depend on Christ for our forgiveness and freedom from sin, we can walk away from the prison of guilt and experience his freedom and joy.

Confession also gives you the ability and understanding to forgive others more freely (Matthew 7:3). Confession ultimately yields authenticity and intimacy with God, freedom from perfectionism, and reliance on Christ to transform and restore you (Hebrews 4:14–16).

As you take your faults to him through confession and declare your dependence on him, he will lead you to repentance. Then trust and follow the voice of your Great Shepherd. As you abide in him, he will continually prune those branches that are not bearing fruit so that you can grow. This is a lifelong process.

Jesus knows your humanity; he recognizes your shortcomings. He is not shocked by your failures. He is not ashamed of you. He understands. When you fall and are hurting, Jesus is there to help you, not condemn you.

Recognizing your weaknesses can be one of your greatest strengths when you see it as a door to depending on Jesus. ONWARD!

Key Treasure

Recognizing your weaknesses can be one of your greatest strengths when you see it as a door to depending on Jesus.

VIDEO SESSION NOTES

Session 4
FREEDOM
Mark 2–3

Videos located online at www.nourishbiblestudyseries.com

Chapter 5
SEEDS OF SECURITY

DAY 1

Nourish Scripture: Mark 4:1–5:20

PRAY.

Begin your time with God in prayer.

2 MEDITATE ON GOD'S WORD.

Using your Anchor of Truth Card* from last week's Nourish Notes, renew your mind on that truth. Quiet and focus your thoughts. Pray the truth. Say the truth. Meditate on God's truth.

3 TAKE THE *REVEAL* STEP OF THE NOURISH™ BIBLE STUDY METHOD.

Connect with Jesus by studying the Weekly Nourish Scripture and allowing the Holy Spirit to reveal truth in those verses. Prayerfully read over and reflect on the passage. Mark any phrases, verses, or words that catch your attention. Journal and learn as the Lord leads you.

---

*Anchor of Truth Cards are available at www.TreasuredMinistries.com/shop

DAY 2

Nourish Scripture: Mark 4:1–5:20

① PRAY.
Begin your time with God in prayer.

② MEDITATE ON GOD'S WORD.
Using your Anchor of Truth Card* from last week's Nourish Notes, renew your mind on that truth. Quiet and focus your thoughts. Pray the truth. Say the truth. Meditate on God's truth.

③ TAKE THE *RESPOND* STEP OF THE NOURISH™ BIBLE STUDY METHOD.
Respond to activate truth in your life. The acronym **IMPACT**™ provides questions to help you apply the truth from your weekly Nourish Scripture. **Sometimes you may not have answers for all six questions.**

IMAGE OF GOD TO TRUST? An attribute of God, Jesus, or the Holy Spirit to trust.

MESSAGE TO SHARE? A word of encouragement, truth, or prayer to share.

PROMISE TO TREASURE? A promise in the Bible to believe.

ACTION TO TAKE? A specific step God is calling you to take.

CORE IDENTITY IN CHRIST TO AFFIRM? A truth about how God sees you to affirm.

TRANSGRESSION TO CONFESS? A sin to acknowledge for help, healing, and restoration through Christ.

---

*Anchor of Truth Cards are available at www.TreasuredMinistries.com/shop

DAY 3

Nourish Scripture: Mark 4:1–5:20

1 PRAY.

Begin your time with God in prayer.

2 MEDITATE ON GOD'S WORD.

Using your Anchor of Truth Card* from last week's Nourish Notes, renew your mind on that truth. Quiet and focus your thoughts. Pray the truth. Say the truth. Meditate on God's truth.

3 TAKE THE *RENEW* STEP OF THE NOURISH™ BIBLE STUDY METHOD.

Like an anchor that secures its vessel, biblical meditation secures truth to transform your life. Take five minutes to *renew* your mind by focusing on one word, verse, or truth that the Holy Spirit revealed through the Bible during your week of study. Record your truth below and on your Anchor of Truth card.* Quiet your thoughts. Focus on the truth. Read the truth. Pray the truth.

My Anchor of Truth

4 UTILIZE YOUR *ANCHOR OF TRUTH* CARD AS A BOOKMARK TO CULTIVATE A DAILY PRACTICE OF BIBLICAL MEDITATION.

Place your Anchor of Truth Card* in your Bible study workbook to bookmark tomorrow's day of study. Let your Anchor of Truth bookmark remind you to pause and renew your mind on God's Word. Repeat this process daily, continuing to reflect on your Anchor of Truth to start your quiet time until the next week, when God reveals another truth to you.

*Anchor of Truth Cards are available at www.TreasuredMinistries.com/shop

DAY 4

"The mind of sinful man is death, but the mind controlled
by the Spirit is life and peace." —*Romans 8:6*

Like a canvas covered with brushstrokes of various colors, shapes, and sizes, our minds are filled with the fears, heartaches, joys, and victories of our life experiences. Each experience adds a new brushstroke, and pictures begin to form. These pictures shape the way we think and then determine how we act. While some of our brushstrokes are beautiful, others swirl together to build confusion and deception in our minds.

Jesus used the brushstrokes of parables to paint pictures of the kingdom of God. God's kingdom operates differently from this world. Rather than being molded by the world, we need to allow the Word to transform our minds. Jesus knew we would face battles and taught kingdom principles that would equip us to navigate through this world—his way. His parables provided new brushstrokes, painting pictures to renew the canvas of his bride's mind.

The Parable of the Sower and the Seed

The women who had decided to support Jesus out of their own means were among those by his side as he spoke about the sower and the seed (Luke 8:1–8). As you stand by your Bridegroom's side, soak in the words of this seed parable. It is foundational to your walk with him. "Listen!" he exclaimed to the multitudes listening by the lake that day. Jesus told his disciples that if they did not understand this parable, they would not be able to understand the other parables that would follow. The lessons it contained would lay a foundation for the fundamentals of faith in Jesus.

Be Careful What You Hear and How You Hear

Bride of Christ, be so careful what you hear and how you hear. Your mind is the canvas. The way you choose to think determines your soil condition and ultimately shapes your soul.

The brushstrokes from our Bridegroom are the truths that will set us free. When we accept our Bridegroom's proposal, we become a new creation in Christ—born again (John 3:7; 2 Corinthians 5:17). However, when we are born again, our minds are not instantly cleared of those bad brushstrokes from our past—the ones that cloud our convictions and blind us from seeing the truth. If we choose to listen to and trust Jesus above all others (including ourselves), the truths in his Word will begin to transform our minds. His brushstrokes of love and peace will gradually overshadow the haunting brushstrokes of the past. But if we continue to trust our own understanding instead of his, our dance will continue along the destructive path of the world instead of into freedom in Christ (Proverbs 3:5–6).

"Be careful," Jesus cautions his bride, "what you hear and how you hear it."

Transformation of your mind is a process. The more you listen to and depend on your Bridegroom, the more truth he can entrust to you. Allow your Bridegroom to paint new pictures through the imperishable seeds of his Word.

Good Soil Produces Good Fruit

It was early fall and a frost was in the forecast. Joe, a family friend, called me to come and get the last of the vegetables from his garden before the cold ruined the remaining tomatoes and cucumbers.

I love the fresh produce Joe gives me. I appreciate even more the lessons this follower of Christ and his family have taught me over the years.

Joe grew up on a farm, and so he knows about seeds and soil. When I arrived at his house, I found him digging in his garden, sputtering about the soil. "Look!" he exclaimed as he dug under the roots of a tomato plant. "This hard clay soil sure does make things difficult to grow."

While many towns in North Carolina have fertile dark soil, Raleigh is not one of them. Our clay-like soil makes it more difficult for seeds to sprout and the roots to grow deep. While Joe was showing me how important good soil is, he was also teaching me the importance of having a childlike faith to allow the truth in God's Word to take deep root and produce fruit.

One Vital Key to Good Soil: A Noble Heart

What exactly is good soil? Luke's Gospel offers a little more detail on the subject. Read Luke 8:15 and Mark 4:20. What are the keys for good soil that allow the seed of God's Word to produce good fruit?

_____

_____

_____

Perseverance and a good, noble heart that hears and accepts the Word are keys to good soil that will allow the Word to produce fruit in our lives. Today we will focus on a good and noble heart. That word _heart_ comes from the Greek word _kardia_. Kardia means "the centre and seat of spiritual life, the soul or mind, as it is the fountain and seat of the thoughts, passions, desires, appetites, affections, purposes, endeavors."[1] The heart is the inner man—our thoughts, the core of our being, our canvas.

A good heart turned to Jesus results in a mind that will allow God's Word, the seed, to make an impression by trusting him completely. A mind that is willing to change the way we think is a mind that will allow the Word to make an IMPACT! When we hear the Word and accept it in our inner man through faith, we are choosing to put the brushstrokes of God's thoughts on our minds. We are allowing God to paint new pictures in our minds, pictures formed by his perfect design for our lives.

Your Soil Condition Is Up to You

God has given you the freedom and ability to choose your thoughts. Your soil condition is under your control because you can choose what you listen to and how you respond. A good heart will believe in God's goodness and trust him completely. Listening and believing will cultivate the seeds of the Word God plants in your heart.

"Consider carefully what you hear," he continued. "With the measure you use, it will be measured to you—and even more. Whoever has will be given more; whoever does not have, even what he has will be taken from him" (Mark 4:24–25).

We must choose carefully what we listen to. We can listen to the demeaning lies of Satan. We can listen to other people's negative opinions of us. We can listen to our own voice reminding us of past failures and trying to convince us there is no hope for change. Or we can listen to what God says about us through His Word. We can listen to the Bridegroom's words of love and hope. These words of Jesus motivate me to allow truth to be a part of my life by staying in God's Word and believing his truth about me and my life over the lies that have harassed me.

Jesus encourages us to till our soil by having childlike faith that trusts in him completely. Think about that. When we are young, our minds have a clean canvas that makes it easier to believe in the goodness of God. Our past can harden our minds to the truth through negative brushstrokes that have been layered over the years. A healthy mind requires that childlike faith. We are not born with fear—it is learned through the years. Fear hardens our soil, but God's perfect love can drive out our fear (1 John 4:18).

The seed of God's Word endures forever. Truth is truth and it never changes, but we can choose to accept it or reject it. Hearing and receiving God's Word sounds so simple, yet as we saw in this parable, sometimes the harvest does not come easily.

Satan Comes to Steal and Destroy

Satan knows the Word is our offensive weapon and would love nothing more than to steal it away before it has a chance to take root (Ephesians 6:17). Jesus gives us a picture of how Satan works (Mark 4:15). Like a blackbird that descends on a field to take the seed away before it has time to grow, the enemy will intercept the seed taking root through the lies he feeds us.

Those seeds that Satan took had fallen along the path. That Greek word for path is *hodos* and literally means "a traveled way." Metaphorically, hodos also means "a course of conduct or a manner of thinking."[2] Negative brushstrokes in our lives can create pathways and patterns of thinking that do not line up with God's truth. We've been traveling down those roads for so long that the paths have become familiar and deeply ingrained. Thinking differently can be daunting, unfamiliar, and uncomfortable. But God promised us that we can do it. He created us with the ability to renew our minds (Romans 12:2).

God's Word is a lamp to our feet and a light on our path (Psalm 119:105). When we bring the lamp of his Word into our lives, it exposes pathways of wrong thinking and gives us a new roadmap to follow (Mark 4:21–25).

Building New Paths Based on the Word

Come with me, my bride. I want to take you down roads less traveled. Trust in me with all of your heart and don't lean on your own understanding. In all your ways acknowledge me, and I will direct you to new paths. (See Proverbs 3:5-6)

> What new pathway has the Holy Spirit highlighted for you as a result of your study on the Gospel of Mark?
>
> _____
>
> _____
>
> _____

Even when God's Word is showing us a better path, a path leading to freedom through the Word, we sometimes stay on the old paths because they are comfortable and familiar, even though they are destructive to our lives.

Like an unrelenting crow, Satan will try to steal the seeds of the Word from your life. However, you can choose to keep the seeds on good soil by assuming accountability for how you think, renouncing the devil's lies, and accepting the truth in God's Word.

Neil Anderson in his book *Restored* writes this:

> "You choose; you don't passively let your old patterns of thinking decide. You take every thought captive in obedience to Christ and choose His truth. This is how we renew our minds—by knowing and choosing the truth, and by letting the Word of Christ richly dwell within us." (See Romans 12:2; Philippians 4:8; Colossians 3:16)[3]

It took time to create the destructive paths of wrong thinking in your life, and it will take time for you to renew your mind to God's truth. This is where the Renew Step of the Nourish Bible Study Method comes into play. Gradually, new brushstrokes will replace old, and the truth of God's Word will dominate the canvas of your mind.

Allow God's Word to paint new pictures. Just like the parable of the farmer who has no idea how his harvest comes, I cannot tell you how the seeds grow (Mark 4:27). All I can tell you is that sowing seeds of the Word into your life through taking time to read, meditate, and act on God's Word works!

All day long thoughts come our way. God has given us the ability to think and choose. We have control over our canvas. We can accept which brushstrokes we will keep and which ones do not belong. Choose life and freedom by choosing thoughts that line up with God's truth. As you study each week, allow those seeds to make IMPACT! Persevere in building new paths to the abundant life Jesus has provided.

Bride, you are beautiful and so worthy of the abundant life God has called you to live. Each minute is a new moment, a new opportunity to create new pathways of thinking by hearing and accepting the truth. Plow up that field by believing in God's love. Choose faith over fear. You have the ability to change your brushstrokes by changing your thinking. Create new and beautiful pictures on the canvas of your mind!

Key Treasure

Bride of Christ, be so careful what you hear and how you hear. Your mind is the canvas. The way you choose to think determines your soil condition and ultimately shapes your soul. The brushstrokes from our Bridegroom are the truths that will set us free.

DAY 5

"Let us not become weary in doing good, for at the proper time we will reap a harvest if we do not give up." —*Galatians 6:9*

Another key to developing good soil is perseverance (Luke 8:15). Don't give up! Patiently continue to meditate on those scriptures that will set you free. Your responsibility is to submit to God in your thoughts. When you do, the devil will flee (James 4:7). Beginning a new pattern of thinking can be a challenge, but with perseverance and God's help, you can do it.

A Bride Who Persevered

Elizabeth Clarkson found satisfaction for her soul by moving her hands through soil to garden the Lord's earth and make it glorious. When her husband told her they were moving from Dallas, Texas, to Charlotte, North Carolina, she made one request—a beautiful garden.

In 1927, when her husband brought her out to their new home on Ridgeway Road in Charlotte, Elizabeth was disappointed as she gazed out over a desolate three-acre plot and saw nothing but some grass and a few trees. As she put her hands in the soil, her fingers felt that North Carolina hard clay.

Some people might have given up right then, but Elizabeth saw beyond the desolate scene before her. She embraced a vision for a garden sanctuary where songbirds and weary souls could find solace as they sat and soaked in the beauty.

As the story goes, the next day Elizabeth set her hands to tilling the soil. She began to plant seeds and with great patience set about breaking up the hard clay ground. Day by day, year by year, seed by seed the garden grew. Patiently she stayed her course and the roots grew deep beyond the clay to drink from richer soil. Azaleas, camellias, and magnolias grew proud and tall, forming what is now known as Wing Haven Gardens. Along the pristine pathways, there are plaques of Scripture to feed the hearts of those attracted to the beauty of the garden.

Elizabeth's gardener, Uncle John, who helped her for twenty years, asked her if she was the one who started the garden. "Yes," she replied. "Haven't I shown you the pictures?" Uncle John looked over pictures of what had once been three acres of nothingness and hard clay soil. "Just like a barn in an old field, that's the way you want your soul to grow and get more beautiful every day."[4]

Wing Haven is a picture of the power of patience in our lives as moment by moment and year by year we wait in expectation for the seeds planted in our soul to become a "display of his splendor" (Isaiah 61:3). Elizabeth must have said something like this to her earthly husband when she first came to Charlotte: "I thought you promised a garden. Where is the glory when all I see are a few trees?" Sometimes as we survey our lives, we might want to ask our Bridegroom the same question. But we must remember that patience and perseverance despite opposition are keys to a harvest. Here is how *The Message* puts it: "But the seed in the good earth—these are the good-hearts who seize the Word and hold on no matter what, sticking with it until there's a harvest" (Luke 8:15).

The Greek word for patience is *hypomoné* and means "the characteristic of a man who is not swerved from his deliberate purpose and his loyalty to faith and piety by even the greatest trials and sufferings."[5]

Persevere Through the Trials

Read Mark 4:5–6 and 16–17. What happened to the seed that fell in rocky places and what did that mean?

_____

_____

_____

An IMPACT moment is when the Holy Spirit speaks to you through God's Word. You must hold on to those seeds for dear life with perseverance and patience in faith, waiting for them to grow. During that waiting time, you need to live by faith and not by sight (2 Corinthians 5:7).

Nothing gives me more joy than hearing from God through his Word! That is the thrilling part. I can identify with hearing the word and at once receiving it with joy (Mark 4:16). The hard part is the patience and perseverance as I wait for the seed to grow.

Read Hebrews 6:11–20. What do these scriptures teach you about perseverance and patience?

_____

_____

_____

God promised Abraham at an old age, when Sarah his wife was too old to have children, that he would have many descendents and be the father of a great nation. Abraham received his promise seed with joy. But the years passed, and he saw no sign of the answer, so he took matters into his own hands. With Sarah's encouragement, he slept with her maidservant, Hagar, to help speed up God's promise. Hagar gave birth to Ishmael, which would cause trouble in his life and for generations to come (Genesis 16). Impatience can cause us to fall away before the harvest.

God's seed still made its way to harvest, but it came through faith and perseverance. When Sarah was 99, she gave birth to Isaac, a child born of a promise and the power of the Holy Spirit (Galatians 4:29). Abraham, through faith in the seed, became a father to many nations. What does Romans 4:18–21 teach you about God's promises?

Don't Give Up!

If God has given you a promise, remember that it may take years for the seed to grow. We cannot give up. We must continually believe that God has spoken to our heart and that he is faithful to bring his promise to pass.

Mark 4:17 tells us that it was "because of the word" that persecution came. In other words we can be living right in the center of God's will and suddenly find ourselves under the fire of persecution. Those plants in shallow soil were scorched under the heat.

I have often heard it said that when God plants a seed in your life—it could be a promise for your family, a vision for a new ministry, a breakthrough in your marriage, or a new direction to travel—you can expect waves of opposition from the enemy. As we allow the Word to make an IMPACT, we cannot allow waves to break us. We must remain steadfast and immovable, abounding in the work the Lord has given us (1 Corinthians 15:58).

Increasing Problems Might Signal a Breakthrough Coming

Sometimes just before a breakthrough, we are bombarded by waves. The enemy is desperate to get us to leave our seed.

After Jesus gave his disciples this teaching about the sower and the seed, he said to them, "Let us go over to the other side." On the other side of the lake was a man possessed by a legion of demons and evil spirits. None of the people there was strong enough to help this man. Not even chains could subdue him. Only the power of Jesus can drive away demons. We can treat symptoms, but only Jesus can transform hearts.

As the disciples and Jesus were crossing to the other side, a furious squall erupted with waves so large they broke over the boat (Mark 4:37). The storm was enough to rattle the faith of the disciples. They cried out to Jesus, who was sleeping soundly in the stern, "Don't you care?"

That is exactly what the enemy wants us to do—doubt God's love for us and pull us away from his presence, pull us away from prayer, pull us away from his power, and open the door for unbelief to seep in. The enemy wants us to give up. Don't allow the waves to define God's love for you.

> "I have told you these things, so that in me you may have peace. In this world you will have trouble. But take heart! I have overcome the world." (John 16:33)

Mark 4:39 gives us a key to persevering even during persecution. Jesus rebuked the waves and they were still. Brave heart, don't ever forget that those waves that threaten to capsize you are subject to your God. Cry out to your Bridegroom, "Tell those waves to be still!"

Jesus Is Always Bigger than the Waves

Jesus knew about the storm, but he also knew that on the other side there was a man only he could help. When you are serving Jesus, expect storms. But also expect him to pull you through—in his own way and time. And when you are on the other side, your roots of faith will have grown a little deeper because you will have experienced firsthand your Bridegroom's love and faithfulness.

Perseverance is the key. Jesus is bigger than any wave of opposition you may be facing. If you are walking out God's plan for your life, don't let storms stop you from arriving at your destination. Have the courage to go on. Have faith that the Lord can bring you through anything that comes your way.

Teaching … Testing … Growing

The disciples were taught through the seed parables, and then they were tested in the storm. Oh, I can so identify with that sequence—more times than I care to admit! Sometimes learning by going through a storm is the best teacher. You may be hanging on to a mustard seed of faith. But as we learned this week, that is enough for God to grow great things in our lives. Just like the mustard seed parable, God can do the extraordinary when we are faithful to the smallest of seeds in our lives. Day by day, moment by moment, those seeds will grow into something extraordinary.

Storms of Life Can Bring Deep Roots of Faith—and Fruit

The storms in life can uproot us, but if we will stand in patience through the storms, the roots of our faith will grow deep. Keep your eyes focused on that original seed God gave you. Speak it aloud repeatedly to remind yourself of his promises. Then wait and watch your garden grow.

When we are patient and persevere, the Lord takes us to destinations and uses us to help others experience their freedom in Christ. Don't miss what is "on your other side." Someone else is in chains and needs the love and truth of Jesus.

One day not long after teaching these parables, Jesus willingly endured pain beyond our comprehension on a cross and laid down his life. He endured so you and I could get to the other side. The Bible tells us he was able to endure because of the joy set before him. Resurrection was on the other side! (Hebrews 12:2–3)

God places his trust in women to bring forth life through birth. On the other side, as we hold a child in our arms, we realize the blessing is well worth any struggle we may have had. But it's not just physical life he asks women to bring forth. Jesus continually scatters seeds among women to birth great things for God. Just as with physical birth, we must be patient to wait and endure labor. When we persevere to do what God has called us to do, we may suffer various difficulties. But when we get to the other side, we know the blessings, the fruit, are well worth the wait and the struggle.

I am so glad that women at Providence Baptist Church in Raleigh, North Carolina, had a vision for a women's conference, for that is where I received Christ as my Savior. I am so glad that Miss Whetheral Johnston persisted in her calling to create Bible Study Fellowship because that is where I got my foundation in God's Word. I will always remember the dedication of my mentor, who taught me that I could hear from God through his Word and encouraged me to serve the Lord with excellence. I am thankful for the perseverance of Nancy Alcorn, founder of Mercy Ministries. Through her, God taught me what a life surrendered to the Holy Spirit can accomplish for his glory.

I am so thankful for Jesus, who patiently continues to sow seeds of his Word into my life and change me from the inside out.

The Harvest Will Come

Another wonder of Wing Haven Gardens was Elizabeth's vision to make it a bird sanctuary. Elizabeth loved birds and went to great lengths to make sure they felt secure in the tree branches of Wing Haven. Many birds found their rest perched in the trees, shrubs, and flowers that grew there. Bluebirds. Cardinals. Robins.

Elizabeth loved the birds so much she left the windows of her home open so her friends could come in and out of the house.

One day Elizabeth rescued a robin that had been injured. The robin found rest in the branches of Wing Haven and Elizabeth's care. After nursing it to health, she realized it needed to go free. It was winter, so she took the bird on a plane to Florida, bringing it to its final destination of freedom. So like the heart of our Savior. He brings us freedom so we can guide others to the freedom that only he can give. A harvest of blessing for us—and others.

It was one of those beautiful North Carolina summer days when the sun beams against the backdrop of a Tar-Heel-blue blue sky. I was visiting Mom in Charlotte. Wing Haven, one of Mom's favorite spots, was within walking distance from her house, so we set out on a journey to visit the gardens. As soon as I walked through the gate, I was lost in the wonder of a garden that seemed to capture the beauty and peace of Christ. Dotted along the paths were exquisite flowers—a harvest from many seeds planted in good soil and cultivated through perseverance. Scriptures on plaques spoke praises to God. Warbling of birds filled the air as if to worship their Creator. When I left, I felt refreshed by the beauty and peace I found there.

Mustard Seeds Can Make a Lasting IMPACT

Elizabeth Clarkson's vision lives on. Although she has gone on to be with her heavenly husband in glory, her garden is still a sanctuary amid the bustle of a large city. In a Myers Park neighborhood in Charlotte, North Carolina, Wing Haven Gardens is a haven of discovery and peace that was built through seeds of patience and perseverance.

God's Word is like a seed that creates a harvest in our life to nourish others. Don't ever give up! Allowing Christ to redefine our identity and the purpose for which we were created impacts not only our lives—but also the lives of those around us.

ONWARD!

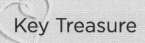

Key Treasure

When you are serving Jesus, expect storms. But also expect him to pull you through—in his own way and time. And when you are on the other side, your roots of faith will have grown a little deeper because you will have experienced firsthand your Bridegroom's love and faithfulness.

DAY 6

"Break up your unplowed ground and do not sow among thorns." —*Jeremiah 4:3*

Brides, beware! Thorns can grow in good soil to choke the harvest of God's Word in our lives. Inside all of us are desires with the potential to cloud our thoughts and choke the seed of the divine Word sown in our minds.

The thorn and the harvest can live together side by side—but they do not live in harmony. Thorns can overtake the harvest. If we are not careful, those thorns can suffocate the life out of God's Word.

What thorns does Jesus tell us to beware of in Mark 4:18–19?

_____

_____

_____

Worries. Wealth. Wants. These all have the potential to suffocate the seeds God has planted in our lives. I don't care how great your faith is, if you have a heartbeat, you have thorns in your garden. Thorns are those triggers in our flesh that can monopolize our thoughts, suffocating the Word right out of us.

One of the most powerful things we can do to defuse the thorns in our lives is to identify them. Then we can deal with them by taking the control away from those appetites by bringing them to Jesus. It's time to get real so we can deal! When you say no to your flesh, you take away the thorns' power.

Worry Is Unproductive and Deadly

Worry is a deadly way of thinking that can monopolize our minds. Worry indicates we have placed our faith in something or someone other than God. Worry thorns can grow so thick in our heads, we no longer see the Word. Worry causes us to be double-minded and confused. Worry is a waste of time. Worry wreaks havoc on our health. Worry will suck the life out of us. Worry prevents us from stepping out in faith to try anything new.

So if I know all that, why do I worry?

My flesh loves to be in control, and surrendering to God's plan feels a little like free-falling. But little by little, I am learning to let go.

Recently God revealed he was giving me permission not to worry. He was not merely suggesting that I not worry—he was commanding. What a gift he gives his brides. We do not have to worry anymore! Getting caught up in the "what ifs" and the "tomorrows" is mentally exhausting—let go. Always ask God for help. There is freedom in letting go. There is freedom when we stop trying to control something we have no control over.

You cannot control your circumstances, but you can control how you react to them. When you worry, fear is in control. According to this passage, worry can choke the fruit of God's Word in your life. Worry blocks the flow of faith in your life by consuming your thoughts with fear. Worry often leads you to place your faith in something or someone other than your Bridegroom.

Now, that is some serious motivation (not condemnation) for this bride to let go of worry and trust my Bridegroom! How about you?

Wealth Cannot Buy Happiness and Security

The deceit of wealth can also choke out the Word. Wealth can be a good thing. It can be used in good ways for kingdom purposes. The women who walked with Jesus in Luke 8:3 supported him out of their own means. Money is needed to take care of our needs and the needs of others. However, when we look to money for happiness and security, we buy into the great deception fed to us by the media. This deception says that money can buy happiness and security—but the truth is that joy and security can be found only in our Bridegroom's arms. When we depend on money instead of our Lord, greed takes over, and the Word is choked in our lives.

Be on your guard, bride. You do not have to have a lot of money for it to control you. Are you jealous of another person's bank account? Do you believe if you just had more money, you would be happy and secure? If so, you have turned the keys of your happiness over to a piece of paper with a dollar sign on it (1 Timothy 6:10).

Avoid being controlled by money by deciding to be a generous giver. Happiness comes in giving. When you give, money loses its control over your life. Your motivation to be prosperous is fueled by a desire to give more, not to have more. Ask the Lord to send someone in your path to bless each day. Imagine if we all lived this way! Be creative. In a fast-food line, pay for the order placed by the car behind you. Anonymously give to someone in need. I have heard it said many times that when you live to give, you will be able to control your wealth instead of your wealth controlling you.

Wants Can Overtake Our Lives

Finally, we have to be on guard for a variety of desires for things of this world (1 John 2:17). An unhealthy desire to get our needs met apart from God is a prickly thorn. Unhealthy appetites dominating our thoughts can drown out God's Word in our lives. I believe God is good and wants to bless us, but when we focus on those blessings instead of on the one who blesses us, we give control over to the gift instead of the Giver. Focusing on one unhealthy desire with such intensity will anchor our thoughts in a destructive way and can suffocate our harvest. When we give into those kinds of thoughts, the thorns have power over our lives.

When our desires are anchored in our Bridegroom alone, we are truly free. Liberty comes when our heart lives for his glory. Our Bridegroom wants us to know we are loved and accepted by him. He wants us to know we can find true security only in him. If we are not careful, we can cling to appetites for security instead of our Bridegroom. Jesus wants us to enjoy the blessings he bestows in our lives, but if we are not careful, even good things can create unhealthy appetites that control us.

All of us have desires that can overtake our thoughts and actions. Healthy desires can quickly turn into unhealthy demands that destroy our thinking. What is your appetite? Is it reasoning obsessively and gaining knowledge? Do you need everyone's acceptance in your life to feel good about yourself? Do you have to always be in control to feel secure? Do you believe marriage or a baby would complete your happiness? Do you try to escape problems through food, alcohol, shopping, or drugs? Do you need to always be right? Are you flirting with thoughts that the answer to your happiness lies outside your marriage? Are you hanging on to bitterness and unforgiveness? Do you feel secure only if you have a title or if your children are a success in the world's eyes?

What do you think you need to feel secure, happy, significant, and accepted?

_____

_____

_____

When desires, however innocently they may begin, become demands in your life or create unhealthy needs, they can cloud the truth from your view.

Learn to Say No When Your Flesh Screams Yes

Once you have identified your thorn triggers, it is easier to recognize your flesh desires over your Spirit-led desires (Galatians 5:22–23). Lean on Jesus to say no when your flesh screams yes! This can only be done through the power of the Holy Spirit, relying on his strength for self-control. Choosing to say no to your feelings and emotions. I have found that choosing to say no to feelings and emotions is the hardest part. However, God is so faithful as we submit to him that peace will follow (Romans 8:5–11; James 4:7–8).

When we are led by the Spirit, we cannot be controlled by another appetite—other people's opinions, material possessions, or anything else. Instead, we are free to love people unconditionally and use and enjoy possessions for his glory. Now, that is true freedom!

There is great freedom when you learn you can say no to your flesh. One of the greatest blessings of fasting is learning you can say no to a basic desire of the flesh. When you learn you can say no to hunger, you experience confidence in your self-control.

No matter what our thorns are, it helps to remember that immediate gratification of desires of the flesh only brings temporary satisfaction—and often does harm. Only Living Water from Jesus can forever quench the thirst in our souls.

Take a good look at your thorns and consider the cost. They are not worth blocking the harvest your Bridegroom wants to bring forth. Don't sacrifice the harvest in your marriage, your family, your ministry, or your career for a thorn. Identify the thorns and starve them of nutrients by feeding your spirit instead of your flesh.

Bring your desires to Jesus (Psalm 37:3–6; Philippians 4:19). He is ultimately the only one who can empower you to stay away from the thorns in your life. When do you need to say no? Saying no to yourself and your impulses will help you gain self-control so you can consistently say no to your flesh and yes to your Bridegroom. What you do today will ensure the good soil of your mind so that you will see a harvest of abundant living tomorrow.

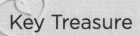 Key Treasure

When our desires are anchored in our Bridegroom alone, we are truly free. Liberty comes when our hearts live for his glory.

VIDEO SESSION NOTES

Session 5

SEEDS OF SECURITY
Mark 4:1–5:20

Videos located online at www.nourishbiblestudyseries.com

Chapter 6
ROCK OF AGES

DAY 1

Nourish Scripture: Mark 5:21–8:30

PRAY.

Begin your time with God in prayer.

MEDITATE ON GOD'S WORD.

Using your Anchor of Truth Card* from last week's Nourish Notes, renew your mind on that truth. Quiet and focus your thoughts. Pray the truth. Say the truth. Meditate on God's truth.

TAKE THE *REVEAL* STEP OF THE NOURISH™ BIBLE STUDY METHOD.

Connect with Jesus by studying the Weekly Nourish Scripture and allowing the Holy Spirit to reveal truth in those verses. Prayerfully read over and reflect on the passage. Mark any phrases, verses, or words that catch your attention. Journal and learn as the Lord leads you.

*Anchor of Truth Cards are available at www.TreasuredMinistries.com/shop

DAY 2

Nourish Scripture: Mark 5:21–8:30

1 PRAY.

Begin your time with God in prayer.

2 MEDITATE ON GOD'S WORD.

Using your Anchor of Truth Card* from last week's Nourish Notes, renew your mind on that truth. Quiet and focus your thoughts. Pray the truth. Say the truth. Meditate on God's truth.

3 TAKE THE *RESPOND* STEP OF THE NOURISH™ BIBLE STUDY METHOD.

Respond to activate truth in your life. The acronym **IMPACT™** provides questions to help you apply the truth from your weekly Nourish Scripture. **Sometimes you may not have answers for all six questions.**

IMAGE OF GOD TO TRUST? An attribute of God, Jesus, or the Holy Spirit to trust.

MESSAGE TO SHARE? A word of encouragement, truth, or prayer to share.

PROMISE TO TREASURE? A promise in the Bible to believe.

ACTION TO TAKE? A specific step God is calling you to take.

CORE IDENTITY IN CHRIST TO AFFIRM? A truth about how God sees you to affirm.

TRANSGRESSION TO CONFESS? A sin to acknowledge for help, healing, and restoration through Christ.

---

*Anchor of Truth Cards are available at www.TreasuredMinistries.com/shop

DAY 3

Nourish Scripture: Mark 5:21–8:30

1 PRAY.

Begin your time with God in prayer.

2 MEDITATE ON GOD'S WORD.

Using your Anchor of Truth Card* from last week's Nourish Notes, renew your mind on that truth. Quiet and focus your thoughts. Pray the truth. Say the truth. Meditate on God's truth.

3 TAKE THE *RENEW* STEP OF THE NOURISH™ BIBLE STUDY METHOD.

Like an anchor that secures its vessel, biblical meditation secures truth to transform your life. Take five minutes to *renew* your mind by focusing on one word, verse, or truth that the Holy Spirit revealed through the Bible during your week of study. Record your truth below and on your Anchor of Truth card.* Quiet your thoughts. Focus on the truth. Read the truth. Pray the truth.

4 UTILIZE YOUR *ANCHOR OF TRUTH* CARD AS A BOOKMARK TO CULTIVATE A DAILY PRACTICE OF BIBLICAL MEDITATION.

Place your Anchor of Truth Card* in your Bible study workbook to bookmark tomorrow's day of study. Let your Anchor of Truth bookmark remind you to pause and renew your mind on God's Word. Repeat this process daily, continuing to reflect on your Anchor of Truth to start your quiet time until the next week, when God reveals another truth to you.

*Anchor of Truth Cards are available at www.TreasuredMinistries.com/shop

DAY 4

"So trust in the Lord (commit yourself to Him, lean on Him, hope confidently in Him)
forever; for the Lord God is an everlasting Rock [the Rock of Ages]." —*Isaiah 26:4 AMPC*

"Who do you say I am?"

I imagine Jesus must have held Peter's gaze as he posed this question to the disciple
who had left his nets to follow him. The adventure that began the moment Peter dropped
his nets was amazing for him. I wonder if during the time between Jesus' question and
Peter's response, memories of miracles played back through Peter's mind. So much had
happened over the last months. Walking on water, healing the sick, feeding the multitudes.
The living water surged freely. Divine provision and restoration flowed from the compassionate hands of this carpenter. Peter's response came quickly and simply:

"You are the Christ."

Those days were great and glorious, but Jesus knew the cross was on the horizon. If Peter
based his faith on circumstances, offense and unbelief could invade his heart when trouble
came. Looking deeply into Peter's soul, Jesus was inviting him to search his personal
convictions and define his faith.

Who Do You Say Jesus Is?

"Who do you say I am?" Allow that question to linger in your thoughts. Peter was already
a disciple, but Jesus paused to ask him about his personal faith.

Take a deep breath, bride. We are getting ready to go deep into the waters of faith. So
great is the love of Christ that it goes beyond our understanding. Only by faith can we dive
into the wide and deep in the ocean of his love and experience the arms of one who will
never let us go. Jesus, your Bridegroom, has been pursuing you, but it is only through faith
that you will turn around and fall into his embrace.

What Is Faith?

Let's take a look at faith itself. The Bible tells us that "faith is being sure of what we hope
for and certain of what we do not see" (Hebrews 11:1). Faith is complete trust. Believing in
something we can see and understand does not require faith. Faith is complete confidence
in something or someone we cannot see or necessarily understand.

Every day all of us act by faith in something or someone. What we believe drives our actions and determines our steps. I don't understand how flipping a switch can turn my lights on, but by faith I flip the switch and the room lights up. If I don't have faith that the lights will turn on by using a switch, I will never flip the switch and will fail to see the light. Although the power source is there, I will live in the dark.

Our Savior is our power source. His power is always available. Power to heal. Power to give us strength for anything we face. Power to carry out what he has called us to do. Power to overcome our weaknesses. But we won't experience his power in our lives unless we "flip the switch" by trusting him. By having more faith in his power than in our own abilities or understanding. By having more faith in him than in what we see. "We live by faith, not by sight" (2 Corinthians 5:7).

The Object of Our Faith

The object of our faith is as important as the depth of our faith. If I trust a water faucet to turn the lights on, my house will remain dark. If we trust anyone or anything other than Jesus with our lives, we will live in frustration and never become all God has designed us to be.

Our faith in Christ alone is fundamental to experiencing his power in our lives. We "live by faith in (by adherence to and reliance on and complete trust in) the Son of God" (Galatians 2:20 AMPC). Rest your expectations in Jesus alone. He is eternal and everlasting. He is constant and never-changing, an anchor of hope (Hebrews 6:19). It's not enough to know who Jesus is. To experience all that he brings requires having faith in him. "The Bible calls God's part of the relationship 'grace,' and our part, 'faith.' Grace has been called 'the divine adequacy.' Faith is the human response to our Father's adequacy."[1]

The object of Jairus's faith was Jesus, not religion. He fell at the feet of Jesus and trusted him to bring life to his daughter (Mark 5:22). Out of money, out of resources, a woman's faith pushed her to touch the cloak of Jesus to find her freedom from 12 years of suffering (Mark 5:29). Faith in Jesus, not in his own abilities, caused Peter to walk on water (Matthew 14:29). Faith in Christ brings power to our lives.

The Purpose of Our Faith

Faith is not a means to get our way—it is a force to help us line our lives up with God's perfect, pleasing will and is necessary to do the work of God (John 6:28–36). Faith makes the impossible, possible. Faith moves mountains. Without faith, we cannot do the work God calls us to do.

Jesus wants us to be motivated to faith by our love and devotion to him, by our desire to serve him. Jesus wants us to focus on him—not on the blessings he can bring. Blessings are always temporary. Jesus cautioned, "Do not work for food that spoils" (John 6:27).

Don't cling to the gift—cling to the Giver. Continue to hold on to Jesus so when it is time for you to lay down the blessing, you will not hesitate. You will follow him through the difficult times, as well as the good ones.

Jesus sighed deeply at the requests of the Pharisees for another sign (Mark 8:12). Signs and wonder addicts have their faith in the wrong place. They will always be looking for more. True faith does not demand a sign or feel entitled to blessings, but places its trust in the firm foundation of faith: Jesus. This is the secret of true contentment (Philippians 4:12–13). When your faith is in Christ, it is on a rock-solid foundation that cannot be shaken.

Your Bridegroom Wants You to Search Your Heart

Who do you say Jesus is?

Your Bridegroom beckons you to explore your heart. He says you are his beautiful, beloved bride, but who do you say he is? Your answer is of utmost importance to a sure foundation of faith. Turn your eyes to your heavenly husband. Listen to his heart as he calls you to search yours.

> Review your Nourish Notes from this week. From the first IMPACT question in the Respond step, which attribute of Christ is the dearest to you and why?

> _____
>
> _____
>
> _____

Christ Jesus. Messiah. Healer. Defender. One name above every name. The Author of our salvation. The Bread of Life, the Light of the World, the Lover of our souls. Our Anchor in the storm. Emmanuel—God with us. Jesus, our Kinsman Redeemer, the Alpha and Omega, Beginning and End. Jesus is our strength when we are weak. He is meaning. He is breath. He is life.

Jesus is the Cornerstone of our faith. He is the Eternal Rock and the only one worth putting our faith in. Jesus is everlasting, the Rock of Ages. The bride—the church—is built solely on the foundation of faith in Christ. When Peter confessed, "You are the Christ, the Son of the Living God," I wonder if Jesus' heart leaped with joy. You've got it, Peter! "I tell you that you are Peter, and on this rock I will build my church, and the gates of Hades will not overcome it" (Matthew 16:16–18).

Jesus Is Always the Answer

The gates of hell cannot overcome your faith in Christ. Think on that for a moment. Whatever you are facing today, whatever life brings you tomorrow, Jesus, your Bridegroom, is the answer. We know that our salvation comes by faith. But our faith walk should not stop there. As we choose to trust in Jesus in every area of our lives, we will walk in obedience to the promptings of the Holy Spirit.

Years later under the divine inspiration of the Holy Spirit, Peter wrote his second letter "to those who through the righteousness of our God and Savior Jesus Christ have received a faith as precious as ours" (2 Peter 1:1). Faith in Jesus is precious. "See, I lay a stone in Zion, a chosen and precious cornerstone, and the one who trusts in him will never be put to shame" (1 Peter 2:6).

Get Out of the Boat

Read Matthew 14:22–33. Peter could have stayed in the comfort of the boat, depending on it to protect him from the storm. But he chose to trust Jesus—not the boat, not his own abilities. He stepped out of the boat and his world opened. He walked on water.

> How can you apply this passage to an area of your life where the Holy Spirit is prompting you to get out of your boat of comfort to walk on water?

Similar to Peter's experience, recently Jesus stood out in the water and invited me to come out of a boat of safety I had been sailing in for some time. Because of past hurts, I had decided to keep my heart safe and secure by not allowing myself to love anyone new. My wounded heart had determined to love those friends I already had—but no one else. I placed my faith in my own efforts to hold others at bay instead of trusting Jesus to defend me. I was kind and friendly, but I refused to open my heart again for fear of being hurt. While I remained in this boat of false security, I was missing out on the freedom to love others unconditionally.

The Lord revealed to me through this passage that I could only find freedom by stepping out on the open waters. Finally one day I stepped out of the boat of self-protection and walked out on water because I knew Jesus wanted me to love again, and I was determined to trust him. But when my toes hit the water, the waves of "what if" came, one after another. *What if I get hurt again? What if this is not a relationship you want me to have? What if I look to someone else to be my god? What if, what if, what if . . .*

"Aliene!"

"Yes, Lord?"

"Who do you say I am?"

As my feet were sinking and the waves of "what ifs" raged, I looked at Jesus. With tears welling up in my eyes, I reached out and held tight to my Bridegroom's hand.

"You, Jesus. You are my Rock of Ages," I whispered with only a mustard seed of faith. "Can you promise me that this will be OK and that I won't get hurt?"

"No, Aliene. But I promise never to abandon you. I am with you always to the end of time. You of little faith, why do you doubt? Put your faith in me, not in others or yourself, and you will be free to love."

And in that moment, I held tightly to my Savior's hand. I understood that my faith in Jesus is all I need. I saw how in the past I had great faith, but it was placed in other people and in myself—not in my Bridegroom. With my faith placed in Christ, I am free to love, free to live, free to give.

We can miss out on walking on water by making other people, things, and even ourselves the object of our faith. Living by faith in Christ is downright scary, but I would not want to live my life any other way. True security is found only by placing our faith in Christ alone.

You belong out of the boat, walking on water. Your faith belongs to your Bridegroom. Step out of the boat and take his hand. Put your faith in the Rock of Ages. Only then will you begin to live as God intended.

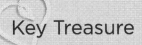

Key Treasure

True faith does not demand a sign or feel entitled to blessings, but places its trust in the firm foundation of faith: Jesus. This is the secret of true contentment.

DAY 5

"Then Jesus answered, 'Woman, you have great faith! Your request is granted.'"
—*Matthew 15:28*

Jesus asked his disciples, "Do you still not understand?" (Mark 8:21). Don't you get it? I blessed your five loaves for more than five thousand and your baskets overflowed with leftovers. And again I took seven loaves and blessed them and your baskets overflowed with more than enough to satisfy. Yes, you only have one loaf with you, but I am the Bread of Life. Stop looking at what you don't have and keep your expectations of faith in me for I am the source of all you need. My supply is limitless for "the earth is the LORD's and everything in it" (Psalm 24:1). By your faith, you will find me an unlimited source from which every good and perfect gift flows.

Inspired to "get understanding" about faith in Christ, I began to pray, *Lord Jesus, teach me more about faith in Christ.*

As I read through the scriptures this week, my Bridegroom sat me down and brought fresh insight into my faith in him. Life is too short to waste on unbelief. So buckle up, brides, and hang on—it's time we sit in on Faith 101 to get understanding of our faith in Christ!

GET UNDERSTANDING:
Faith Is Not a Method

Faith is not a method. Faith is a way of life that listens for the promptings of the Holy Spirit and follows them. There is nothing wrong with traditions, but if we rely on tradition instead of following the voice of the Holy Spirit, we are placing our faith in tradition—not Jesus. "You nullify the word of God by your tradition that you have handed down" (Mark 7:13).

Our traditions can give us security because there are concrete actions to take. It's comforting to think that if we do steps xyz, the problem will be solved. But it takes faith to follow the Holy Spirit and to get out of the boat. God is always doing a new work, and faith says, *I will follow the Holy Spirit and stay away from religious formulas.*

GET UNDERSTANDING:
God Will Meet All Our Needs

Have faith that God loves you, cares about your needs, and wants to bless you so you can be equipped to bless others (Philippians 4:19). If you don't believe God wants to meet your needs according to his perfect will through Christ Jesus, you will place your faith and expectations elsewhere to get your needs met.

Splashed all over this week's scriptures are signs of a Savior who cared for those around him. From Jairus's daughter to the blind man, Jesus paused in his travels to relieve people from suffering. He called his disciples away for the time of rest they needed (Mark 6:31). When he sent his disciples out, he blessed them supernaturally to empower and equip them for what they would need to fulfill their calling (Mark 6:7). He looked out over the crowds that were following him and fed them spiritually and physically. When they ate, all were satisfied. He met their needs.

Jesus is a giver. He is generous in his very nature. Just as he cared about the people during his ministry on earth, he cares about your cries and sees your deepest needs. His love knows no bounds. Place your faith in him. He will meet your needs—in his way and in his time.

Jesus is our daily bread. "Then Jesus declared, 'I am the bread of life. He who comes to me will never go hungry, and he who believes in me will never be thirsty'" (John 6:35). Jesus is the Bread of Life and compared himself to manna. Manna was the daily food the Lord provided to the Israelites in the wilderness. God used manna to teach the Israelites to depend on him daily—that he would meet their needs.

> He humbled you, causing you to hunger and then feeding you with manna, which neither you nor your fathers had known, to teach you that man does not live on bread alone but on every word that comes from the mouth of the LORD. Your clothes did not wear out and your feet did not swell during these forty years. (Deuteronomy 8:3–4)

When Jesus sent the disciples out two by two, he asked them to travel lightly. "Take nothing for the journey except a staff—no bread, no bag, no money in your belts. Wear sandals but not an extra tunic" (Mark 6:8–9). Often the Lord will send you out with little in your hands—little talent, little time, little treasure—to teach you to depend on him.

Just like the woman who had spent all she had on her illness, sometimes we have to come to the end of our resources before we turn to his.

Jesus taught his disciples to pray, "Give us this day our daily bread" (Matthew 6:11). Proverbs 30:8 says, "Give me neither poverty nor riches, but give me only my daily bread." The danger that has the potential to come with abundance is depending too much on ourselves and not on our Bridegroom.

GET UNDERSTANDING:
Jesus Turns a Little into a Lot

When Jesus challenged his disciples to feed more than five thousand people with five loaves and two fish, he was teaching them to give what they had to him and trust him to turn it into a lot. Many times Jesus will lead us into circumstances where we have little and

will ask us to do a lot. In this way, he shows us and teaches us how to live with moment-by-moment faith and trust in him. Through faith, we can bring our little to Jesus and he can make it a lot. I believe Jesus repeated the miracle of feeding multitudes twice because he wanted the disciples to get understanding of this kingdom principle of faith.

What is in your hand today? What are your five loaves and two fish? If you give your little to Jesus, you can depend on him to make it a lot.

GET UNDERSTANDING:
Unbelief Limits Jesus' Work in Us and Through Us

Read Mark 6:3–6. How did the people in Jesus' hometown respond to his ministry and how did this affect Jesus' ability to work?

_____

_____

_____

Jesus was amazed at the lack of faith among the people in his hometown and could not perform many miracles among them. These verses struck me to the core this week. I wondered, _Is there any area of unbelief or offense that is limiting Jesus' work in my life?_

The people from Jesus' hometown knew about the miracles and they heard his powerful teaching, but they "took offense" in this carpenter who claimed to be the Christ—and this affected their faith. They were looking for a Messiah to establish an earthly kingdom and restore Israel's place of prominence. How could this come from a carpenter's son?

Prayer is God's channel to depend on Jesus and defeat unbelief as we learn to trust him. Take your needs to him, lay them at his feet, and wait expectantly. Journal and reflect on the ways he has answered your past prayers and watch your hope soar.

GET UNDERSTANDING:
"Bad Company Corrupts Good Character"
(1 Corinthians 15:33)

Faith is contagious—but so is unbelief.

Have you ever noticed how the attitudes of people you are close to can affect your faith? Jesus knew this. He ignored the men at Jairus's home who said, "Why bother?" Instead Jesus told Jairus, "Don't be afraid—just believe!" When the people laughed at Jesus for speaking in faith that Jairus's daughter was not dead, Mark 5:40 says he put them out of the house before he healed her. I don't believe that Jesus wanted the crowd's unbelief to affect the faith of Jairus and his wife—or the disciples with him.

I want to surround myself not with perfect people, but with those who believe God is good all the time and trust him no matter what the circumstances. Beware of the company you keep—complainers, worriers, and faultfinders can have a negative effect on your faith in Christ.

GET UNDERSTANDING:
Victim Mentality Hinders Faith

In Day 4 we discussed the dangers of getting addicted to signs and wonders. I believe, as mixed up as it sounds, we can also get addicted to suffering and become reluctant to receive the blessings Jesus offers us. When you have been suffering for a long time, an unhealthy belief can settle in your mind that says, "Things will always be this way" or "I don't deserve any better." A victim mindset can settle into your heart.

If we belong to the Bridegroom, we are not victims. Faith believes God is always working on our behalf. Faith wakes us up every day and looks expectantly for Jesus to bring goodness into our lives. "And without faith it is impossible to please God, because anyone who comes to him must believe that he exists and that he rewards those who earnestly seek him" (Hebrews 11:6). We need to have that same persistent faith the Greek woman had when she begged Jesus to heal her demon-possessed daughter (Mark 7:24–30).

Sometimes we can enter unbelief through words that we carelessly allow to fly out of our mouths. "I am just not any good at anything. I am a loser. Life will never get better. I wish I had . . ." and on and on we go.

Watch your words (James 3:3–12). They should be full of faith in Christ. *This is hard, but I know that I can do all things through Christ who gives me strength* (Philippians 4:13). *I can tell my child is struggling, but I know the plans God has for my child—they are plans to prosper him, plans to give him a hope for the future* (Jeremiah 29:11). *I feel as though I have no time or money to get this project done, but I am glad I serve a Savior who can take my little and bless it to make much* (Mark 8:1–10). *I am weak in this area, but whenever I am weak, that is when the power of Christ rests on me* (2 Corinthians 12:8–9). *Because I belong to the Bridegroom, I will speak about myself the way that Christ speaks about me* (Psalm 139:14).

Brides, we need to get rid of any "not-enough thinking" that would cause us to say we don't have enough to give. You belong to the Bridegroom. However little it is, it is enough to do great things in a God-ordained vision.

Our words are an overflow of our hearts. The words we say can tell us a lot about what we believe. Keep speaking faith-filled words. Try it for one day and see the difference it makes in your life. Jesus said, "What comes out of a man is what makes him 'unclean.' For from within, out of men's hearts, come evil thoughts, sexual immorality, theft, murder, adultery, greed, malice, deceit, lewdness, envy, slander, arrogance and folly. All these evils come from inside and make a man 'unclean'" (Mark 7:20–23).

We need to wake up every day and say with confidence, "This is the day the Lord has made. [I will] rejoice and be glad in it" (Psalm 118:24). I *will* rejoice. *Will* indicates there is a choice involved. Choose each day to keep your hope alive by having a faith that says, "God is for me and loves me beyond my understanding."

It Is Time for Us To Get Understanding!

It is easy to lose our faith in Christ when we ask God for something and don't see it happen. Don't take offense. Don't lose your faith. Trust your Bridegroom by deciding in your heart that he loves you. Keep your faith placed in Christ.

> From our Faith 101 class, where do you have new understanding and how will you apply it to your life?

....

....

....

Faith perceives the invisible and depends on God to achieve the impossible. Jesus will provide you with the resources to accomplish what he is calling you to do. He is your only true security. He is your only true source. Walk by faith in him. Live by faith in, reliance on, and complete trust in him.

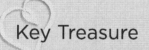

Key Treasure

Faith perceives the invisible and depends on God to achieve the impossible. Jesus will provide you with the resources to accomplish what he is calling you to do. He is your only true security. He is your only true source. Walk by faith in him. Live by faith in, reliance on, and complete trust in him.

DAY 6

"I have been crucified with Christ [in Him I have shared His crucifixion]; it is no longer I who live, but Christ (the Messiah) lives in me; and the life I now live in the body I live by faith in (by adherence to and reliance on and complete trust in) the Son of God, Who loved me and gave Himself up for me." —*Galatians 2:20 AMPC*

The scar was on her arm. *Forgotten*. She had engraved the word in an effort to relieve her pain through self-harm. Cutting herself, she had written on her skin what the enemy had written on her mind. Forgotten.

The day she walked through the doors of Mercy Ministries, the scar was hidden behind a long-sleeved shirt. However, this young woman was on her way to healing at this ministry where young women with life-controlling issues find freedom from their scars.[2]

Forgotten. Perhaps you too have scars that are hidden. Pushed down are those times in your past when you faced evil and you felt forgotten by God and everyone else in the world.

Although Jesus is our Rock of Ages, sometimes we can stumble in our faith because of scars formed in our past. Our scars may not be visible, but the scars on our hearts are just as real as the scar on this young woman's arm. We want to believe that Jesus is our Defender, our Comfort, and our Provision, but our wounds tell us otherwise. We feel forgotten. If we are not careful, those scars can become stumbling blocks to our faith.

Yesterday's Scars Can Hinder Our Faith

It was hard for me not to stumble as I read the story of John the Baptist's beheading. Right in the middle of this faith-filled passage, the death of John the Baptist was like a terrible scar among so many miracles.

John boldly proclaimed Christ as Messiah, but when he landed in prison, doubt settled in his heart. Matthew's Gospel tells us John sent his disciples to ask Jesus, "Are you the one who was to come, or should we expect someone else?" (Matthew 11:3).

I think that is a legitimate question, don't you? I can only imagine John the Baptist felt forgotten. If Jesus was the Messiah and John had served him so passionately, why was he in prison?

Jesus didn't condemn John for the question. "Go back and report to John what you hear and see: The blind receive sight, the lame walk, those who have leprosy are cured, the deaf hear, the dead are raised, and the good news is preached to the poor. Blessed is the man who does not fall away on account of me" (Matthew 11:4–6).

In other words, *John, I know you don't understand, but trust me, I have not forgotten you.*

John had been faithful to Jesus. He had fulfilled his role on this earth by preparing the way for Jesus' ministry. He was ready to decrease so that Jesus could increase. He took no offense, and only sought a confirmation of truth from Jesus.

Sometimes scars in our yesterdays can hinder our faith in Christ for tomorrow. Those memories of when we felt Jesus was not there in our lives, if not addressed, can surface in unbelief. You can know a lot about Jesus but still not believe him because of past pain that leaves you feeling he is not trustworthy. Following the example of John the Baptist, we need to ask Jesus to show us where he is working in our lives and choose to trust a plan beyond our understanding.

The scars ran deep for Cathy. A good friend of mine had buried her child and her feelings of sorrow. Unanswered questions that were pushed away resurfaced one day to bring new birth to her faith in Christ.

In John 16:33, Jesus tells us, "In this world you will have trouble. But take heart! I have overcome the world." Before 1998, I never knew what real "trouble" was. But in September of that year, I learned what the worst of that could mean.

On September 1, 1998, my husband and I took our two girls, Elizabeth, who was 3, and Sarah, who was 4 months old, for their well-checks at the pediatrician. What was supposed to be a routine visit turned into an almost five-month nightmare. Our entire world was turned upside down in a matter of minutes. Sarah was diagnosed with infantile leukemia. We were immediately sent to Duke Hospital where Sarah received chemotherapy and eventually a bone marrow transplant. After a long and valiant battle, she passed away in my arms as my husband and I whispered soft lullabies in her ear. We knew she was with Jesus and there would be no more suffering for her in this world. We rejoiced for her, but our hearts were broken. Through this time, God was so faithful. He brought so many people around us that loved us and cared for us; he comforted us in so many tender ways. But there were scars that ran deep, scars I didn't even realize I was carrying until eleven years later.

I knew God was calling me into a counseling ministry. One day just before this started to become a reality, I was having my quiet time with the Lord. I was writing in my journal all the things God was for me: my Savior, my Redeemer, my Defender, my Provider. "My Protector" came to mind ... but I couldn't write it. I didn't trust God to be my Protector! But why? I realized that I had a fear deep inside me that caused me to worry a lot about my children's health, my husband's health, and even my own health. I would feel panic every time we had checkups. I would worry for days before and even days after that we would get some bad medical news stemming from these doctor visits. I felt God urging me to surrender this to him. But how was I ever going to do that? I dropped to my knees and cried out to him to help me give it all to him … everything. I held out my tightly clenched hands and then, by the power of his Holy Spirit, I slowly opened them, releasing it all to him. I cannot begin to tell you the weight that was lifted from me in that moment, as tears streamed down my face. Gone were years of trying to "control" something that I really never had any control over anyway. Gone were the burdens of worry and anxiety. I felt completely free!

Cathy has a heart for bringing healing to the scars from people's past in a biblical counseling ministry. She shared with me that one of the most powerful things we can do is to ask Jesus to show us the footprints of his faithfulness during the painful parts of our past. It can clear those stumbling blocks in our faith. "Search me, O God, and know my heart; test me and know my anxious thoughts. See if there is any offensive way in me, and lead me in the way everlasting" (Psalm 139:23–24).

We are not forgotten. God did not cause the scars in your life or the wrong choices others made that brought you sorrow and pain. We all have pain in our past, but the truth in God's Word tells us that Jesus never leaves us or forsakes us (Hebrews 13:5). The Holy Spirit reminds us of everything Jesus said to us (John 14:26). You can find comfort and healing by asking Jesus to help you remember all the ways he was there for you during those times you felt forgotten. Allow the Lord to take your scars and turn them into a story to share of his restoration and redemption!

Scars Are Healed When We Bring Them into the Light of Jesus

With her carved scar "forgotten" still secretly hidden behind her shirtsleeve, the young woman listened intently along with other girls from Mercy Ministries to a gifted guest speaker. Not only on her arm but also in her mind were scars that stole her faith—but this would soon change. The speaker narrowed her focus from the group of girls to settle on this young woman's face. Without knowing the word engraved and hidden on her arm, the speaker spoke four words that would communicate the love of Jesus louder than the lies of the enemy.[3]

"You are not forgotten."

In that moment, those words moved a mountain of unbelief. The young woman finally knew she was not forgotten. She rolled up her sleeve to show the speaker. As she made this move to bring her scar out into the light of Jesus, she was forever changed. She believed he loved her, and her faith soared.

Remember the Faithfulness of Jesus
During Past Storms

Bride, you were never forgotten. Your Bridegroom was there when your heart was broken. You are never alone. Jesus will never abandon you.

During the time I wrote this chapter, Cathy encouraged this bride to read Psalm 31:1–5 aloud and ask Jesus to show me how, in the darkest times of my past, Jesus never abandoned me. And so I stopped and sat before Jesus in prayer and invited him into places of my past that were dark and broken. And as I traveled to those times that created scars in my life and allowed the Holy Spirit to lead me, I saw Jesus. He was there holding me. He was there through people he brought along my path. He was there as he kept me safe when I turned to destructive ways to handle the pain in my life during my young years. He was there even when I left him and pushed away his protective boundaries. Jesus was there and rescued me from unhealthy relationships. He was there!

As Cathy encouraged me, I encourage you to go back in your past and ask Jesus to show you his faithfulness in the midst of your pain. This was life-changing for me and I believe you will be blessed as well. Spend some time with your Bridegroom. Journal what the Lord reveals to you. As you begin to see the hand of Jesus in your life, your faith will increase.

Let's pray.

> Lord, I cry out to you. "In you, O LORD, I have taken refuge; let me never be put to shame; deliver me in your righteousness. Turn your ear to me, come quickly to my rescue; be my rock of refuge, a strong fortress to save me. Since you are my rock and my fortress, for the sake of your name lead and guide me" (Psalm 31:1–3). Jesus, I invite you to show me all the ways you were there for me in the past. Show me how you were there to catch my tears as they fell. Show me how you defended me when others committed evil against me. Show me how you never left my side when others abandoned me. Show me how you were working a greater miracle those times when I could not see the answer to prayer. Lord Jesus, help me in any area of unbelief in your love for me so I can trust you completely. I want to have the freedom to fall into the arms of my Bridegroom, for I know that is where I belong. Show me all the ways you have been faithful in the past. "Free me from the trap that is set for me, for you are my refuge. Into your hands I commit my spirit; redeem me, O LORD, the God of truth" (Psalm 31:4–5).

Journal below as the Holy Spirit reveals footprints of your Bridegroom's faithfulness in your past.

_____

_____

_____

_____

_____

_____

_____

_____

_____

_____

_____

_____

_____

Bride of Christ, God has never forgotten you. Jesus knows all the hurts and pain in your past. Jesus came to bring justice to the injustices done in your life. He wants to make that which is broken into something beautiful. When you were hurt, when you were broken— your Bridegroom was broken too. He saw your tears, he heard your weeping. Because you are his bride, it was as if he was hurt too. If you will allow him, he will bring you beauty from your ashes. Freedom is found when you trust your Bridegroom. You belong in his arms.

VIDEO SESSION NOTES

Session 6
ROCK OF AGES
Mark 5:21–8:30

Chapter 7
THE DANCE

DAY 1

Nourish Scripture: Mark 8:31–9:50

 PRAY.

Begin your time with God in prayer.

MEDITATE ON GOD'S WORD.

Using your Anchor of Truth Card* from last week's Nourish Notes, renew your mind on that truth. Quiet and focus your thoughts. Pray the truth. Say the truth. Meditate on God's truth.

TAKE THE *REVEAL* STEP OF THE NOURISH™ BIBLE STUDY METHOD.

Connect with Jesus by studying the Weekly Nourish Scripture and allowing the Holy Spirit to reveal truth in those verses. Prayerfully read over and reflect on the passage. Mark any phrases, verses, or words that catch your attention. Journal and learn as the Lord leads you.

*Anchor of Truth Cards are available at www.TreasuredMinistries.com/shop

DAY 2

Nourish Scripture: Mark 8:31–9:50

1 PRAY.

Begin your time with God in prayer.

2 MEDITATE ON GOD'S WORD.

Using your Anchor of Truth Card* from last week's Nourish Notes, renew your mind on that truth. Quiet and focus your thoughts. Pray the truth. Say the truth. Meditate on God's truth.

3 TAKE THE *RESPOND* STEP OF THE NOURISH™ BIBLE STUDY METHOD.

Respond to activate truth in your life. The acronym **IMPACT**™ provides questions to help you apply the truth from your weekly Nourish Scripture. **Sometimes you may not have answers for all six questions.**

IMAGE OF GOD TO TRUST? An attribute of God, Jesus, or the Holy Spirit to trust.

MESSAGE TO SHARE? A word of encouragement, truth, or prayer to share.

PROMISE TO TREASURE? A promise in the Bible to believe.

ACTION TO TAKE? A specific step God is calling you to take.

CORE IDENTITY IN CHRIST TO AFFIRM? A truth about how God sees you to affirm.

TRANSGRESSION TO CONFESS? A sin to acknowledge for help, healing, and restoration through Christ.

*Anchor of Truth Cards are available at www.TreasuredMinistries.com/shop

DAY 3

Nourish Scripture: Mark 8:31–9:50

 PRAY.

Begin your time with God in prayer.

 MEDITATE ON GOD'S WORD.

Using your Anchor of Truth Card* from last week's Nourish Notes, renew your mind on that truth. Quiet and focus your thoughts. Pray the truth. Say the truth. Meditate on God's truth.

TAKE THE *RENEW* STEP OF THE NOURISH™ BIBLE STUDY METHOD.

Like an anchor that secures its vessel, biblical meditation secures truth to transform your life. Take five minutes to *renew* your mind by focusing on one word, verse, or truth that the Holy Spirit revealed through the Bible during your week of study. Record your truth below and on your Anchor of Truth card.* Quiet your thoughts. Focus on the truth. Read the truth. Pray the truth.

My Anchor of Truth

 UTILIZE YOUR *ANCHOR OF TRUTH* CARD AS A BOOKMARK TO CULTIVATE A DAILY PRACTICE OF BIBLICAL MEDITATION.

Place your Anchor of Truth Card* in your Bible study workbook to bookmark tomorrow's day of study. Let your Anchor of Truth bookmark remind you to pause and renew your mind on God's Word. Repeat this process daily, continuing to reflect on your Anchor of Truth to start your quiet time until the next week, when God reveals another truth to you.

*Anchor of Truth Cards are available at www.TreasuredMinistries.com/shop

DAY 4

"And he died for all, that those who live should no longer live for themselves but for him who died for them and was raised again." —*2 Corinthians 5:15*

Jesus invited her to live forever. All she needed to do was respond, "I do." As she said those words with her heart, he forgave her. She then sat at the table of the new covenant to feast freely on her spiritual inheritance. She was a bride and she belonged to her Bridegroom—yet she sensed there was more.

A Dance Proposal

A second invitation came. Jesus wanted her to dance closely with him—and let him lead. He called her to follow his steps—not those of the world. He asked her to be willing to step out on a limb to leave a legacy of his love. He asked her to bravely spread the gospel and fight with the most powerful weapon: love. She would need to get lost in his lead. "Surrender to me," he called to her. He did not move the way the world moved; she would need to follow his steps, to live differently. He called her to love the way he loved. "Surrender to me," he invited.

Following the steps of her Savior would mean losing her life to find his. It was a risk. "Surrender to me, my bride. If you want to come after me and follow my dance, lose yourself and find yourself in me." Her Bridegroom was a gentleman and would never force her to follow him, but as she spent more time in his presence, his love engulfed her. And as she learned more about the gospel message, her love grew deeper. Slowly her fear turned to faith. As he held out his hand, she looked back over the worn paths of her life and then returned to his eyes of love. She decided to love and never look back.

She armed herself with a new attitude filled with Christlike courage! She followed her Savior fearlessly. As she danced, great delight filled her heart. Her happiness was not temporary like the joy the world offers. It was a continuous flow of living water. As she surrendered her life and gave her heart completely to him, she was set free to live and love others just as he does. The world no longer mattered—his embrace was enough. She was not afraid for him to lead, and for the first time in her life, she truly lived. As she yielded herself completely, the Holy Spirit filled her with his love and grace in indescribable ways. And as she loved and lived her life only for him, a force of love was released—a force so strong that others would be rescued as her life revealed the gospel.

A new attitude released her soul to soar on the heights of her Savior's love. She was fearless and free. She followed him so closely that her footprints were engulfed in his.

Lose Your Life and Find It

Lose your life to find it. This phrase seems like a paradox, and yet often kingdom principles go against our natural thinking. Jesus began clarifying what discipleship means. Words like suffering, denying self, servanthood, being last, and losing your life would unsettle many who contemplated surrendering their lives to Christ.

Read the following scripture aloud and record in the blanks below some of your first thoughts about Jesus' "dance proposal."

> "Anyone who intends to come with me has to let me lead. You're not in the driver's seat; I am. Don't run from suffering; embrace it. Follow me and I'll show you how. Self-help is no help at all. Self-sacrifice is the way, my way, to saving yourself, your true self. What good would it do to get everything you want and lose you, the real you? What could you ever trade your soul for?" (Mark 8:34–37 MSG)

Attitude Is Everything

Attitude—the way we think about things—is everything. In his epistle, Peter wrote, "Since Christ suffered in his body, arm yourselves also with the same attitude" (1 Peter 4:1). This week we are going to look at arming ourselves with the right attitude about sacrifice, suffering, and separation. Today we will look at having a right attitude about sacrifice.

When Christ was here, he never wavered from God's will for his life. He was relentless in his calling even when it led to sacrifice. He left the glory of heaven and the riches of gold-paved streets. He became fully man. He left comfort and walked on earth to give us the gospel.

Jesus trusted God to the point of being led to the cross. He told his disciples to count the cost (Luke 14:28). He was asking them to explore their thoughts, their attitude, about sacrifice. Following Jesus means being willing to make sacrifices. Arming ourselves with a Christlike attitude says we are not going to shrink back from following God's will in our lives, regardless of the sacrifices.

The enemy will try to stop us from fulfilling God's plan by getting us so self-focused that we are afraid or unwilling to sacrifice. He feeds us lies telling us we will lose if we give, but God's way is to gain by first losing. Self-centeredness will not fulfill us. That is a lie from the enemy.

The Bible says we can overcome the enemy by the blood of the Lamb, the word of our testimony, and by not loving our lives so much that we shrink from death (Revelation 12:11–12). If we are worried about staying safe, we will pull back and miss God's plan for our lives. Instead of complete surrender to Jesus, we will put our self-interests above God's will for our lives. Fear puts limits on what God can do through us. This fear is not from God. Arming ourselves with an attitude of Christ requires radical trust in his love.

We Can Trust God's Love for Us

Read Mark 10:17-22. Why do you think Jesus asked the rich young ruler to sell his possessions?

There is no fear in love (1 John 4:18). Jesus loved the rich young ruler (Mark 10:21) and asked him to let go of his treasure. If your Bridegroom asks you to surrender some treasure to him, it is always because he loves you. Choosing to trust his love, no matter what the circumstances, is the key to abundant living.

The rich young ruler had it all according to world standards. He said he wanted to follow Jesus, but he saw his wealth—not Jesus—as his security. There is nothing wrong with wealth. God uses wealth in the hands of his believers to do great things for his glory. However, when we look to our wealth to provide our security, significance, and happiness, our hearts are captive and we are not truly free.

Only Jesus can give us eternal life. The rich young ruler pridefully asked Jesus what he could do to inherit eternal life. Jesus pointed him back to the Ten Commandments, which no person can keep perfectly. He was showing the young man that he could not save himself (Romans 3:23; James 2:10). Salvation is only possible through faith in Jesus Christ (Mark 10:27; Ephesians 2:8; Romans 10:11–12). However, the young man's self-sufficiency blinded him from seeing any faults in his life.

God Wants Our Hearts Captive to Him

Salvation is so much more than just our entry into heaven—salvation is restoration in every area of our lives. I have heard it preached many times that Jesus is far more concerned about our character than our comfort. Your Bridegroom will go to great lengths to have your whole heart.

Learning to Let Go

The love of God and the harvest of the gospel should motivate us to live the "let go" life. It was Jesus who asked the rich young ruler to let go of his riches. It is always for the kingdom that we are called to let go. Be careful that you are not letting go for the sake of letting go with a religious mindset. This will not bear fruit. It's when we listen and heed the promptings of our Bridegroom that letting go becomes fruitful.

The Bible says the rich young ruler went away "sad." I wonder ... if he had known Jesus as "Savior" and the "one who loved him greatly," would he have let go of his riches and found everlasting joy?

Read John 12:23–26. What happens when we let go and live for Christ?

How do these scriptures free you from the fear of letting go of any possession or habit or relationships and living fully for Christ?

Mark 8:35

Mark 10:29–31

What harvest have you seen as a result of letting go of a "seed"? Or like the rich young ruler, are you sensing that your Savior is challenging you to surrender in some area of your life?

You don't get to choose what to surrender, but you can choose your attitude by seeing Christ not just as your teacher but also as your Savior, the one who loves you beyond human understanding. If you have his love—and you do—you have all the security you need.

Unfortunately, the rich young ruler did not surrender his treasure. Consequently, he missed God's blessings in his life—and eternal life. The key to kingdom living is to hold everything God gives us loosely in our hands, never afraid to let go when he asks—but always holding tightly to his love.

Letting Go Brings Freedom and Reward

In God's kingdom, the way up is down. Don't be afraid to lose anything in this life that Jesus asks you to lose for him. You will find freedom and great reward when you are willing to submit every area of your life to him. Surrender by arming yourself with the right attitude about God: God is love. If he asks you to let go of something, it is because he loves you and has something better in store for you. Jesus said whatever he asks you to release in this life, he will give back to you one hundred times in "this present age" (Mark 10:30).

When you follow Christ, allow him to call all the shots. When you wake up each morning, decide to believe that God loves you. Then, when the Holy Spirit prompts you to lose something, arm yourself with childlike faith that says, "Lord, because I trust your love for me, I am willing to let go and live for you." God's dreams for our lives are so much greater than our limited thinking can contain. It's only when you let go that you can truly live to find yourself in the great expanse of his perfect plan. Believe in the goodness of God. It's through our faith in his love and in the gospel message that we can let go to live.

Key Treasure

God's dreams for our lives are so much greater than our limited thinking can contain. It's only when you let go that you can truly live to find yourself in the great expanse of his perfect plan.

DAY 5

"For our light and momentary troubles are achieving for us an eternal glory that far outweighs them all. So we fix our eyes not on what is seen, but on what is unseen. For what is seen is temporary, but what is unseen is eternal." —*2 Corinthians 4:17–18*

She was armed and dangerous. A brave bride of Christ. Aware of the amazing adventure and abundant living, she felt alive! As she glanced back, the worn paths were gone. She was blazing a trail of his love to the world. It was not a straight road—it was mountainous, filled with ups and downs. Plenty of unexpected turns and free falls into valleys. Sometimes she identified with the sufferings of her Savior, but she smiled for she had determined to enjoy the dance. She sailed into the storms with confidence that the Holy Spirit was filling her sails. And so at every turn, she let go of all her fears, and in faith she followed her Bridegroom. Dancing with him was where she belonged.

In India lives a brave bride of Christ. She has left friends and family to be a missionary and spread the gospel of Jesus Christ. She has faced rejection—all for his glory. She is filled with joy.

In Uganda lives a brave bride of Christ. Her name is Marilyn Skinner. She has a passion to restore the hearts of the forgotten children and abused women of Uganda. She has faced death but continues to live fearlessly for the cause of Christ as she battles injustice for his glory. She is passionate about training the children of Uganda to lead the future in the ministry she and her husband founded called Watoto.

In Iran live two brave brides of Christ. They were imprisoned for leading the underground church and endured unspeakable suffering inside a prison in Tehran but never relented from their faith. During that time, they led many prisoners to Christ.

This same bravery to stand against injustice and for the gospel of Jesus Christ exists inside you because the Holy Spirit lives within you. God may never call you to Uganda or India, but he may call you to take an unpopular stand, step out in faith to begin a local ministry, speak to a group when you are terrified of public speaking, get out of your comfort zone to use your gifts more effectively. Your courage to follow his lead in every situation may be buried in layers of fear. Take heart knowing that the Holy Spirit will give you courage to take any dance step your Bridegroom asks you to take when you need to take it. As his bride, you have the chance to live fearlessly, boldly share the gospel, and leave a legacy.

Therefore I remind you to stir up the gift of God which is in you through the laying on of my hands. For God has not given us a spirit of fear, but of power and of love and of a sound mind. Therefore do not be ashamed of the testimony of our Lord, nor of me His prisoner but share with me in the sufferings for the gospel according to the power of God. (2 Timothy 1:6–8 NKJV)

When was the last time God called you outside of your comfort zone to do something for his glory, something that terrified you but you did it anyway? How were you able to press through your fears? What were the results?

_____

_____

_____

Share in Christ's Sufferings—and His Glory

As we battle against injustice and endure hardship to share the gospel, we will identify with the sufferings of Christ and share his glory (Romans 8:17; 2 Corinthians 2:15; Philippians 3:10). There is a relationship between suffering and glory (Romans 8:15–18; 1 Peter 4:1–2, 12–14; 5:6–10).

In our passage this week, Christ revealed to his disciples on several occasions that he would suffer and die before the glory of the resurrection (Mark 8:31; 9:12, 30–31; 10:32–34). Suffering before the glory. I believe Jesus wanted his disciples to be armed with the right attitude. He taught them in Mark 10:29–30 that they would encounter persecution—but also blessing.

Don't Doubt God's Love for You

Don't ever doubt God's love for you in the face of suffering! Your suffering does not necessarily mean you are out of his will. Christ was in the center of God's will—but he suffered more than we can imagine. As we walk through suffering, we must always remember—as Jesus did—that the resurrection and the glory are on the other side.

As I look back at the cross, the hardship of whatever Christ asks me to do pales in comparison. We can embrace any suffering that Jesus asks us to bear with great courage if we remember God loves us and is using us to bring the light of the gospel to a dark world. Our attitude must be the same as Christ's. We must be willing to go anywhere and let go of anything for the sake of the gospel. He gave us freedom, and now we must fight fearlessly for others. Our motive must be the same as his—love. Love for him. Love for others.

Fearlessly Spread the Good News

We are called to be courageous in sharing the gospel and never to be ashamed of it (Mark 8:38). Fear of suffering will keep us from complete surrender. Jesus needs his brides to set the world on fire by fearlessly spreading the good news (2 Timothy 1:11–12).

Peter was armed and dangerous for the kingdom. Thousands said yes to the Bridegroom because Peter was bold and brave for the gospel's sake (Acts 2:38–41; 3:11–16; 4:18–20). It was the filling of the Holy Spirit and God's glory that gave Peter boldness in his calling. Peter also prayed for boldness (Acts 4:24, 29–30). Christ will give you courage to do

whatever he is calling you to do as you walk away from fear by relying on his Spirit through prayer.

However, Peter had not always been this bold. His bravery was once buried in layers of fear. When Jesus first talked about suffering, Peter was not armed with the right attitude.

In our passage this week, when Jesus first mentioned that he would suffer, Peter decided to have a come-to-Jesus meeting—with Jesus! Peter loved Jesus. Hearing that his Master would have to suffer must have pulled at Peter's heart. But I also believe Peter did not want to hear of his Savior dying because the disciple shared Israel's dream of overturning the Roman Empire and the prophecy of a restored earthly kingdom. Israel had waited so long to see their Savior as promised through the prophets. Their Messiah who would restore Israel's greatness. They had waited days, weeks, years, and generations for their suffering to end. It was as if Peter was saying, "Enough of suffering! I thought you were going to rescue us from Roman control."

This bride can identify with Peter. Oh my, am I happy there was a disciple named Peter who wavered in his faith and fell in fear. If there was hope for Peter, I know there is hope for me!

I must admit I don't want to hear about suffering when it seems as though my sisters are already surrounded by it. I am tired of hearing about the injustice that women suffer. I am tired of hearing about the abuse and neglect of their hearts. Sometimes it seems as though my sisters in Christ who shine the brightest are hit the hardest. My heart is heavy as I think of my sisters who have been bruised in battle. Sisters all around the world who are hurting. Like Peter, I want to cry out, "Enough! I want to come to you to end my suffering—not to identify with your suffering. Restore your kingdom and bring justice to all the injustice in this world."

Evil and the results of evil are not from God. Christ is not asking us to embrace the injustice in this world, nor is he asking us to seek suffering for suffering's sake. He is not asking us to be a doormat. He is not asking us to choose something to lose for him—it all has to be directed by the Holy Spirit and driven by God's love. Losing or suffering for any other reason is serving self—not serving Christ. False humility and self-abasement do not bring glory to God.

Walk Confidently in Your Calling— No Matter What the Circumstances

Christ is calling us to walk confidently in our calling, no matter what the circumstances. The adventure of following Christ is a bit like riding a roller coaster. There are unexpected twists and turns and plenty of free falls. You cannot choose the path of the roller coaster, but you can choose your attitude. Identifying with the sufferings of Christ is a part of the ride. Pride comes with a sense of entitlement and demands only glory, but humility surrenders to servanthood. Like Peter, we don't like hearing that part of surrender, but there is great freedom in trusting Christ with a fearless attitude.

Trust God—Even in the Face of Suffering

I smile when I think of Peter who, just moments before resisting God's plan, claimed Christ as Messiah with childlike faith. Surrender is easy as long as my Bridegroom is asking me to do something I want to do. When my Bridegroom asks me to lose to live, I suddenly feel that those next dance steps are precarious.

Jesus did not condemn Peter, and he does not condemn us. Jesus attacked Satan and then stated Peter did not have in mind the things of God but the things of men. God does not give us fear (2 Timothy 1:7). Satan can use fear to keep us from following Christ. Jesus wants us to live beyond our expectations, trusting him with childlike faith (Mark 10:15). It's an attitude that says, "I trust you even in the face of suffering."

Christ will give us the courage we need for our callings at just the right time. Don't get caught up in tomorrows. Decide that you will trust Christ, and through the Holy Spirit he will give you the courage and boldness to take whatever dance steps you need to take (Acts 4:24, 29–30).

If you live your life with an "I could never" attitude, you never will! Instead, say to yourself, "Lord, I trust you and believe your Holy Spirit will give me the courage to do whatever you ask me to do and follow you in the dance."

Sometimes, especially in the face of suffering, God's plan may not make sense to you. When that happens, ask him to give you his mind so you can arm yourself with his attitude. Ask him to show you a glimpse of his glory and fill you with the Holy Spirit.

A Glimpse of God's Glory Helps Through the Hard Times

Jesus gave Peter a glimpse of his glory as he was transfigured on the mountain. Jesus was no longer a simple carpenter—he was revealed in dazzling glory. Peter's eyes must have been wide in awe. Before him stood his Savior in all his glory with Moses and Elijah. These were celebrities in his day. Moses represented the Law and Elijah represented the prophets. Jesus fulfilled both law and prophecy. Peter was so overjoyed by the glory of God, he wanted to set up camp and stay there! I believe Jesus was giving him a glimpse of the glory of heaven to hang on to during the hard times to come.

Remember your mountaintop experiences—they are glimpses of the glory of heaven. They are reminders of God's amazing love and will encourage you in the valleys. His glory sustains us as we lay our lives down so others can see his goodness.

Express your gratitude to God by praising him for those glimpses of glory. Andy Stanley, pastor of North Point Community Church, once said that felt gratitude is not expressed gratitude.[1] Verbally reviewing glimpses of his glory in your life as you walk through this

fallen world is a key to arming yourself with the right attitude. Glimpses of glory can be found in a sunset or a hug from your child. In a powerful worship service or an answer to prayer. In the filling of his Holy Spirit as you spend time in his presence through prayer. And one of the greatest glimpses of his glory comes when someone you love comes to know Jesus as Lord and Savior. It is vital to your survival in the valleys for you to praise God aloud for those glimpses of glory.

Keep Your Focus Heavenward, Not Earthbound

When I had my children, the labor was intense, but the entire time I focused on the blessing of having a baby and bringing a new life into this world. Likewise, Jesus wants our focus to stay heavenward, not earthbound (2 Corinthians 4:17–18).

Choose every morning to believe in God's goodness. Celebrate those glimpses of glory he gives you. When you feel as if you are free-falling, hang on to your faith with all your might. Every day in your life can be a gift if you will arm yourself with a Christlike attitude by focusing on Jesus and his glory.

Which determines your attitude—your suffering or your Savior? Fall into the arms of your Savior and you will be a fearless force for the gospel. You were created to bring significance to this world. Living in safety and avoiding risks will hold you back from the remarkable adventure God has planned for your life (Hebrews 10:34–39).

Will you be brave for your Bridegroom? He is calling his brides into battle for his glory. Arm yourself with an unstoppable attitude by focusing on the gospel and God's glory.

> *She was armed and dangerous. A brave bride of Christ. Aware of the amazing adventure and abundant living, she felt alive! As she glanced back, the worn paths were gone. She was blazing a trail of his love to the world. It was not a straight road—it was mountainous, filled with ups and downs. Plenty of unexpected turns and free falls into valleys. Sometimes she identified with the sufferings of her Savior, but she smiled for she had determined to enjoy the dance. She sailed into the storms with confidence that the Holy Spirit was filling her sails. And so at every turn, she let go of all her fears, and in faith she followed her Bridegroom. Dancing with him was where she belonged.*

DAY 6

"Therefore, since we are surrounded by such a great cloud of witnesses,
let us throw off everything that hinders and the sin that so easily entangles,
and let us run with perseverance the race marked out for us." —*Hebrews 12:1*

As she set out to follow her Savior, she found that at times her feet became entangled. Her steps were not as nimble and her feet felt heavy; she began to stumble. Frustrated, she sat down. It was that same old sin that stalked her like a shadow. She wanted to follow her Bridegroom in the dance. She wanted to surrender, but she could not shake this particular sin. She realized it was not just fear that would keep her from following her Savior—sin would entangle her and weigh her down. She fell down, broken, before her Bridegroom. He did not condemn her. He held her and then began to help her. He spoke these words: "My bride, I did not die for you to stay in your sin. I am calling you to a life of liberty and freedom that you will find only when you deny yourself and take up your cross daily and follow me."

Anything More Important than Jesus in Your Life Is an Idol

You belong to the Bridegroom. Don't entangle yourself by tying your soul to anything or anyone but Jesus. As our Bridegroom points out, it's useless to gain even the whole world at the price of our souls (Mark 8:36). Following Jesus means you put him first. You must let go of anything that prevents you from following him. Things or people that cause us to sin are not necessarily bad in themselves. But when they become more important to us than Jesus, they become idols.

She was brought to a place of brokenness where she armed herself with a new attitude about the sin in her life. "Let your will be done in me, Jesus. Cleanse me. Fill me with your Holy Spirit so I can be free to follow you without any hindrances. Lord Jesus, empty me of anything that stands in the way of my freedom. I want to walk in your love."

Her Bridegroom wanted her to be free. There were mountains he wanted her to climb. He needed her to set the world on fire with his love. He wanted her to be salt to a world that was bland with its ways. He was serious about the sin in her life because it was keeping her from the abundant life he died to give her.

Sin Will Entangle Our Dance Steps with Jesus

"Therefore, since we are surrounded by such a great cloud of witnesses, let us throw off everything that hinders and the sin that so easily entangles, and let us run with perseverance the race marked out for us." (Hebrews 12:1)

There is liberty when we follow the Holy Spirit, throwing off our hindrances and sin. A wise bride knows sin will entangle her—tripping up her dance steps with Jesus and robbing her of the adventure Jesus has called her to live.

For us to be free to follow Christ and strong enough for the battle, we cannot lose our salt by staying entangled with sin. "Jews were not allowed to put leaven or honey on their sacrifices, but they were required to use salt (Leviticus 2:11,13). Salt speaks of purity and preservation."[2] The fire of the Holy Spirit rested on the disciples to empower them in their walk (Acts 2:3). The Holy Spirit brings us transforming power for purity in our lives.

Jesus Takes Sin Seriously, and So Should We

Review Mark 9:42–47.

How does this scripture point to the seriousness of the sin in our lives?

_____

_____

_____

New Testament scholars interpret this passage in various ways, but one truth that cannot be ignored is that Jesus is serious about the sin in our lives. Why would he not be? Freedom from sin is a gift to us, but God paid a very great price. Our sin is bondage that creates destruction in our lives and the lives of others. Grace is not a license to indulge in our sin (Galatians 5:13). Grace was given so that through our abiding relationship with Jesus the fruit of the Spirit grows in us, and the sin in our lives shrinks, its entangling vines withering away.

Through his sacrifice, Jesus saves all who put their faith in him from the horrors of hell. Hell is complete separation from God for all eternity—a place of total darkness and utter death. Because of Jesus, you and I never have to experience those horrors if we have received his forgiveness and gift of life. (If you have not accepted this gift, I encourage you to go back and read Day 4 of chapter 2, and say "I do" to all Christ has done.) When I think of the truth that I will never be apart from God—simply because of the grace of God through Jesus Christ—my heart fills with gratitude, and any separation or sacrifice seems to pale in comparison in light of what Jesus has done for me (Romans 12:1–2).

Whatever Causes Us to Stumble Must Be Removed

Warren Wiersbe, in his commentary on the New Testament, writes this about Mark 9:42–47:

This solemn message about hell carries a warning to all of us to deal drastically with sin. Whatever in our lives makes us stumble, and therefore causes others to stumble, must be removed as if by surgery.[3]

Jesus was not advocating self-mutilation; he was making the point that a wise bride will recognize her weaknesses and temptations and remove anything or anyone enticing her to sin. Jesus is teaching an effective strategy to avoid sin—it is better to sever ourselves from anything that separates us from him than to keep it and sin. For a time you may need to lose something valuable, essential, and beneficial so you can find your life in him.

This is not legalism—this is a smart strategy to preserve your liberty and spread the gospel through the testimony of the fruit in your life. When we prune away the things that have control over our lives, we make space for the Holy Spirit to change and mold us. The Spirit of God is still what transforms us, but when we separate, we say no to what has been controlling us to surrender to the one who loves us beyond measure.

Sin always promises glory first and then results in bondage later. Conversely, separating ourselves from sin might be difficult but will result in freedom (1 Peter 1:4–6; Isaiah 1:24–25; 37:19).

Sometimes we get pruned (John 15:2). Pruning is messy and it hurts, but the results are beauty, growth, and freedom. I see the glory and the grace in the way God loves us enough to free us from those things that entangle our lives.

Jesus is serious about sin because it hurts us and it hurts others. The sin in my life did not affect just me; it affected others around me whom I cared for deeply. Precious brides, it is better for us to cut off what causes us to sin than to cause others to sin with us. God is love. The law is summed up in one command—love your neighbor as yourself (Galatians 5:14). Sometimes love means letting go.

Whether it's an attitude or an addiction or an idol, sometimes pruning is necessary so our hearts can be free again to love the one who will never leave us or forsake us. It is because he loves us that he calls us to cut off anything that would hinder our ability to absorb the nourishing water of his love into our hearts.

For example, be careful in choosing what you see, the places you go, and what you do. The world pulls hard at our minds. Satan is always on the prowl tempting us to stray from God. He knows where we are weak. You are flirting with fire when you allow your eyes to rest on temptations through the media or other avenues. You may find yourself dancing with the wrong partner.

Alcohol, work, shopping, food—these things are not bad in themselves, but when they have control over our lives, they can create problems. Our hands become entangled when we hold on to idols.

Relational Entanglements

Unhealthy relational entanglements have destroyed many of Christ's strongest branches. In her book *When Godly People Do Ungodly Things*, Beth Moore, who has ministered to the church for years, points out how some of the most committed Christians have fallen into "messy" relationship entanglements.

Our souls can become entangled with unhealthy relationships that will destroy us no matter how determined we may be to make them work. Relationships, like our eyes, hands, and feet, are good and necessary in our lives, but some relationships are not healthy. Brides, beware! Satan loves to prey upon our need for intimacy and offer counterfeits for healthy relationships.[4] Our fragile hearts that thirst for love can settle for poor substitutes. Not all ties and relationships are healthy.

But aren't we called to minster to those who need Jesus? Absolutely! Aren't we made to be in relationship and community with one another? You bet! But there is a difference between ministering to someone who needs the Lord and tying your soul to someone who is unhealthy. There is a difference between loving others and deeply enmeshing yourself with them. God is the only one who can be God (it's not our job!) and when he is, we are free to love others and let go of those unhealthy entanglements.

We all understand the overt signs of an unhealthy relationship—signs like physical, verbal, emotional, or spiritual abuse, and infidelity. But what about the more subtle signs? In her book *When Godly People Do Ungodly Things*, Beth Moore talks about the importance of discerning clean versus messy ties in relationships. How can we discern a messy tie? Beth provides some warning signs. Do these describe any of your relationships—either friendships or romantic ties?

- Unhealthy dependency on each other.

- Temptation to engage sexually with the person outside of marriage.

- Someone in the relationship becomes a false Christ figure, spiritually guiding the other person more than Jesus.[5]

Is there a relational tie in your life that needs to be severed? Don't ignore those red flags and warning signs, no matter how strong your emotional attachment is and how well your desires are being satisfied. Anyone who is influencing you to sin is not worth keeping around, no matter how valuable the relationship may be to you. The situation may be sticky, and the severing may be painful, but you must cut it off. Instead of depending on this relationship, take your desires to God, who can fulfill every one of them.

Identify What Is Causing You to Sin

Are you unsure of what tempts you to sin? Do you need wisdom? The Bible tells us there are three main sources of wisdom available to us: Scripture (Psalm 119:105), wise counsel (Proverbs 19:20), and the Holy Spirit (James 1:5).

Stop and think for a moment about a sin you struggle with repeatedly. Pray and ask the Holy Spirit for wisdom. Is there something connected with that sin that is causing you to struggle? Are you involved in an unhealthy relationship? After you spend some time in prayer, write what God revealed to you.

_____

_____

_____

What practical steps can you take to remove from your life whatever is tempting you to sin? If you are unsure, which wise and godly person in your life will you ask for insight?

_____

_____

_____

Making Changes Brings Freedom to Ourselves and Others

As you enter a relationship with Jesus, he will help you overcome anything that is hindering you. You are powerless in your own might to live a sin-free life, but as you obey Jesus, including cutting off anything he asks you to separate yourself from, you will experience glory. Out of your relationship with him, you will be transformed day by day. Becoming more like Christ is a lifelong process. A wise bride will make courageous choices so she can leave her old ways and take up her new identity in Christ.

And as she surrendered to her Bridegroom and got serious about her sin, she saw a change. Those old temptations faded away. She belonged to the Bridegroom and knew he would give her the strength to separate from anything or anyone he asked her to. With every step of surrender through separation, she danced a little lighter, free to be graceful, free of entanglements. She loved, laughed, and lived the adventure he was calling her to live.

It is only in complete trust and surrender that we become effective for the kingdom. It's a risk, but one that comes with great reward. When we cut off our old ways, we see the growth of the glory of God sprouting in our lives and in the lives of others.

VIDEO SESSION NOTES

Session 7

THE DANCE

Mark 8:31–33

Videos located online at www.nourishbiblestudyseries.com

Chapter 8
HER HEART

DAY 1

Nourish Scripture: Mark 10:1–45

1 PRAY.

Begin your time with God in prayer.

2 MEDITATE ON GOD'S WORD.

Using your Anchor of Truth Card* from last week's Nourish Notes, renew your mind on that truth. Quiet and focus your thoughts. Pray the truth. Say the truth. Meditate on God's truth.

3 TAKE THE *REVEAL* STEP OF THE NOURISH™ BIBLE STUDY METHOD.

Connect with Jesus by studying the Weekly Nourish Scripture and allowing the Holy Spirit to reveal truth in those verses. Prayerfully read over and reflect on the passage. Mark any phrases, verses, or words that catch your attention. Journal and learn as the Lord leads you.

*Anchor of Truth Cards are available at www.TreasuredMinistries.com/shop

DAY 2

Nourish Scripture: Mark 10:1–45

1 PRAY.

Begin your time with God in prayer.

2 MEDITATE ON GOD'S WORD.

Using your Anchor of Truth Card* from last week's Nourish Notes, renew your mind on that truth. Quiet and focus your thoughts. Pray the truth. Say the truth. Meditate on God's truth.

3 TAKE THE *RESPOND* STEP OF THE NOURISH™ BIBLE STUDY METHOD.

Respond to activate truth in your life. The acronym **IMPACT**™ provides questions to help you apply the truth from your weekly Nourish Scripture. **Sometimes you may not have answers for all six questions.**

> **I**MAGE OF GOD TO TRUST? An attribute of God, Jesus, or the Holy Spirit to trust.

> **M**ESSAGE TO SHARE? A word of encouragement, truth, or prayer to share.

> **P**ROMISE TO TREASURE? A promise in the Bible to believe.

> **A**CTION TO TAKE? A specific step God is calling you to take.

> **C**ORE IDENTITY IN CHRIST TO AFFIRM? A truth about how God sees you to affirm.

> **T**RANSGRESSION TO CONFESS? A sin to acknowledge for help, healing, and restoration through Christ.

*Anchor of Truth Cards are available at www.TreasuredMinistries.com/shop

DAY 3
Nourish Scripture: Mark 10:1–45

1 PRAY.

Begin your time with God in prayer.

2 MEDITATE ON GOD'S WORD.

Using your Anchor of Truth Card* from last week's Nourish Notes, renew your mind on that truth. Quiet and focus your thoughts. Pray the truth. Say the truth. Meditate on God's truth.

3 TAKE THE *RENEW* STEP OF THE NOURISH™ BIBLE STUDY METHOD.

Like an anchor that secures its vessel, biblical meditation secures truth to transform your life. Take five minutes to *renew* your mind by focusing on one word, verse, or truth that the Holy Spirit revealed through the Bible during your week of study. Record your truth below and on your Anchor of Truth card.* Quiet your thoughts. Focus on the truth. Read the truth. Pray the truth.

4 UTILIZE YOUR *ANCHOR OF TRUTH* CARD AS A BOOKMARK TO CULTIVATE A DAILY PRACTICE OF BIBLICAL MEDITATION.

Place your Anchor of Truth Card* in your Bible study workbook to bookmark tomorrow's day of study. Let your Anchor of Truth bookmark remind you to pause and renew your mind on God's Word. Repeat this process daily, continuing to reflect on your Anchor of Truth to start your quiet time until the next week, when God reveals another truth to you.

───────

*Anchor of Truth Cards are available at www.TreasuredMinistries.com/shop

DAY 4

"Immediately the boy's father exclaimed, 'I do believe;
help me overcome my unbelief!'" —*Mark 9:24*

For six days God spoke the world into being. Majestic mountains appeared and his glory filled the world with creatures of all kinds. From dust, God created man. God's breath filled his lungs with air and gave him life. His creation was "good"—but not complete. From Adam's rib, with the Creator's final stroke, love and beauty burst forth into creation. Woman was born and the Master finally rested his hand. His creation was complete with Eve.

Eve's heart was at rest—she was safe and secure in the garden. Surrounded by the surreal beauty, she knew perfect love, security, and significance as she strolled with her God through a pristine creation. God's arms of acceptance seemed to hold her tightly. She slept in peace and walked naked and unashamed in fellowship with her God. She depended on him, and her heart was free.

Eve was created and wired to love and depend on God. Named the mother of all living, Eve's soul was designed to nurture those in her care; she had great capacity to love. Eve did not look to Adam to complete her for she found her completeness in God. She looked to Adam in her desire to love and help him.

Life in the garden was as God intended, but the one who came to kill, steal, and destroy would ruin this perfection (John 10:10). Satan, disguised as a snake, deceived Eve and stole her security and peace.

Read Genesis 3:1–15. How did Satan trick Eve and what result is described in verse 15?

_____

_____

_____

How did Adam and Eve cover themselves? (verse 7)

_____

_____

_____

Why did they cover themselves and hide? (verse 10)

_____

_____

_____

What covering did God provide to replace the fig leaves? (Genesis 3:21)

_____

_____

_____

How do you think this new covering points to Christ?

_____

_____

_____

Satan stood in the shadows and surveyed Eve's beauty. Perhaps he resented her beautiful soul destined to nurture others—or her perfect relationship with God. If he could convince her not to trust God for her needs, he could take her away from her destiny. He could start a cycle of unbelief about God's goodness toward her. He could shut down her heart, and she would never find the everlasting joy that comes only from worshiping God and serving others.

With masterful manipulation and carefully crafted lies, Satan convinced Eve to stop trusting God and take matters into her own hands. _Don't trust God. He is lying to you. You don't need him. Depend on yourself to meet your needs._

Eve listened to the devil's lies. She stopped resting in God's loving care and chose to depend on herself. Adam was also there but kept silent and did not interfere. They both turned away from God by eating from the forbidden tree. Sin, death, and suffering entered the picture, and Eve's once secure world was no more.

Eve turned away from God and inward to herself to find satisfaction for her desires . . . and the human race has been doing that ever since. Self-protection. Self-preservation. Self-interest. Self-centeredness. Self-sufficiency. Self-righteousness. Satan pushed us to be our own gods. He tricked us into getting our legitimate needs met in illegitimate ways. We stopped looking upward to God for protection, and a cycle of self-reliance and selfishness was born.

John and Stasi Eldredge explain what happened to Eve—and what happens to us—in their book _Captivating: Unveiling the Mystery of a Woman's Soul._

For as we all know personally, something in Eve's heart shifted at the Fall. Something sent its roots down deep into her soul—and ours—that mistrust of God's heart, that resolution to find life on our own terms. So God has to thwart her. In love, he has to block her attempts until wounded and aching, she turns to him and him alone for her rescue . . .

Jesus has to thwart us too—our self-redemptive plans, our controlling and our hiding, thwart the ways we are seeking to fill the ache within us. Otherwise we would never fully turn to him for our rescue. Oh we might turn to him for our "salvation," for a ticket to heaven when we die. We might turn to him even in the form of Christian service, regular church attendance, a moral life. But inside our hearts remain broken and captive and far from the One who can help us.[1]

Like Eve, we close off certain parts of our hearts to prevent getting hurt again. We no longer use our energy to depend on God in serving others—we spend it on desperate attempts to preserve ourselves. Tempted by Satan, taught through the world, and trained by our past hurts, we fall for the mirage of self-focus. We falsely believe we need to be in control to get our needs met instead of trusting God. We think we have to depend on ourselves to find our salvation. These beliefs create self-focused behaviors that ultimately leave us alone and empty inside, and lacking the love we are trying to gain.

Eve listened to the lies and began wearing fig leaves. She thought they would cover her shame. She thought they would protect her and help her find the security and love she had lost. And so it has gone through the centuries. We still try to use "fig leaves" to protect ourselves. We often hold back love, our greatest gift to others, because we focus inward instead of outward. Our self-protectiveness blocks our love-flow to one another. Self-preservation begins to play itself out in many destructive ways. Self-reliance keeps us from doing all he has called us to do.

What Are You Wearing?

For our lesson this week, FIG stands for Focused Inward instead of on God. The "root" of every FIG leaf is unbelief in God's love, resulting in a desire to be our own gods. The "tree" is self-focus, which displays itself in various "species" of leaves. Behaviors include jealousy, perfectionism, control, workaholism, manipulation, and people pleasing.

But God has a better solution—one that came through the sacrifice of his Son, Jesus.

In the garden of Eden, God covered Adam and Eve with animal skins (Genesis 3:21). This act pointed to his plan of redemption through the sacrifice of his Son, Jesus Christ. Forgiveness comes only through sacrifice. Jesus was the blameless Lamb sacrificed so you and I can have freedom from our sins (John 1:36; 1 Corinthians 5:7; 1 Peter 1:18–19; Exodus 12:21). Remember from chapter 2 that God has given us a new garment to wear.

"I delight greatly in the LORD; my soul rejoices in my God. For he has clothed me with garments of salvation and arrayed me in a robe of righteousness, as a bridegroom adorns his head like a priest, and as a bride adorns herself with her jewels." (Isaiah 61:10)

You do not have to hide under FIG leaves of self-righteousness and self-dependence. Find your security, love, and worth in the Bridegroom as you wear his garments of salvation and robe of righteousness. It is out of this abundance that you can give to others.

In the following scriptures, how did the disciples focus inward? What solution to their self-focus did Jesus give?

Mark 9:33–37

_____

_____

_____

Mark 9:38–41

_____

_____

_____

Mark 10:35–45

_____

_____

_____

The disciples were close to the Bridegroom yet displayed FIG leaves like manipulation and jealousy among themselves because they did not trust him fully. They should have been thinking of ways to make Jesus' name great. Instead they wasted time arguing about who among them was the greatest (Mark 9:33–34). They displayed an attitude of superiority when they pushed the children away (Mark 10:13). They worried about their position in heaven instead of focusing on introducing people to the kingdom of God (Mark 10:37). They were jealous of others' success in ministry (Mark 9:38). The disciples wanted to control who sat where in the kingdom of heaven. Peter wanted to control Jesus instead of surrendering to God's plan (Mark 8:32). Instead of praying and depending on God, the disciples tried to heal in their own strength.

Jesus was preaching others-focused love, and his disciples were completely missing the point! While the disciples were busy clamoring for position and promotion, Jesus was honoring children, widows, the unclean, sinners, and others who had no social standing in their culture. Jesus depended on God for his meaning and worth, while his disciples were comparing themselves and fighting one another for empty human praise.

Jesus gave his disciples a whole new way of thinking that would challenge them as it challenges me today. The solution to their self-focus was to rely on God and focus outward by serving others.

When Jesus' disciples were concerned about their position in heaven, Jesus taught them about humility: anyone can be given a title and lord it over others, but it's servants who are remembered (Mark 10:42–45). Jesus was teaching his disciples that greatness does not come with a title but by helping those people God puts in our path, one by one. Jesus recognizes our acts of love, however small they may be, and has a reward for us in heaven. It does not matter if others appreciate us here on earth. Servants do not focus on doing things to be seen or thanked. When we forget about who gets the credit and roll up our sleeves to do God's work in the world—when we live to serve instead of living for ourselves—only then will we truly live.

Self-focus, in any FIG leaf form, creates division in our relationships with others and causes a distraction in our relationship with God. Just as strife entered the disciples' relationship with one another when they argued about who was the best and competed for position in heaven (Mark 9:33–34; 10:41), so strife enters women's relationships when they enter self-focused rivalry.

What examples of this inward focus and division do you see among women in today's world?

_____

_____

_____

Although we were made to love and nurture others, why do we sometimes choose words ever so carefully to turn a compliment into a jab? We gossip and tear one another apart instead of building one another up. Instead of accepting our identity in Christ, we fight for our own position and identity—and a spirit of competition arises. We reject others by hiding behind walls. We fear anything that would make us vulnerable. In our insecurity, we fix FIG leaves of protection over our hearts.

RELY ON JESUS: Exchange Self-Preservation for God's Loving Care

All behaviors brought about by FIG leaves of self-preservation are influenced by the lies Satan has fed us—lies that push us to depend on ourselves instead of on God. Satan has tricked us, ladies, causing us to shut down our most powerful gift to others: love.

Self-focus is not the answer. What brings fulfillment is relying on Jesus, and then out of that abundance, serving others. You were created to nurture. Inside every woman is a great capacity to love and serve others. Because we belong to the Bridegroom, we have all the love, security, and significance we will ever need. From that place of abundance we can trust God to take care of us and help us reach out to others.

You cannot serve others unconditionally until you rely on your Bridegroom completely. You cannot rely on your Bridegroom completely until you believe he loves you. Until then you will be looking for more from others. Therefore, believing in God's unconditional extravagant love for you is the ultimate solution to self-centeredness.

Be clear: serving others is not worshiping others, pleasing others, or enabling others. Our worship belongs to God alone. Serving others should always be done with the goal of pointing others to Christ, not to ourselves. Enabling others does not serve them. Playing the role of a victim or showing false humility does not glorify God. These are acts of pride because they put the spotlight on you. Pleasing others is *conditional* love. Love is not to be used as a tool for manipulating or controlling others. Love does not give only to get someone's approval, favor, or reconciliation.

Radical Love

Real love—God's unconditional love—is different from love that demands return. First Corinthians 13 is a famous passage in the Bible that describes this beautiful, radical love.

Read 1 Corinthians 13. When compared with the kind of love we learn in our culture, what in this passage do you find most radical?

_____

_____

_____

What aspect of real love do you find most challenging personally?

_____

_____

_____

Because you belong to the Bridegroom, you have a great capacity to love. From the beginning of time back in the garden of Eden, you were created to nurture and to serve. The solution to focusing inward is to trust God and focus outward.

While Jesus was on the earth, a group of women followed him and ministered to his needs (Matthew 27:55). The Greek word for ministered is *diakoneō*, which means "to serve, wait upon."[2] It is the same word Jesus uses for *serve* in the following scripture.

"Whoever wants to become great among you must be your servant, and whoever wants to be first must be slave of all. For even the Son of Man did not come to be served, but to serve, and to give his life as a ransom for many." (Mark 10:43–45)

Isn't it fascinating that this group of women who followed Jesus around understood about servanthood? They must have truly loved him. They must have seen the great value in his ministry, so much so that it became their ministry to support him and his efforts! What a striking contrast to the group of men who followed Jesus around. The disciples somehow missed not only Jesus' message about servanthood but also plenty of opportunities to love and serve him! They must have thought they were too great to be servants. Ironically, Jesus himself indicated it was the serving women who were great. This brings up a great question: would we rather be great in our own eyes, or in Jesus' eyes?

There is nothing like unity among sisters in Christ as we stand against the injustices in this world. We can be a mighty force when we stand together with Christ-centered servant hearts. When Jesus prayed his final prayer before going to the cross, he prayed for many things among believers—including unity (John 17:22–23). A bride who is walking in love and unity with her sisters in Christ is an unstoppable force. There is an anointing and a blessing when believers stand in unity (Psalm 133). When we walk in love, we walk in the fullness of the Holy Spirit (Romans 5:5; Ephesians 4:30–31).

You do not have to hide under FIG leaves of self-righteousness and self-dependence. Find your security, love, and worth in the Bridegroom! Out of that great abundance you will be able to give abundantly to others. When we do not walk in love and unity, we grieve the Holy Spirit and weaken our effectiveness for the kingdom. We fight the wrong battles and waste our energy by spending it in the wrong places (James 4:1–3).

It's time the bride of Christ declares love and never looks back. If we trust God with our hearts, we can walk in love with one another. Don't deny yourself one of the greatest gifts in this life—believe in God's unconditional, amazing love for you, focus outward, join together, and show the love of Christ by serving others!

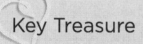

Key Treasure

You cannot serve others unconditionally until you rely on your Bridegroom completely. You cannot rely on your Bridegroom completely until you believe he loves you. Until then you will be looking for more from others. Therefore, believing in God's unconditional, extravagant love for you is the ultimate solution to self-centeredness.

DAY 5

"I trust in you, O Lord; I say, 'You are my God.'" —*Psalm 31:14*

"Everyone who loves has been born of God and knows God" (1 John 4:7). This passage tells us that love is from God. The key to walking in love is our own love relationship with the Lord. God is love. We need to "know" God before we can experience and share his unconditional love with others. *Ginōskō* is the Greek word for *know* in this passage. It means to "know intimately."[3] In other words, the Word tells us God's love for us must not be just information—it must become experience.

In our Nourish Scripture from chapter 7, a man came to Jesus confused because the disciples could not drive out the demon that had possessed his son's body (Mark 9:18). Jesus responded in what I think was a bit of frustration. "O unbelieving generation," Jesus replied. "… How long shall I stay with you?" (Mark 9:19). I think nothing frustrates Jesus more than our failure to believe in his greatness, goodness, and love. When we don't believe God is for us, we will not trust him. We will look elsewhere for our value and security, resulting in selfishness.

As our study of Mark unfolds, God is weaving a common thread through every chapter: his love for his bride and his desire for her to find security in him in a fallen world. You belong to the Bridegroom. You can find your security only in his loving arms. Part of this journey to our freedom involves identifying our FIG leaves and then shedding them as we change our beliefs and begin to rely on Jesus.

We all have FIG leaves. Don't take on condemnation because of your leaves—but determine to do something about them. If we just change our behavior, we are only putting a temporary Band-Aid on the problem. We must first change what we believe. We must believe that Jesus, and only Jesus, can provide for our needs.

This is a lifelong process. We release some leaves, only to add others along the way. This is a chapter you can revisit from time to time as needed. The important thing is to continue drawing closer to our Bridegroom—day by day and year by year. We must continually learn to rely on him for our security, love, and worth. We must allow him to continually transform us so we will accomplish the purpose of our journey (Romans 12:1–2).

I still struggle with shedding my share of FIG leaves! But I am learning to stop and ask myself when those leaves rear their ugly heads, "Where am I not trusting you, God? What is my area of unbelief?"

Because I belong to the Bridegroom, I so want to trust God to the point where I can let go of worrying about me and focus on others. I see that the leaves will fall not simply by my wanting them to, but through identifying, confessing, and forming new beliefs so I can trust my Bridegroom to take care of me. Out of the abundance of God's blessings, I can walk in love for others.

CONFESSION: Bring Our Sins into the Light

How can we change our beliefs and let go of FIG leaves? Jesus told his disciples some things can only be driven out by prayer (Mark 9:28–29). Our FIG leaves can be removed only with the help of Jesus. We need to bring our sins into the light by confessing them (1 John 1:9).

The presence of Jesus gives the gospel its power. When the people came into the presence of Jesus, they were "overwhelmed with wonder" (Mark 9:15). When the spirit saw Jesus, it "threw the boy into a convulsion" (Mark 9:20). Ultimately Jesus drove out the spirit with his words (Mark 9:25–26). Never underestimate the power of the presence of Jesus and his Word. When you come into the presence of Jesus and bring him emotions like jealousy that are controlling you, he can begin to heal you.

Because we know we should be walking in love, sometimes we push down selfishness and jealousy instead of taking them to Jesus and asking him to drive them out. Suppressing sin will not help us. In Capernaum, when Jesus asked the disciples why they were arguing, they failed to confess they were arguing over who was the greatest. I imagine they were embarrassed to share with Jesus the pettiness of their argument. The irony is that Jesus already knew their hearts, just as he knows our innermost thoughts (Mark 9:35). Keeping our sins to ourselves does not solve things; we must share them with Jesus and trust him to set us free.

REPENTANCE: New Beliefs Bring New Behavior

After confession comes repentance. To repent means to turn around and walk in the opposite direction. In this case, it means to change your mind or your thinking. When we feel those urges to tighten our FIG leaves and not trust God, we need to cry out as the man with the afflicted son did, "Help me overcome my unbelief!" (Mark 9:24).

Our beliefs mold our behavior. If we change our beliefs, we change our behavior. If we believe only God can meet our needs and that he loves us extravagantly and unconditionally, we will depend on him.

When you pray, ask him to give you courage to trust him to take care of you. Ask him to feed you where you are hungry for acceptance and security. Ask him to help you recognize when you begin to add new FIG leaves and give you the courage to turn to him instead.

The father brought his son to Jesus, wanting the Lord to set the boy free from an evil spirit (Mark 9:20–27). When the spirit sensed the presence of Jesus, it convulsed the boy's body, but Jesus drove out the spirit and set the boy free. When Jesus removes FIG leaves, you may experience some temporary storms or "convulsions" as you bring the leaves into his presence because you are dealing with issues that have been suppressed.

Surrender can be scary, especially when we've lived in our negative cycles for a long time and have grown comfortable in them. It's difficult to break old belief patterns and walk in new ones. However painful it may be to address those hidden hurts, you can be confident Jesus will set you free as you bring them into the light.

Identify, Confess, Trust

In the charts on the next few pages, I describe some of the ways women protect their hearts instead of trusting God. This is a short list representing just some of the many FIG leaves we use to cover ourselves. I then suggest a way to confess the unbelief and form new beliefs, allowing dependence on God.

As you read through these descriptions, mark any behaviors you sometimes employ and circle the FIG leaves that relate to you personally. Spend some time in prayer and meditation, bringing your FIG leaves into the light through confession. There is a journal page to record any thoughts you may want to remember.

Changed Beliefs Open the Door for Love

We belong to the Bridegroom. When we believe that, we will live free and love others. Let's not be like the "unbelieving generation" that irked Jesus, but a believing generation that believes in God's goodness. What a blessing to know we can find freedom from our FIG leaves through confession and repentance. As we change our beliefs, we can change our behavior and walk in love.

🍂 Control

SIGNS TO IDENTIFY	The control FIG leaf seeks security by trying to control other people and other things through tactics such as manipulating, flattering, controlling. This leaf plays politics to protect position because of fear of trusting God. Control is a false sense of security. This leaf decides it's safer to be my own god and get my own needs met.
CONFESS UNBELIEF	I confess I am afraid you won't take care of me, God, so I need to be in control.
TRUST MY BRIDEGROOM	I believe God is good, has the best plan for my life, and will see that plan through for me. I can trust him completely. I can let go of my life and my agenda. As I trust God, he will lead me and take care of me. As I pray and seek him first, he will take care of my needs.
RELATED SCRIPTURES	Jeremiah 17:7–8; Jeremiah 29:11; Isaiah 41:13–14; John 10:1–21; John 14:27; John 21:17–19; Luke 17:33; Proverbs 3:5–6; Psalm 91:2; Philippians 4:19; Mark 10:29–30; Isaiah 40:11.

Shame

SIGNS TO IDENTIFY	Beating myself up with negative self-talk and possibly self-harm. Lacking in confidence, hiding, fearing punishment from God.
CONFESS UNBELIEF	Lord, I confess I don't believe what Jesus did on the cross is good enough or complete enough, and so even though I am a Christian I must still pay for my mistakes and rely on myself to cover my sin.
TRUST MY BRIDEGROOM	God has covered all my sin and shame through Christ. I rest under his banner of love and the cover of his righteousness by faith in the finished work of the cross.
RELATED SCRIPTURES	Romans 8:1; Romans 4:7; Lamentations 3:22–23; Galatians 2:20–21; 1 John 1:9; Isaiah 61:10; Romans 10:10–11; Hebrews 10:10–14.

Victim

SIGNS TO IDENTIFY	Playing the victim and using circumstances to gain attention. Expecting bad things to happen and believing they only happen to me. Remaining the victim to avoid taking responsibility for my actions.
CONFESS UNBELIEF	Lord, I confess I believe you are not looking out for me, and sometimes I even believe you are against me. I derive identity from being the one bad things happen to.
TRUST MY BRIDEGROOM	Although I live in a fallen world and bad things may happen, God will use them for my good. Nothing will happen to me today that I cannot handle with God's help. I am more than an overcomer because Christ overcame. Jesus will not abandon me to the winds of fate. He walks with me daily. I get my identity from God.
RELATED SCRIPTURES	1 Peter 5:7; Psalm 61:2; Romans 8:28; Romans 8:37–39; John 10:10; Psalm 23; James 1:17; Proverbs 3:5–6; Luke 8:24–25; 1 John 4:4.

🍂 Performance

SIGNS TO IDENTIFY	The performance FIG leaf says this: I must be the greatest or best at everything because I need to hear you say I am good so I can feel good about myself. I get my worth and value from what I do so I need to prove myself. I need a title to be important. I have to be special for others to love me. I have a competitive spirit and criticize others. I have misplaced priorities and workaholism. Try to do everything myself, have a superior attitude, and feel threatened by another person's success.
CONFESS UNBELIEF	Lord, I confess I believe your love for me is based on what I do and how I stack up to others. I look to and believe the world's standards to achieve value.
TRUST MY BRIDEGROOM	God loves me just as I am and thinks I am special because I am his child. I can't earn his love—I just rest and receive it through faith. I look to God and not the world's standards to affirm me. I already have a position as Christ's ambassador and his child. I am chosen and loved by him so I don't need to promote myself. I can rest and be obedient where God has called me.
RELATED SCRIPTURES	Ephesians 1:3–6; Matthew 11:28; 1 Peter 2:9; Jeremiah 29:11; Romans 12:3–8; Philippians 2:3–9; 1 Corinthians 12.

🍂 Idolatry—Codependency

SIGNS TO IDENTIFY	The idolatry FIG leaf looks to people to fill us and give us what only God can bring in our lives. Putting unrealistic expectations on my children, friends, or husband, demanding that they be my gods. Prone to enmeshment. Double mindedness. Unforgiveness. Needing to be needed to feel important.
CONFESS UNBELIEF	I confess I falsely believe people have more power than you, God, and so I should look to people for my worth, value, and identity. I confess I have become deeply attached to others in an unhealthy way.
TRUST MY BRIDEGROOM	Peace and security come through Christ alone. Everlasting joy is found in trusting the Lord and from that place of abundance I give to others. My soul is tied to God so I can walk away from unhealthy relationships.
RELATED SCRIPTURES	Jeremiah 17:5–9; Isaiah 44:6; Galatians 5:1,14; John 4:13–18; Matthew 6:31–34; Nehemiah 8:10; Philippians 2:13; Zephaniah 3:5.

Isolation

SIGNS TO IDENTIFY	Pulling back from loving others. Pulling away from people and God, isolating myself, rejecting others, convincing myself I have nothing in common with my peers.
CONFESS UNBELIEF	Lord, I confess I don't believe I can trust you to defend me so I seek to rely on myself by closing off my heart completely from anyone.
TRUST MY BRIDEGROOM	I can trust God to protect me so my heart can stay open to love others. God gives me love I can give to others. The more love I give to others, the more I receive. I entrust myself to God completely, and trust is a gift I give to others as God leads me.
RELATED SCRIPTURES	Psalm 91; Joshua 23:3; Isaiah 61:7–8; Hebrews 10:24–25; Luke 8:21; Luke 6:31, 38; 1 John 1:7; Psalm 5:11; Galatians 5:13.

People Pleasing

SIGNS TO IDENTIFY	Constantly striving to please others with the expectation of getting something in return. Identity based in what others say about me. Serving not out of love but to get praise. Instead of contributing gifts to the body and depending on others to use theirs, never saying no (which robs others of the chance to serve). Becoming exhausted from trying to do it all, getting angry because no one is helping. A fear of rejection so great that confronting others or speaking the truth in love is very difficult.
CONFESS UNBELIEF	I confess I don't believe what you say about me so I need to seek approval from others to gain my identity and worth. I need everyone to be happy with me and to approve of me in order to feel good about myself. If one person is upset with me, I am not OK.
TRUST MY BRIDEGROOM	I believe Christ gives me my identity. I live to serve and follow him and no one else. I don't have to worry anymore about getting others' approval. I concentrate on following Christ and seek to love others unconditionally and not to live to please them.
RELATED SCRIPTURES	1 Corinthians 7:23; Galatians 1:10; Proverbs 29:25; Psalm 27:10; Hebrews 13:5; Psalm 139:13–14.

Jealousy—Envy—Greed

SIGNS TO IDENTIFY	Feeling threatened by another person's success, belongings, life story, and more. Feeling jealous, envious, or unable to be happy about another person's blessings. Critical of their gifts or talents.
CONFESS UNBELIEF	I confess I believe you have not given me enough and what I have is not good. I confess I am afraid you will not take care of me.
TRUST MY BRIDEGROOM	God gives me exactly what I need when I need it so I can rest in his perfect care being content with what I have. God blesses me in ways the world cannot. As I walk in gratitude, his blessings in my life are amplified and my heart is at rest.
RELATED SCRIPTURES	Matthew 6:33; Psalm 24:1; 1 Timothy 6:18–19; Philippians 4:19; Luke 11:10–12; Philippians 4:11–13; Romans 12:6; James 4:2; Luke 6:38.

Perfectionism

SIGNS TO IDENTIFY	This FIG leaf carries the desire to be perfect, insistence that others be perfect, no tolerance for weakness in others or myself, unrealistic expectations of others and myself, depression or anger caused by unrealistic expectations, fear of taking risks, over-analysis of decisions for fear of making a mistake, passive-aggressive comments about others who are gifted in areas I am not in an effort to pull them down to make myself feel better.
CONFESS UNBELIEF	I confess I don't believe you will love and accept me if I am not perfect and so I rely on myself.
TRUST MY BRIDEGROOM	I rest under Christ's perfection alone. When I am weak, the power of Christ rests on me. If I were perfect, I would not need Jesus. My weaknesses allow me to depend on Christ and trust God. When I make mistakes, I can accept my failure and go to Jesus to get help. When I fall down, he'll pick me up and teach me from my mistakes so I can learn new things. He loves me no matter what.
RELATED SCRIPTURES	2 Corinthians 12:9–10; Lamentations 3:22–23; Psalm 37:23–24; Hebrews 4:14–16; Psalm 40:1–3; 37:24; Hebrews 7:11; Galatians 3:3–6; Romans 3:21–24; Philippians 3:8–9; Romans 8:1; Hebrews 12:10–12.

FIG LEAF JOURNAL

DAY 6

"A man will leave his father and mother and be united to his wife,
and the two will become one flesh." —*Mark 10:7–8*

God designed the marriage relationship before the fall. He takes it seriously, for it is not just a relationship. Quoting Genesis, Jesus reminded the Pharisees who came to test him, "At the beginning of creation God 'made them male and female.' For this reason a man will leave his father and mother and be united to his wife, and the two will become one flesh" (Mark 10:6–8).

In marriage, God created a relationship like no other. It goes beyond any friendship. It is a covenant in which two lives intertwine to become one. With the purpose of providing a reflection of the relationship between Christ and the church, the marriage relationship was designed to reveal God's heart for intimacy with us.

God's plan was that, inside the marriage relationship, family would grow against the backdrop of a framework divinely designed by the Author of family himself. Like a carefully constructed canvas, this framework provides a place for God to paint a beautiful picture, an illustration of the type of relationship he desires with us on many levels. Indeed, the two—our earthly families and God's family—are so closely related that our own experience with family has a direct effect on how we see God and relate to him.

Understanding our relationship with Jesus through the lens of marriage is the very foundation of this Bible study. So whether you are single, married, divorced, or widowed, marriage provides a reference point for your relationship with God.

Sadly, under the weight of a broken world, the experiences most of us have with families is fractured rather than whole, distorted rather than ideal. Every woman has an imperfect family. While God's framework for family is perfect, we are not. The perfect family does not exist because there are no perfect people.

Read Matthew 19:1–10, Ephesians 5:21–25, and 1 Corinthians 7:10–16.
What do these scriptures reveal about God's framework for family?

What do these scriptures reveal to you about God's heart for women inside the family?

_____

_____

_____

Because there are no perfect families, we have all experienced brokenness within our family structures. How has this impacted your life? How has it affected the way you relate to God?

_____

_____

_____

God's design for family establishes a framework that creates a place of rest, solace, and love—a refuge from the storms of life. His boundaries establish a place where we are free to make the mistakes necessary to uncover our true potential and thrive, free to become who God created us to be. Wives are to be loved as Christ loved the church. Husbands are to leave the nest of their mothers to create their own family, putting their wives first. Daughters are to be valued and raised without anger through unconditional love.

This love, family love, is sacrificial. It is costly. It brings beauty.

Just after Paul's description of God's family framework in the book of Ephesians, he writes about the armor of God and our war with the enemy (Ephesians 5:21–6:20). This order in Scripture is no accident. The enemy knows there is strength in family and would love nothing more than to destroy God's design, because then he can distort our perception of our relationship with him. But Satan's attack on family goes beyond just us; it is an attack on the gospel itself, since God's family framework communicates the reflection of his desire to have a relationship with all people.

Don't believe the enemy's lies that God's framework for family doesn't work. If marriage and family have failed to satisfy your own needs or the needs of society, it was not God or his plans that failed. It was people, fallen and imperfect, who were not there to fulfill their God-given role so that you could have the security you needed. It was people, fallen and imperfect, who did not love and nurture you the way God designed you to be cared for.

But even in the brokenness of our own family frameworks, the gospel message pierces through those cracks when we look to Jesus. Redemption. Forgiveness. Adoption. Unconditional love. From our Nourish Scripture this week, we see the heart of Jesus toward women inside fractured families. Let the imperfections in your family drive you straight into the arms of the only source of perfect love—Jesus. Let the fractures be the very parchment upon which Jesus writes his story of redemption, illustrating it with your life.

God wants to fill every relational need you have. He can be your heavenly husband (Revelation 21:9), your ultimate promise keeper (2 Corinthians 1:20), your perfect provider (Philippians 4:19), your protector and defender (Romans 8:33–39). He is your Abba Father (Romans 8:15), the Good Shepherd who guards and guides you perfectly (John 10:10–27). He is your nurturing mother (Isaiah 49:15; Matthew 19:14) and best friend (John 15:15). He is your trustworthy guide (John 10:27), your wise counselor (John 15:26), your healer (Matthew 9:35), your loving and wise teacher (John 16:12–15), your righteous Savior (2 Corinthians 5:21), your Great High Priest (Hebrews 4:14). Every area of your relational needs can be met in the Lord.

Redemption

What happens if your husband has broken his covenant with you by leaving you for another or abusing you? God's Word calls a man to love his wife as Christ loved the church. I believe our Lord grieves over marriages where abuse of any kind exists.

As women, we have to realize that we cannot control others. We can pray for our husbands to change. We can focus on our God-given responsibilities. But these things provide no guarantee that our husbands will change. We can live in peace insofar as it depends on us. But if an unbelieving husband chooses to leave, the apostle Paul tells us to let him go (1 Corinthians 7:10–16). If he commits adultery, God's Word gives the woman freedom to leave because the man has broken a covenant. (However, we know from other scriptures that God wants us to reconcile with our spouses whenever possible.)

If you have experienced the pain of abuse and adultery, then remember this: Jesus is your Bridegroom, and God will provide for you as he provided for the children of Israel in the desert. Jesus knows your whole story. He knows your heart; he knows how much you so desperately want to be loved. He is willing to be your Bridegroom, to meet those needs, and to never leave you.

Also know this: the fact that your marriage failed does not mean that you are a failure.

Don't look to your past. Don't blame God for imperfect people. Bride of Christ, it's time to trust Jesus and move forward. Step by step, commit your ways to the Lord, and he will lead you into his perfect plan for you.

Finding Freedom from the Past

Heather experienced the pain of adultery, divorce, and shame. Here is her story about finding freedom from her past—and God's redemption for her future.

> Mine is not a unique story. I was raised in a Christian home, saved at an early age, and hardly ever missed a Sunday in church. However, by my early twenties, I began to head for that faraway country of partying and making terrible decisions, one of the

worst being marrying "the wrong guy." As one can imagine, ours was a rocky relationship from the beginning, and no matter how hard or often I prayed, and regardless of the fact that I saw a Christian counselor, my marriage was not saved. My ex-husband never did become that faithful man I so desperately wanted, and in the end, he chose the "other woman" over me.

Naturally, I was crushed and hated the fact that I had become a statistic. I prayed that the Lord would restore the years that the locust had eaten (Joel 2:25), so when I later married a wonderful Christian man, I thought that was the end of the story. Not even close!

The real healing had to come from within, and it took not only my forgiving those who had hurt me but also forgiving myself. It was a long road to this realization. I had not only been rejected by a man, but also later I had been told by the church that I could not serve in a certain capacity because of my divorced status, so I felt rejected by the church too. That was a blow.

So despite my new, wonderful, equally yoked Christian marriage, I walked around broken, insecure, and with "the big D" on my back, which I had, of course, put there. But because I knew the Bible says, "God hates divorce," I cleverly hid all of these feelings behind the "happy Christian wife mask." It was exhausting.

Then one day, after completely falling apart, I finally began to believe that despite it all, Jesus really did love me. Yes, even ME. He had been with me through everything. He had held me close and cried with me. And yes, he absolutely hates divorce. Who doesn't? He hates it because it hurts his children. And he hurts with them.

I know that God hated my going through the divorce. It certainly wasn't his desire for me, but it never meant that he loved me any less because I did go through it. In fact, I now know that he loves this bride so much that he has set her free to throw away the mask and tell her story.

If you have gone through a divorce, you can allow the pain of your divorce to make you either bitter or better. If you were at fault in your divorce, just take that to the Lord. Take it to the cross through confession, and then move forward, believing God is able and willing to do great things in your life.

When we move forward, God can use our story to continue painting a picture of Christ's relationship with the church through redemption. Heather is married now to a wonderful man, and they have adopted two beautiful children from China.

Your Role Is Vital

Our world offers women no applause for motherhood or for being a supportive wife. So we may not understand the difference women can make within the family.

In the beginning, when life was as it should be, Eve was given to Adam to help him. Don't misunderstand what the Bible means when it tells us that. The Hebrew word for "helper" used in Genesis to describe Eve is *ezer*.[4] It's not a word that describes a cute little maidservant who helps her husband by bringing him his favorite drink on a hot day while he changes the wheel on the chariot. This is a robust word that refers to life-saving help without which Adam might die. Outside of the two references to Eve, it is used only nineteen other times in the entire Bible—and then, only to describe God. So fear not—your role is not boring, nor is it an unimportant luxury addition. It is indispensible to your husband's very life and vital to the created order.

But this is not how women see their roles. We are surrounded by so many misconceptions, even from Christians, about a woman's role. Submission and respect are poorly understood; respecting our husbands should never require disrespecting ourselves or disobeying God. Yet examples of abuse are all around us. And the enemy uses such circumstances to lie to us that God's ways don't work and that his system results in weak women, not strong ones.

In my own marriage, I operated for years from a framework that was completely out of alignment with the truth—and I didn't even know it. When life was easy sailing, I got by. But then a major storm hit our lives, and my need to be in control slipped into high gear. And that's when my marriage faced its greatest challenge.

Fortunately, a friend introduced me to April Cassidy's ministry (www.peacefulwife.com), and my eyes were opened to God's truth. God never wanted me to just get by—he wanted so much more. He wants more for you too! April, author of *The Peaceful Wife*, shares this insight in her book:

> What many wives don't realize is that we don't lose power and influence when we obey God's Word and His commands for us as wives. The only power we lose is our sinful power to destroy, tear down, and harm. We gain the power of heaven! We gain the power of Christ![5]

Many women, because of emotional wounds they have received in life, are suspicious of the words *submission* and *respect*. My own hurts needed the healing of Jesus first before I was truly able to begin to embrace my God-given role as a wife. And I am still on that journey today. If we take the hand of Jesus, who knows everything about us, he will lead us in creating new legacies in our family, no matter how damaging the legacies of past generations and even our own earlier years may have been. Reestablish God's framework in *your* family, and leave blessings in your wake for future generations.

Above all, remember that a man can never complete you. Although our husbands have the ability to love *like* Christ, they cannot—no matter how wonderful they are—*be* Christ. To expect Christ's perfection from our husbands is unrealistic and unscriptural. But society has given us expectations that *are*, in fact, unrealistic and unscriptural. From the time we are toddlers, watching with wonder those fairy tales where handsome princes come to rescue the damsel in distress, we are taught that we can be completed by a man. Then when we do marry and our husbands fail that impossible expectation we have placed on them, we continue to live with unsettled souls.

Within the marriage relationship, God gives us the opportunity to love and be loved, to experience deep significance, to put another above ourselves, to serve sacrificially. In a marriage, both partners are called to give … and give … and give some more. We are called to serve each other. If we can find our life only by laying it down, marriage can provide that opportunity.

Bride of Christ, let's begin to look at marriage as a God-given opportunity to reflect Christ's relationship with the church. By leaning on him to meet all our needs, let's grow closer to Christ. From that place of abundance, let's grow to be the women God created us to be. And during times of challenge, let's remember our marriage covenant as God remembers the covenant of love he made with us.

Our goal should not be perfect families but rather families and lives that reflect God's perfect love toward others within our fallen, fractured world. Could there be any greater blessing in life than that?

VIDEO SESSION NOTES

Session 8
HER HEART
Mark 10:17–22

Videos located online at www.nourishbiblestudyseries.com

Chapter 9
MY FATHER'S HOUSE

DAY 1

Nourish Scripture: Mark 10:46–11:26

 PRAY.

Begin your time with God in prayer.

MEDITATE ON GOD'S WORD.

Using your Anchor of Truth Card* from last week's Nourish Notes, renew your mind on that truth. Quiet and focus your thoughts. Pray the truth. Say the truth. Meditate on God's truth.

TAKE THE *REVEAL* STEP OF THE NOURISH™ BIBLE STUDY METHOD.

Connect with Jesus by studying the Weekly Nourish Scripture and allowing the Holy Spirit to reveal truth in those verses. Prayerfully read over and reflect on the passage. Mark any phrases, verses, or words that catch your attention. Journal and learn as the Lord leads you.

*Anchor of Truth Cards are available at www.TreasuredMinistries.com/shop

DAY 2
Nourish Scripture: Mark 10:46–11:26

1 PRAY.
Begin your time with God in prayer.

2 MEDITATE ON GOD'S WORD.
Using your Anchor of Truth Card* from last week's Nourish Notes, renew your mind on that truth. Quiet and focus your thoughts. Pray the truth. Say the truth. Meditate on God's truth.

3 TAKE THE *RESPOND* STEP OF THE NOURISH™ BIBLE STUDY METHOD.
Respond to activate truth in your life. The acronym **IMPACT™** provides questions to help you apply the truth from your weekly Nourish Scripture. **Sometimes you may not have answers for all six questions.**

IMAGE OF GOD TO TRUST? An attribute of God, Jesus, or the Holy Spirit to trust.

MESSAGE TO SHARE? A word of encouragement, truth, or prayer to share.

PROMISE TO TREASURE? A promise in the Bible to believe.

ACTION TO TAKE? A specific step God is calling you to take.

CORE IDENTITY IN CHRIST TO AFFIRM? A truth about how God sees you to affirm.

TRANSGRESSION TO CONFESS? A sin to acknowledge for help, healing, and restoration through Christ.

*Anchor of Truth Cards are available at www.TreasuredMinistries.com/shop

DAY 3
Nourish Scripture: Mark 10:46–11:26

 PRAY.

Begin your time with God in prayer.

 MEDITATE ON GOD'S WORD.

Using your Anchor of Truth Card* from last week's Nourish Notes, renew your mind on that truth. Quiet and focus your thoughts. Pray the truth. Say the truth. Meditate on God's truth.

 TAKE THE *RENEW* STEP OF THE NOURISH™ BIBLE STUDY METHOD.

Like an anchor that secures its vessel, biblical meditation secures truth to transform your life. Take five minutes to *renew* your mind by focusing on one word, verse, or truth that the Holy Spirit revealed through the Bible during your week of study. Record your truth below and on your Anchor of Truth card.* Quiet your thoughts. Focus on the truth. Read the truth. Pray the truth.

 UTILIZE YOUR *ANCHOR OF TRUTH* CARD AS A BOOKMARK TO CULTIVATE A DAILY PRACTICE OF BIBLICAL MEDITATION.

Place your Anchor of Truth Card* in your Bible study workbook to bookmark tomorrow's day of study. Let your Anchor of Truth bookmark remind you to pause and renew your mind on God's Word. Repeat this process daily, continuing to reflect on your Anchor of Truth to start your quiet time until the next week, when God reveals another truth to you.

*Anchor of Truth Cards are available at www.TreasuredMinistries.com/shop

DAY 4

"And as he taught them, he said, "Is it not written: 'My house will be called a house of prayer for all nations'? But you have made it 'a den of robbers.'" —*Mark 11:17*

"Get out of here! How dare you turn my Father's house into a market?" The Bridegroom was beside himself. Anger surfaced to the brim and boiled over. The temple—the house of God—was designed to be a place for praying in the peace of God's presence. The constant swirl of activity must have stung his heart because it robbed the people of God's presence and the gift of prayer. Prayer was lost in the constant shuffle of money changing hands. The clutter of commerce distracted people from the beautiful blessing of a place filled with prayer.

> This was not the first time Jesus cleared the temple. Read John 2:13–17. Put yourself in the disciples' shoes. How would you respond if you saw Jesus tear through the temple with a whip in his hand?

> _____

> _____

> _____

Immediately after Jesus turned the water into wine at the wedding in Galilee, he went to Jerusalem. There he found his Father's house had been invaded by businessmen who had traded a place of prayer for a marketplace filled with frenzy and extortion. A holy anger arose in Jesus. The disciples watched their Savior's usually calm demeanor fade. He cleared away the confusion by using a whip he made himself. The manipulative money changers had pushed him to take drastic measures.

I imagine the disciples looked wide-eyed with wonder as Jesus tore through the temple. Their recall of Scripture gave them insight into his fervor for his temple to be a place of his presence (John 2:17; Psalm 69:9).

God's Temple Today

> Read 1 Corinthians 3:16. What is God's temple today? What fills today's temple?

> _____

> _____

> _____

After Jesus' death and resurrection, our bodies became his temple. The Holy Spirit lives in every believer. Jesus breathed on the disciples and said, "Receive the Holy Spirit" (John 20:22). If you are a Christian, you have received the Holy Spirit (Ephesians 1:13). Bride of Christ, the Spirit of the Living God lives inside you! You are God's temple and Jesus still has a consuming passion for his temple to be a place of prayer. Why? Because linking us with the Lord in an intimate relationship, prayer is the prescribed pathway to God's presence. We need the peace, power, and joy that come through prayer. The power of prayer produces fruit in our lives.

Out of his love for his Father—and for the people—Jesus overturned the tables to clear the path for prayer. Because he loves us, he may turn over some tables in our lives if they rob our prayer life and the blessings it brings. I can think of plenty of clutter I need to clear out of my temple. How many days have I chosen to worry instead of trusting the Holy Spirit to guide me? Instead of lifting my request to God and asking him to take care of a problem, my mind grapples with a million ways to fix it. My ways—not his. How about you? What is cluttering your temple and robbing you of your prayer life?

Let's peek into this passage to explore some potential prayer stealers and ask Jesus to overturn the tables so we can enjoy the blessing of being filled and fruitful!

A Religious Mindset Will Rob Your Prayer Life

You do not have to retreat to a private place or get in a certain posture to talk to God. You just have to pause and remember he is always with you and wants to be involved in every area of your life. He wants an intimate relationship with you. Understanding this can free you from the religious mindset that prayer can happen only during a "morning quiet time."

Continual prayer prompted by the Holy Spirit throughout the day keeps us connected with a God who loves us with a passion beyond the scope of our human understanding. In chapter 3 we talked about the importance of pulling away to be alone with Jesus and communing with him through prayer and Bible study. We also need to be sensitive to the Holy Spirit throughout each day as he prompts us to pray. First Thessalonians 5:17 says, "Pray continually."

You may say, "I don't have enough time to pray." But praying continually doesn't require hiding away in your prayer closet for hours at a time (although some are called to do that).

Thinking we need to pray for x amount of time can keep us from praying at all. Complicated prayer formulas and religious hoops are not of God. They distract us and will eventually wear us out. Most of the prayers recorded in the Bible are short and do not follow a set pattern.

God does not measure the length of our prayers. He doesn't look for flowery language (Matthew 6:7). He is not about pride or pretense—but faith and love. It's those bold, unpretentious prayers backed with our faith in God that move mountains.

Condemnation Can Rob Your Prayers

Self-condemnation will distract you from continual prayer. Remember that Christ covers us with his robe of righteousness. God sees Jesus' righteousness when you pray. You need to see yourself that way too.

When Bartimaeus prayed, he asked for mercy because he knew he was guilty of sin and needed forgiveness. His blindness may or may not have been related to his sin, but he knew he needed spiritual healing as well as physical healing, and he was not afraid to get help from Jesus.

Condemnation is one of the devil's primary tools against us because it keeps us from asking God for help. Thinking that God cannot help you because you are not worthy enough is an old-covenant mindset. Bartimaeus threw his outer garments aside and ran to Jesus. Bride of Christ, throw off those outer garments of condemnation and pray with hopeful expectancy of faith in God's goodness in your life.

Only one is worthy—his name is Jesus. He lives to intercede for you (Hebrews 7:25–28). When God looks down, he does not see your sin—he sees the righteousness of the Bridegroom. When you pray in Jesus' name, you are essentially saying, *I am coming to God and presenting my requests based on his name, not mine* (John 15:16).

Let Jesus clear the clutter of your past. Go boldly before the throne in his name. See yourself as God does: forgiven, clothed in the righteousness of Christ.

Other Voices Can Rob Your Prayer Life

Bartimaeus ignored the people who rebuked and tried to silence him.

How have people tried to silence your bold prayers? "Jesus doesn't heal anymore." "You deserve what's happening to you." "Speaking to a mountain—that's ridiculous!"

How has the enemy tried to silence your prayers? "Prayer doesn't work. You don't really need to pray. God is too busy to answer you." "You didn't pray right. God didn't hear you. He doesn't care about you."

When you have a need, great or small, forget about what other people say and cry out to Jesus. Your Bridegroom cares. Prayer is God's will and he wants us to ask for help. If Jesus knows how many hairs are on our heads, he surely knew Bartimaeus was blind. Yet when he cried out, Jesus said, "What do you want me to do for you?" (Mark 10:51). Although Jesus knew his need, *he wanted Bartimaeus to ask*.

The Bible is clear. James 4:2 says, "You do not have, because you do not ask God." Matthew 7:7 tells us to ask, seek, knock, and the door will be opened. Jesus wants us to ask him to meet our needs. God loves it when we ask him about anything (Matthew 7:11).

God will always work through his prescribed ways. Speaking to a mountain in your life and telling it to move may seem ridiculous, but don't let feeling foolish distract you from praying bold prayers. Pray God's way, knowing his ways are so much higher than ours (Isaiah 55:8–9). Take care that your intellect doesn't hinder you from trusting God's plan. "The foolishness of God is wiser than man's wisdom" (1 Corinthians 1:25). I challenge you to respond to the Holy Spirit as he prompts you to lift bold, simple prayers backed by faith—and watch your mountains move.

Bartimaeus did not keep silent. He pressed on. In bold simplicity, he cried out to Jesus. When Bartimaeus shouted, Jesus stopped and called to him (Mark 10:49). Jesus was on his way to Jerusalem for the main part of his earthly ministry, but he took time to stop for the blind man crying out to see! Jesus always cares and always has time for us.

Complaining Robs Your Prayer Life

Sometimes we get distracted by complaining about the mountain instead of speaking to it. Instead of addressing the mountain through prayer, we just walk around it, grumbling all the way. If we find a friend with the same problem, we join forces and complain to each other. Venting to a friend may make us feel good for a while, but it does not solve our problems. Instead, it adds fuel to them because it turns our focus and faith on the problem instead of Jesus. We also pull others down around us because complaining creates what I call a complaining vortex that sucks everyone into the negative.

There is nothing wrong with godly counsel, but watch that you are not going around and around the mountain repeatedly, sharing your complaints with a friend. "But she understands me!" you may want to say. This may be true, but she can't meet your needs. Only Jesus can do that. A good friend will stop you from repeatedly following the trail of complaints around your mountain and encourage you to pray.

Doubt Robs Your Prayer Life

Jesus promises when we speak to the mountain and do not doubt in our heart, the mountain will move (Mark 9:23–25; Matthew 21:21). To activate this promise, we must walk in faith released through our trust in God alone. We may pray boldly, but then quickly doubt when we don't see the mountain move when we think it should. Just because we have not seen the mountain move yet does not mean God is not the mountain mover!

Bride of Christ, what has God spoken to your heart? What promises has he whispered in your ear? Jesus gave his disciples specific instructions about finding a colt to bring to him. Everything happened just as he had described. This promise, this prophecy, was fulfilled quickly. Sometimes his promises take much longer to be fulfilled. More than five hundred years earlier God had prophesied through Zechariah about Jesus riding into Jerusalem on a colt (Zechariah 9:9). Whether a prophecy is fulfilled quickly or thousands of years later—God's prophecies always come to pass.

Fulfillment of prophecy is proof that God's Word is trustworthy. We can count on his promises.

Are you like the prophets? Sometimes they waited for years to see God's promises fulfilled. Sometimes they did not see the answer in their lifetime. But they believed. Not because of what they saw but because of who God is. They did not doubt him. Do you have that kind of faith?

We Need Continuous Filling of the Holy Spirit

Jim Cymbala, pastor of the Brooklyn Tabernacle Church, writes this in his book *Fresh Wind, Fresh Fire*: "Our store of spiritual power apparently dissipates with time. Daily living, distractions, and spiritual warfare take their toll. We need, in the words Paul used in Ephesians 5:18, to 'be always being filled with the Spirit' (literal translation)."[1]

Just as Jesus had to clear the temple repeatedly, we need to return repeatedly to the Holy Spirit to guide us and empower us when we pray.

According to Romans 8:15–17, when did God's Spirit begin living in you?

According to Ephesians 6:18, when should we invite the Holy Spirit to guide our prayers?

According to Romans 8:26–27, how does the Holy Spirit help us pray?

According to 1 Corinthians 2:10–12, why should we pray in the Spirit?

Seek a Fruit-Bearing Prayer Life

Continual communion with God through the promptings of the Holy Spirit keeps us connected with a God who loves us beyond measure and fills us with his presence. When we pray led by the Spirit, we are filled with his presence. When we are filled with his presence, more fruit will naturally come forth as we depend on Jesus for our strength.

> "I am the vine; you are the branches. If you remain in me and I in you, you will bear much fruit; apart from me you can do nothing. If you do not remain in me, you are like a branch that is thrown away and withers; such branches are picked up, thrown into the fire and burned. If you remain in me and my words remain in you, ask whatever you wish, and it will be done for you. This is to my Father's glory, that you bear much fruit, showing yourselves to be my disciples." (John 15:5–8 NIV 2011)

In our Nourish Scripture for this week, Jesus was frustrated with a fig tree that was not bearing fruit. A tree does not have to toil to produce fruit—it happens naturally. The fruit of the Spirit—love, joy, peace, forbearance, kindness, goodness, faithfulness, gentleness, and self-control—come from staying close to Jesus like a vine on a branch.

I found it interesting that Jesus was angry with the fig tree for not producing fruit when it was out of season. Mark 11:20 tells us the fruit tree was "withered from the roots." We cultivate our roots by trusting in the Lord and leaning on him and not our own strength (Jeremiah 17:7–8).

A lack of prayer in our lives suggests we are depending on our own strength instead of God's. The fig tree was often associated with the nation of Israel (Jeremiah 8:13; Hosea 9:10; Nahum 3:12). Israel refused to see Jesus as their Savior, and so they did not bear fruit. Similarly, when we don't see Jesus as our strength, we look to ourselves or another source to help us and do not bear fruit.

I think it frustrates Jesus when we claim to be his disciple but don't bear fruit because we don't have the power that comes from continual prayer and abiding with him. When we depend on God, we bear supernatural fruit without ceasing, no matter what the season (Jeremiah 17:7–8).

Prayer Is a Privilege

Prayer is one of the greatest privileges of being a bride. Be of good cheer. On your feet! Jesus is calling you. He is never distracted and is always available. Sadly, we can be easily distracted from turning to him and don't always make ourselves fully available to him.

Listen! He stands at the door. When we pray, we open that door into his presence through an intimate relationship. Stay filled with the Spirit by keeping this door open all day long. When you are prompted by the Holy Spirit, pause and pray. Don't miss one of the greatest gifts of being a Christian. Keep your temple clear of distractions and pray throughout your day.

Key Treasure

Linking us with the Lord in an intimate relationship, prayer is the prescribed pathway to God's presence.

DAY 5

"Be kind and compassionate to one another, forgiving each other,
just as in Christ God forgave you." —*Ephesians 4:32*

At a women's conference, I was privileged to hear Charlotte Gambill, daughter of Paul Scanlon, the founder of Abundant Life Church in England, speak on the influence and impact of forgiveness. Charlotte's message made a lasting impression on my life. Her candid humor and agile ability to teach the Bible painted a clear picture of the story of Herodias and the devastation that comes when we hold on to a grudge.

Herodias was a woman of great influence. No doubt she was beautiful for she had captured the heart of King Herod. With her wealth and position, she carried power, but she also carried a grudge against John the Baptist. She had left her husband to marry his brother, and John called out the sin in this new marriage. Herodias took offense, clung to unforgiveness, and a grudge was born. Charlotte pointed out that Mark 6:19 tells us that she "nursed" this grudge. Time passed. The grudge continued to grow and finally took control of her life.

At Herod's birthday party when her daughter had danced most provocatively before the guests of high officials, military commanders, and the leading men of Galilee, a delightful opportunity presented itself for Herodias to satisfy her need for revenge. Her handsome husband, Herod, was so mesmerized by the way Herodias's daughter moved, he promised her anything she wanted up to half the kingdom. Imagine the good that could be accomplished for God's kingdom with all that wealth! The dutiful daughter asked her mother what she should request. Charlotte noted that instead of using her influence for good, Herodias let bitterness rule as she asked for the head of John the Baptist.

Nothing Positive Can Come from Nursing a Grudge

When we nurse a grudge and cling to unforgiveness, we come under the influence of evil thoughts and actions. Nothing positive results from a woman nursing a grudge. Nothing. When we nurse grudges, we play into Satan's hands, and our influence is wasted instead of being used for God's glory.[2]

A woman who prays carries great influence. However, carrying unforgiveness or nursing grudges as Herodias did can have a negative impact on our prayer life. Today we are going to look at the connection between forgiveness and our prayer life. We'll also talk about some practical keys to getting out of the prison of bitterness. It's time to stop nursing those grudges and use our influence to bring glory to our Bridegroom!

Pray and Forgive

"Therefore I tell you, whatever you ask for in prayer, believe that you have received it, and it will be yours. **And** when you stand praying, if you hold anything against anyone, forgive him, so that your Father in heaven may forgive you your sins." (Mark 11:24–25, *emphasis mine*)

I think the most powerful and probably overlooked word in this passage is the word *and*. This word links the importance of forgiveness to a powerful prayer life. We know faith is a key to powerful prayer, but forgiveness is essential also. For our prayers to be effective, we need to walk in the righteousness of Christ, faith, and forgiveness (James 5:16; Mark 11:24–25).

In our fallen world, a bride's heart is vulnerable to being hurt by others in her life. Sometimes this hurt can come from the most unlikely places—a trusted friend, a family member, someone in a leadership position. The ones who are called to defend and protect us may let us down. In fact, the closer the person who causes the offense is to us, the deeper the hurt. Bitterness puts us in a prison of torment and shuts down our hearts.

Unforgiveness hurts our health, destroys relationships, is a waste of energy, and grieves the Holy Spirit (Ephesians 4:30–32). Buried bitterness is a terrible poison that spills out into the lives of those around us. I have heard it preached many times: hurting people hurt others, and when we nurse a grudge, we pass on bitterness instead of blessing.

Call Satan's Bluff

Grudges are Satan's tools to destroy our lives. Satan works through people to hurt us and put us in the prison of unforgiveness (Ephesians 6:11–12; 2 Corinthians 2:10–11). Be aware, bride. Unforgiveness is his scheme to keep you from living the blessed life. Want to move mountains? Call his bluff! Paul told the Corinthians this:

"If you forgive anyone, I also forgive him. And what I have forgiven—if there was anything to forgive—I have forgiven in the sight of Christ for your sake, in order that Satan might not outwit us. For we are not unaware of his schemes." (2 Corinthians 2:10–11)

Be wise, bride. Don't allow his schemes to outwit you. You can use your influence as a woman for God's purposes. However, when you pull up to the banquet of bitterness, you are dining with the devil. He's serving anger and strife. The one who comes to kill, steal, and destroy will rob your sleep, your health, your destiny with God, your blessings, and your prayer life.

But God has given us a greater way. Release offenders to God so you can receive peace through forgiveness. Let's be wise and walk in forgiveness.

Forgive as You Have Been Forgiven

What does it mean to forgive? Forgiveness does not necessarily equal trust or a restored relationship. Restoration may result from forgiveness, but forgiveness does not mean you return to the person who abused you. Forgiveness is not saying what the person did was right. God wants you to forgive for your benefit.

> In our fallen world beyond the garden of Eden, we have learned that brides will experience bruises along the way caused by others hurting us. A natural reaction to this hurt is to feel that person owes us something. The debt could be anything. Think about a hurt you cannot seem to release. What does that person owe you? Money? Time? Your childhood? Your self-esteem? An apology? Your health? Your marriage? What has been stolen? Your dignity, self-respect, or self-worth? Your reputation?

_____

_____

_____

Our offender may never be able—or willing—to give us back what they took. However, instead of looking to the offending person to restore what we lost, we need to look to Jesus.

Jesus Is Our Restorer

Jesus, our Bridegroom, has secured spiritual blessing for believers and promises to bring restoration to the hurts in our lives. Jesus brings justice to the injustices in our lives. It is not our job to administer justice and make everything right and fair. Further, the Word tells us Jesus can make up for the hurts in our lives. People cannot restore what has been lost, but Jesus can (Isaiah 61:7). The restoration may not come from the person who owes us, but it will come. Selah!

> Read Luke 17:3–6. How did the disciples pray after Jesus told them to forgive seven times in a day?

_____

_____

_____

Faith Makes Forgiveness Possible

There is a relationship between forgiveness and faith. When Jesus told his disciples to forgive seven times a day, they cried out, "Increase our faith." When we cling to unforgiveness, we are putting our faith in people coming through for us. Jesus said, "Have faith in God" (Mark 11:22). Forgiveness is not saying what happened was acceptable or right. Forgiveness is saying, "I release you so I can receive from God." We may never receive what we are due from that person, but God will take care of us in ways beyond our thinking.

But we must first forgive. As we forgive, we are placing our faith in the King of Kings, who owns everything! (Psalm 24:1).

This past summer I was clinging to unforgiveness in a relationship. One night I confided in a good friend of mine, a wise bride of Christ. I told her about my hurt and that this person would not even admit she had done anything wrong. I wanted the offender to say she was sorry, and I was going to hold her to it. She owed me an apology! I also told my friend about a long-standing prayer request that I had yet to see God answer. This wise bride said, "Aliene, God has much to release in your life, but he is waiting for you to release the one that hurt you."

She was right. After I cried out to God for help, he gave me the ability to release the offender. Jesus has been true to his word—restoration beyond measure. Answers to prayers began to surface.

Perhaps the mountain in your life has not yet moved because you are harboring unforgiveness. Release the debt so you can receive peace and restoration from Jesus.

Think about a tightly balled fist representing unforgiveness and bitterness. When God pours down his blessings, we cannot receive them because our hands are closed. But when we release others, we can open our hands to receive from God. I have always believed faith is one of the most important aspects of prayer. However, after pondering on this passage, my eyes are wide open to the truth that forgiveness opens my clenched hands to receive because it places my faith in God instead of man. This is the relationship between faith and unforgiveness and our prayer life. Life is not fair—and it never will be—but God is faithful to give us more than enough when we consistently walk in forgiveness.

Where do you need a release in your life? Are you holding on to any unforgiveness? Where is your faith? Do you have a personal story of seeing God's release in your life because of forgiveness? Would you be willing to share with the group?

_____

_____

_____

Six Keys to Freedom

God has equipped his brides with the ability to move mountains. However, if you are carrying the burden of unforgiveness on your back, your faith is misplaced and the mountains in your life cannot be moved. Instead of carrying the weight of unforgiveness, carry the keys to forgiveness that open the painful prison doors of bitterness to set you free.

KEY #1: Remember God is your source. The first key to escaping from the prison of unforgiveness is keeping our faith and expectations in the Lord and not man. Jesus kept his trust in God and not man.

"Jesus would not entrust himself to them, for he knew all people" (John 2:24 NIV 2011). Trust is a gift from God. This does not mean we shouldn't trust anyone; it means we should always depend on God. People are people. We all have our faults. No matter how wonderful people are, they have the potential to hurt us because they are not perfect. However, if our faith is in God, we are free.

God is your defender (Joshua 23:10; Exodus 14:14). He is your promise keeper (Joshua 23:14). He is your provider (Matthew 6:33; Philippians 4:19). He is the lover of your soul. God protects your heart. He gives you acceptance and abundance in his love and grace. This is where your trust needs to rest.

KEY #2: **Make praise a prayer priority.** The second key is to remember to keep praise a priority of your prayer life. Praise is thanking God for what he has done.

When Paul and Silas found themselves unjustly put in prison, they began praising God with hymns (Acts 16:25). If you find yourself in a prison of bitterness, may I suggest you crank up your worship music and sing praises!

Spend time in praise and thankfulness for what God has done in your life. The more you reflect on your blessings, the more you will remember God can do greater things than you could ever ask (Ephesians 3:20). As you reflect and remember, you will rest your trust in your Bridegroom and be brave enough to let go of hurts in your life, knowing that God is on your side.

KEY #3: **Consider the debt Jesus paid for us.** A third key is to ask God to show us our personal sin debt. When I look at the sin in my life and God's grace that freely covers it all, how can I hold a debt over anyone else? God's grace through Christ covers all our sin. Grace stands for God's Riches At Christ's Expense. The more we see the sin in our lives, the more we see God's grace and find it easier to show the same grace to others.

Stay humble. Pride and self-righteousness can steal our compassion for others. We don't deserve God's grace, but he gives it. And so we need to give grace to others, even if they don't deserve it.

Jesus offered us grace by paying with his life for our sins. His gift of forgiveness is so much bigger than any forgiveness we may be called to extend to those who have hurt us.

KEY #4: **Choose to forgive.** A fourth key to getting out of the prison of unforgiveness is to realize that forgiveness is a choice. When someone has hurt you, you will probably not feel like forgiving. Don't wait for the feelings to surface—make a choice to obey God. We receive our forgiveness by faith—not feelings—and we must offer forgiveness based on faith, not feelings.

This is a choice you will need to make day after day (Luke 17:3–5). If you choose to forgive someone, don't be surprised if you are tempted to go back into the prison of bitterness.

Say aloud, "I have released that debt to the Lord and I am trusting God. I choose to remain in forgiveness and stay out of the prison of bitterness. I am free in Jesus' name."

KEY #5: Rely on the power of the Holy Spirit. A fifth key is to realize the necessity of relying on the Holy Spirit to empower you to forgive. To hold on to hurts is understandable, justifiable, and natural. To get angry and want revenge is easy. But to forgive is supernatural. God has given you his resurrection power through the Holy Spirit. Cry out for help.

You are not alone. God is with you as you step out in obedience to forgive. He'll equip you to forgive and be free!

KEY #6: Let it go! A final key is to surrender. Forgiveness is not merely a suggestion—it is a command, a dance step our Bridegroom wants us to take. If you belong to the Bridegroom, he is your Savior—but is he your Lord? Let the unforgiveness go!

What Have You Learned?

What is one new truth you learned about forgiveness this week? How will you apply it to your life?

_____

_____

_____

Herodias was beautiful. She had wealth and power, but because she nursed a grudge, she used her influence for evil instead of kingdom purposes. Nursing grudges is simply not worth the torment and bad choices they bring to our lives.

Your Bridegroom loves you radically, and he is asking you to do the same. Part of loving is forgiving.

Freedom from Unforgiveness Brings Freedom in Prayer

Walking in forgiveness is for your benefit. When you hold on to hurts, you put yourself in a prison. Unforgiveness affects every area of your life, including your prayer life.

One of the most important things you can do for your prayer life is to keep your heart clean by walking in forgiveness. When you hold on to hurts, your faith is misplaced. Get up from the table of unforgiveness—it gives you nothing but grief in return. God sees your hurt and he knows your sorrows. Trust in the King of Kings to bring restoration. "The reason the Son of God appeared was to destroy the devil's work" (1 John 3:8). You belong to the Bridegroom. Have faith in God. Release others so you can receive from Jesus. Walk in forgiveness and watch the mountains in your life move.

DAY 6

"Jesus said, 'Father, forgive them, for they do not know what they are doing.'"
—*Luke 23:34*

Inside the temple in Jerusalem was an inner room called the Most Holy Place. Inside the Most Holy Place was the ark of the covenant where the presence of God dwelt (2 Samuel 6:2). If today's temple is our bodies, I believe the Most Holy Place is our hearts. Life flows out of our hearts (Proverbs 4:23). Just as Jesus cleansed the old temple that day, one of the most powerful things we can do in our prayer life is ask the Holy Spirit to search our hearts and see if we are holding any unforgiveness toward anyone. As we clear the clutter of bitterness from our temple by releasing our offenders, God will release his power and blessing in our life in greater measure.

And so today I want to lead you in a prayer of forgiveness. It's time that we take our keys and unlock the dungeon of bitterness. Let's step out of our prison and into God's blessing for our lives. You belong to the Bridegroom, and he wants you to live free, not in a prison of bitterness (Matthew 18:21–35).

The Word tells us we can cry out to God as our "Abba, Father" (Romans 8:15). Go crawl up in your Father's lap and wrap your arms around his strong shoulders. Let the tears fall. He knows about your hurts and is ready to restore. Let us pray.

> *Abba, Father,*
>
> *Thank you that I can cry out to you anytime and get help. Lord, I want to be free from any unforgiveness in my heart. It clashes with your love and clutters my prayer life. This bitterness has brought me nothing but pain. I want my heart to be free from anything that is holding me back from your blessings and hindering my fruitfulness. I take my authority in Jesus' name and ask for protection from the enemy so he cannot steal the freedom I am about to receive. I know unforgiveness of others—and of myself—is one of his greatest schemes. I come to you with a broken heart that has been hurt. I confess I am angry and have put my faith in man instead of looking to you for restoration. I ask right now in Jesus' name through your Holy Spirit that you would reveal to me anyone I am holding a debt over through unforgiveness.*

Write down the names God has revealed to you and the debt they owe you or what they stole from you and how this hurt made you feel. This is an exercise that I learned through Dr. Neil Anderson's Steps to Freedom. (For example, "Susie talked behind my back and she owes me an apology. She made me feel unloved and stole my reputation." Or "John had an affair and wrecked our marriage. He stole my joy, my family, and my peace. It made me feel used, unattractive, worthless, and robbed." Or "My father always expected me to be perfect. He stole my childhood. He made me feel abandoned and never good enough.")

_____

_____

_____

_____

_____

Continue your prayer . . .

It hurt, God. It hurt, and I am still living with the consequences of their sin. But today I choose to let go and forgive so I can turn to you for help. I thank you that you are a King of great riches, and as I turn to you, you will not only restore but redeem and repay twice my former shame.

Now I come to humble myself before you and count on the promise in your Word that tells me the Holy Spirit will empower me to do the supernatural. Forgiveness is supernatural. I ask right now in Jesus' name that you would give me the power and grace and ability to forgive.

For each person you recorded in the blanks above, write and pray . . .

Father, I release (name of person) _____ for (offense or debt to you) _____.[3] It made me feel _____ _____. I now turn to you to receive your reward and trust you to take care of me. I confess holding on to anger and bitterness, but I am ready to release to receive. I release my expectations of (name of person) _____ and put my faith in you to come through for me. In Jesus' name I forgive their wrong and trust you to make things right in my life. Give me the courage to let go of all unforgiveness so I may love and let go.

(Note: Portions of this prayer are taken from Neil Anderson's The Steps to Freedom in Christ. *For more resources visit www.freedominchrist.com.)*

Guess what? If you have prayed this prayer from your heart, you are free! God will begin to restore what has been lost! Glory! The enemy may tempt you to pick up unforgiveness again even after you have prayed. If that happens, open your mouth and say, "I have already forgiven _____. I am out of my prison and I don't want to go back in. I am trusting God to redeem and rebuild."

Another way you can keep your heart cleansed and defeat the enemy's attempts to put you back into the prison of unforgiveness is to pray for the ones who hurt you (Luke 6:27–28). This is the prescription Jesus gave his disciples. In my own life, I have found it hard to pray for someone who has hurt me—but something amazing happens in the spiritual realm when I do. My heart softens and it is easier for me to let go of the hurt and to continue walking in forgiveness.

Let's keep our temples free and clear from any clutter that would distract us from having a powerful prayer life. Nursing a grudge clutters our prayer life, and healing begins with forgiveness. I pray that you have been blessed by praying through areas of unforgiveness. Just as Jesus had to come twice to clear the temple, address any areas of unforgiveness as often as needed to keep you free to pray—warrior style!

God gives you the power to move mountains through prayer. The power of prayer. What an extravagant gift from our Bridegroom. Don't be shy—open it up and enjoy what God has given you. Prayer was meant to be a gift for you to enjoy every moment of every day.

Key Treasure

Just as Jesus cleansed the old temple that day, one of the most powerful things we can do in our prayer life is ask the Holy Spirit to search our hearts and see if we are holding any unforgiveness toward anyone. As we clear the clutter of bitterness from our temple by releasing our offenders, God will release his power and blessing in our lives in greater measure.

VIDEO SESSION NOTES

Session 9
MY FATHER'S HOUSE
Mark 11:12–21

Chapter 10
NO HOLDING BACK

DAY 1

Nourish Scripture: Mark 11:27–13:37

 PRAY.

Begin your time with God in prayer.

MEDITATE ON GOD'S WORD.

Using your Anchor of Truth Card* from last week's Nourish Notes, renew your mind on that truth. Quiet and focus your thoughts. Pray the truth. Say the truth. Meditate on God's truth.

TAKE THE *REVEAL* STEP OF THE NOURISH™ BIBLE STUDY METHOD.

Connect with Jesus by studying the Weekly Nourish Scripture and allowing the Holy Spirit to reveal truth in those verses. Prayerfully read over and reflect on the passage. Mark any phrases, verses, or words that catch your attention. Journal and learn as the Lord leads you.

---

*Anchor of Truth Cards are available at www.TreasuredMinistries.com/shop

DAY 2

Nourish Scripture: Mark 11:27–13:37

1 PRAY.

Begin your time with God in prayer.

2 MEDITATE ON GOD'S WORD.

Using your Anchor of Truth Card* from last week's Nourish Notes, renew your mind on that truth. Quiet and focus your thoughts. Pray the truth. Say the truth. Meditate on God's truth.

3 TAKE THE *RESPOND* STEP OF THE NOURISH™ BIBLE STUDY METHOD.

Respond to activate truth in your life. The acronym **IMPACT**™ provides questions to help you apply the truth from your weekly Nourish Scripture. **Sometimes you may not have answers for all six questions.**

IMAGE OF GOD TO TRUST? An attribute of God, Jesus, or the Holy Spirit to trust.

MESSAGE TO SHARE? A word of encouragement, truth, or prayer to share.

PROMISE TO TREASURE? A promise in the Bible to believe.

ACTION TO TAKE? A specific step God is calling you to take.

CORE IDENTITY IN CHRIST TO AFFIRM? A truth about how God sees you to affirm.

TRANSGRESSION TO CONFESS? A sin to acknowledge for help, healing, and restoration through Christ.

*Anchor of Truth Cards are available at www.TreasuredMinistries.com/shop

DAY 3

Nourish Scripture: Mark 11:27–13:37

1 PRAY.

Begin your time with God in prayer.

2 MEDITATE ON GOD'S WORD.

Using your Anchor of Truth Card* from last week's Nourish Notes, renew your mind on that truth. Quiet and focus your thoughts. Pray the truth. Say the truth. Meditate on God's truth.

3 TAKE THE *RENEW* STEP OF THE NOURISH™ BIBLE STUDY METHOD.

Like an anchor that secures its vessel, biblical meditation secures truth to transform your life. Take five minutes to *renew* your mind by focusing on one word, verse, or truth that the Holy Spirit revealed through the Bible during your week of study. Record your truth below and on your Anchor of Truth card.* Quiet your thoughts. Focus on the truth. Read the truth. Pray the truth.

My Anchor of Truth

4 UTILIZE YOUR *ANCHOR OF TRUTH* CARD AS A BOOKMARK TO CULTIVATE A DAILY PRACTICE OF BIBLICAL MEDITATION.

Place your Anchor of Truth Card* in your Bible study workbook to bookmark tomorrow's day of study. Let your Anchor of Truth bookmark remind you to pause and renew your mind on God's Word. Repeat this process daily, continuing to reflect on your Anchor of Truth to start your quiet time until the next week, when God reveals another truth to you.

*Anchor of Truth Cards are available at www.TreasuredMinistries.com/shop

DAY 4

" 'Well said, teacher,' the man replied. 'You are right in saying that God is one and there is no other but him. To love him with all your heart, with all your understanding and with all your strength, and to love your neighbor as yourself is more important than all burnt offerings and sacrifices.' " —*Mark 12:32–33*

No more holding back. My heart for his glory. I wonder if the widow in the temple heard those words whispered in her soul as she clutched the warm coins in her hand. Pressing the precious metal into her perspiring palm, she held them tightly for the last time. They were all she had to live on—dropping the coins would declare her dependence on God.

Was she tempted to pull back? Did insecurity or intimidation grab her thoughts as she was surrounded by the well-to-do? Did they even notice her? Her two tiny copper coins were so small compared with the heaps of money the wealthy placed in the offering as they paraded by.

But her Bridegroom noticed. Jesus smiled and asked his disciples to study this wise woman. Through his eyes—the only eyes that mattered—her offering was far greater than the vast amounts of money given for show.

She Gave Her All

The widow was getting ready to give her all—no holding back. As she dropped her coins to be captured by the treasure table, did the tapping and clinking ring out in heaven like a symphony? Jesus watched and beheld the beauty of a woman giving her heart without reservation to him, for where her treasure was, her heart was also (Matthew 6:21).

The widow's giving was a picture of the principle Jesus had recently taught to a teacher of the law asking which of the commandments was the most important. Perhaps this scribe was overwhelmed with the hundreds of unnecessary rules invented by the religious leaders and desperately needed some simplification. When did following God become so complicated? What was most important to the heart of God?

Pulling in words spoken to the Israelites in the wilderness on the brink of their Promised Land arrival, Jesus captured the essence of following God: no holding back. " 'Hear, O Israel, the Lord our God, the Lord is one. Love the Lord your God with **all** your heart and with **all** your soul and with **all** your mind and with **all** your strength.' The second is this: 'Love your neighbor as yourself.' There is no commandment greater than these" (Mark 12:29–31, *emphasis mine*).

Was the widow in the shadows when Jesus shared his heart about giving our all? Did she hear it secondhand from others? Perhaps her parents had told her the story about the widow from Zarephath from the days of the prophet Elijah. This widow also gave her all. She let go of the last of her flour in a time of famine to feed Elijah.

> "Elijah said to her, 'Don't be afraid. Go home and do as you have said. But first make a small cake of bread for me from what you have and bring it to me, and then make something for yourself and your son. For this is what the LORD, the God of Israel, says: "The jar of flour will not be used up and the jug of oil will not run dry until the day the LORD sends rain on the land." ' " (1 Kings 17:13–14)

Lasting provision during the famine only came when she gave her all—all the remaining nourishment she had for herself and her son. The widow from Zarephath had only enough food for one more meal. But as she trusted the Lord and gave with no holding back, God was faithful to feed Elijah, the widow, and her son until the rain came (1 Kings 17:7–16).

Jesus said the widow in the temple truly gave because she gave all she had. No holding back. Anyone can give out of abundance, but how much more precious is our offering when we are giving Jesus our all. It's easy to give out of a harvest, but it takes faith to give our last seed when the harvest is yet to come.

Love Him with All Your Heart, All Your Understanding, and All Your Strength

The principle of not holding back does not apply just to widows—but to everyone. The teacher of the law who questioned Jesus had an *aha* moment about giving without limit.

> " 'Well said, teacher,' the man replied. 'You are right in saying that God is one and there is no other but him. To love him with all your heart, with all your understanding and with all your strength, and to love your neighbor as yourself is more important than all burnt offerings and sacrifices.' " Mark 12:32–33

How did Jesus respond to the man in Mark 12:34?

_____

_____

_____

Her Heart for His Glory

Loving God without reservation and loving others brings a bounty of unspeakable joy and blessings as we are brought closer to the kingdom. I believe this is why Jesus did not stop the widow from such radical giving.

As the Bridegroom beheld this sacrificial offering, notice he did not stand in the way of her giving. He did not run toward her, grab her hand, and say, "Are you crazy? This is your very last—your very last! Hold back some to see you through the coming days!"

This passage has always caused me to pause. If our Bridegroom loved the widow, why would he stand back and watch her give everything she had to the temple treasury?

Christine Caine, founder of A21 Ministries, has helped this bride understand why Jesus did not prevent the widow from giving her all. It was not that he did not want her needs to be met. Jesus knew her true needs would be met through her giving. Christine Caine explains that Jesus did not stop the widow from giving her all because "her need was met through her seed."[1] If Jesus can make money come from the mouth of a fish, he can provide for us in creative ways when there seems to be no way (Matthew 17:27).

Jesus knew the widow's giving was not about money. It was about her heart. Jesus did not stand in her way because he knew that those who choose to live for the Lord with no holding back are blessed beyond measure.

Often when we have nothing, we discover he is our everything.

She trusted him with all her heart. Her heart for his glory.

I want to trust like that, Jesus—with all of my heart—no more holding back. Loving you with all my heart and out of that overflow loving others. When I am down to my last mite of money, my last mite of strength, my last mite of time—let me not pull back in fear but press in to trust you with everything.

Your heart has great capacity to love. You can trust Jesus with your all. You were created to worship him with your whole heart and there is no substitute to satisfy your soul. Close today spending some time with your Bridegroom in prayer. Give him your heart today.

DAY 5

"For we are God's workmanship, created in Christ Jesus to do good works, which God prepared in advance for us to do." —*Ephesians 2:10*

Do you know that you are on a special assignment from your Bridegroom? You are God's work of art created to do special tasks that were prepared before you were born (Ephesians 2:10). Think about that. God created you and molded you to make his mark on this world. Inside every bride is the potential to unlock a God-given purpose and passion. Mark 13:34 says, "He leaves his house and puts his servants in charge, each with their assigned task." The King James Version says God has given us "authority" (Mark 13:34). God has given us a job to do in our assigned sphere of influence to serve others and point them to Christ. While we are on this earth, we need to make the most of every minute in that sphere. Just as the stars in the sky have a specific spot and purpose, you have a unique calling. Your uniqueness will intertwine with other brides to make a beautiful tapestry of his love to the world. You are a magnificent masterpiece with the God-given authority and ability to make waves of God's glory.

What Is Your Sphere of Influence?

How does Matthew 25:14–30 also encourage you to live with purpose and passion for your Bridegroom?

_____

_____

_____

I love these verses because they motivate me to walk out my calling. It is exciting to know I have a purpose. How inspiring to know that God has given each of us specific tasks to do while we are here on earth. All brides were created for his glory with unique gifts and callings. God orchestrates our steps, but he calls us to live with passion—no holding back.

God has given me influence in my home. I am a wife, a mom, and the heart of my home. Loving my husband and nurturing my children are my most important ministries. There was a time when this was not my first priority—but God has changed that and I know that my closest and most important neighbor to love is my family. I don't get this right every time and I am still learning, but I am finding making my family my greatest priority brings me joy beyond measure.

Beyond the walls of my home, God has also given me the assigned task of inspiring women to hear from God through his Word so they can discover the freedom and treasure of following Christ. For the rest of my days through Treasured Ministries, I want to tell others they are God's treasure designed for a unique purpose. I want to inspire women to trust God with their whole hearts and live for his glory. He has given me this assignment to pursue, in my writing, and in encounters with every woman he puts across my path.

I want to embrace my authority and live each day with these passionate pursuits in mind, but honestly, there are days when I get distracted from my purpose. I feel overwhelmed and I want to quit! I feel so inadequate and I want to quit. I am afraid of failing and I want to quit. I get weary and wail "what about me?" and I want to quit. I compare myself or listen to the words of others and I want to just sit down and quit!

But then I look at Jesus, who never quit and stayed focused on his mission so that we could live eternally, and I find focus on what really matters. I have given up on being perfect and I rest in the perfection of the One who called me. If he has called me to be a wife, mom, and minister to the hearts of women, he will equip me to carry out the task.

How do you become distracted? It's easy to let your focus become buried by distractions, but as we peer into this passage we'll uncover some key points to staying focused.

Don't Be Distracted from Your Purpose

With so much need in the world around us, it is easy to respond to the needs instead of God's calling. Each bride will find peace as she realizes she is not called to do it all.

It is better and healthier for us to focus on our assigned tasks and do them with excellence than to spread ourselves thin trying to do it all. Only Jesus is omnipresent and omniscient. When we try to do too many things instead of putting our energy in what God has called us to do, we become strung out and stressed out instead of focused and fruitful.

Who Is Lord of Your Life?

Jesus tossed the question of lordship out to the Pharisees and Sadducees who came to spar with him. After quoting Psalm 110:1, Jesus posed a question to them. "David calls himself 'Lord.' How then can he be his son?" (Mark 12:37).

> The Jews believed that the Messiah would be David's son (John 7:41–42), but the only way David's son could be David's Lord would be if Messiah were, *God come in human flesh.*[2]

The Pharisees who were looking for a king had a hard time accepting Jesus as their Lord, and so they missed the Messiah. Jesus is Lord. When we surrender to his leading in our lives, we will find our purpose and assigned tasks. Jesus, our Cornerstone, must be the foundation of all our works (1 Corinthians 3:13; 1 Peter 2:4–5). He is the one who assigns the tasks and gives out the talents. Jesus is our Lord, and we are his servants.

Seek Jesus and ask him to show you your calling. He might reveal your mission a step at a time or all at once, but if you keep seeking Jesus and following the promptings of the Holy Spirit, he will lead you into your calling. He will open doors for you and prepare you. You do not have to push forward—just follow Jesus. As you faithfully walk in obedience, he will give you assigned tasks and continue to expand your boundaries. Don't be impatient—just follow him. When he tells you to wait, be still and know that he is God (Psalm 46:10).

Let Your Bridegroom Lead You

God can and will equip you to do any assigned task he gives you. However, if you travel outside his will and decide to be captain of your own ship, you will have to depend on your own resources. A work of the flesh has to be maintained by the flesh while a work done from the promptings of the Holy Spirit is maintained by the power of the Holy Spirit (John 3:6).

Never compare yourself to another woman! Never think less of yourself because you think one woman can handle more than you can. God gives different anointing for different callings. It's God who gives out the assigned tasks—and the talents to complete them (Matthew 25:14–30). There is no small task in his eyes (1 Corinthians 12:23). We don't choose our callings, but we can choose to surrender and serve Jesus with a passion for fulfilling the purpose to which he has called us.

Motive Is Everything

Watching our motives is a good safeguard to stay on the path of our purpose. Jesus told his disciples to watch out for the Pharisees who were praying, serving, and attending church and fancy banquets simply for show (Mark 12:38–40). We always need to check our motives in our giving and our serving and in all that we do for the Lord. Our motives should be based on the greatest two commands—love of God and love of others. Anything beyond that should bring a check to our spirit. When we are led by pride, a desire to please people, guilt, manipulation, or a desire to be seen, we are giving with an alternative motive and will eventually become frustrated and worn out. Wise brides take their dance steps from their Bridegroom alone (Galatians 1:10).

Every time an opportunity to serve presents itself, pause and pray. *What is my motive for saying yes to this opportunity? Is it love of God and others?*

The Holy Spirit Will Empower You

Feeling overwhelmed can distract us, but we can find our focus again by remembering that it's not up to us. God calls and he equips!

As we pursue the tasks God gives us, we must rely on the power of the Holy Spirit if our work is to be fruitful. "If anyone serves, he should do so with the strength God provides" (1 Peter 4:11). Jesus told his disciples they would do even greater things than he had done.

He promised to leave them the Holy Spirit to help them carry out the tasks before them. After his resurrection, he instructed the disciples to wait until they received the baptism of the Holy Spirit before they began their ministry (Acts 1:4–5).

Although Jesus used Mark 12:26–27 to teach the Sadducees about resurrection, he was also revealing another truth: God does not change.

> "Now about the dead rising—have you not read in the book of Moses, in the account of the bush, how God said to him, 'I am the God of Abraham, the God of Isaac, and the God of Jacob'? He is not the God of the dead, but of the living."

The God of Abraham is my God also. The God who used Abraham to establish the nation of Israel is the same God I serve. The Bible says Jesus is the same yesterday, today, and forever (Hebrews 13:8). The Holy Spirit who moved among the early church is the same Holy Spirit who equips believers today to do even greater things than Jesus did.

God has not changed. We still need his Spirit to fulfill our assignments. Stay in God's presence. I have often heard it said that we don't need more of the Holy Spirit—the Holy Spirit needs more of us. When you face the impossible, see that as an opportunity to depend on the Holy Spirit to empower you to fulfill your calling.

Don't Let Agitators Distract You

When running the race to accomplish your assigned tasks, look straight ahead and focus on YOUR finish line and goals. As soon as you start looking right or left or behind, you will be distracted and begin to lose ground.

You know those sandpaper people God places in your life to "grow" you? They always know just how to push your buttons. They may be sincerely trying to help you. Or like the Pharisees, the Sadducees, and Herodias, they may want to trap and trip you up.

Sometimes outside influences can steal your focus and drain your energy away from your assigned task by making you feel angry, confused, or frustrated. Their interference, even if well-intentioned, may cause you to be sidetracked instead of focusing on what really matters.

In our passage this week, as our Bridegroom walked his path, he was bombarded by a series of ridiculous questions. Our Bridegroom was way too savvy to allow them to steal his focus. He knew their hearts were full of hypocrisy, and he addressed their questions one by one in a way that left them speechless. Jesus addressed his agitators with confident humility. He was not defensive. He was focused on the people he came to save. He remained calm and never allowed himself to be thrown off balance but kept his eyes focused onward and upward.

Satan Is an Accuser—and a Liar

Jesus' authority was attacked, and as you seek to serve him your authority as a believer will also be attacked (Mark 11:28; John 15:20). As a child of God, you have been given authority over anything that would hinder your service to Jesus. You have also been given authority to fulfill your assigned task.

The enemy is our greatest accuser. His goal is to attack our position in Christ. When the devil came to Jesus in the desert, he attacked his sonship (Matthew 4:3). If he can convince us we are not really God's child, we will not be confident enough to enjoy all the provision in our spiritual inheritance. If he can convince us God does not love us unconditionally, we won't follow him radically. A woman who knows she is loved by God is confident and secure in her relationship with Christ.

Satan will also accuse you in your calling. "Who do you think you are, wanting to lead women to Christ? Who do you think you are, wanting to stand against sex trafficking—you can't conquer that problem. Where did you get the idea in your head that God could ever use you to minister to women? Who do you think you are—you are not qualified for that position." And he'll growl and prowl.

We can stop the enemy dead in his tracks by opening our mouths and speaking the truth of God's Word.

Who am I? I am God's child—fearfully and wonderfully made, designed and destined for this purpose. My lack of ability does not faze me—Jesus has given me the Holy Spirit and my faith is in God to do the impossible and move mountains. And by the way, it's not selfish ambition to follow my calling with a passion. God has given me talents and expects me to use them for the glory of the kingdom. So back off this bride because I belong to the Bridegroom. I have a special assignment to fulfill.

The more I talk to women, the more I see that we wear insecurity like an essential accessory (this bride included!). I believe insecurity is the devil's device to divert brides from fulfilling their God-given destiny. Satan crushes us by crushing our confidence. We always need to remember that insecurity is nothing but a tactic of the enemy to shut us down from taking our authority to do our assigned task. Don't waste another minute by allowing the enemy to intimidate you. We need to push past those insecurities because our callings are not about us—they are about loving others and pointing them to Jesus.

Step Up to Your Special Assignment

Step up to your special assignment. God gives believers the ability and authority in a sphere of influence to bring him glory. Make the most of every minute every day. When I see Jesus in glory face-to-face, or when he returns for this bride, I want him to find me passionately focused and pursuing my calling.

Open your eyes wide, bride of Christ. Allow your life to sing of your Redeemer by not getting sidetracked from your special assignment. You are a beautiful child of God built to do the impossible. You are his secret service agent with an assignment to bring influence and impact for his goodness and gospel. You have the authority and ability to make a difference. What are you waiting for?

Key Treasure

Just as the stars in the sky have a specific spot and purpose, you have a unique calling. Your uniqueness will intertwine with other brides to make a beautiful tapestry of his love to the world. You are a magnificent masterpiece with the God-given authority and ability to make waves of God's glory.

DAY 6

"Whatever your hand finds to do, do it with all your might, for in the grave, where you are going, there is neither working nor planning nor knowledge nor wisdom." —*Ecclesiastes 9:10*

My heart for his glory. No more holding back. This is the way I want to live—no more holding back in serving Jesus and others. But I sometimes allow my *tomorrows* to give me an excuse to hold on tight instead of letting go. When I live in tomorrow, I worry and I fear. When I live in tomorrow, I find myself saying, "I can do that another day" to what God wants me to conquer today. When I live in tomorrow, I procrastinate instead of going where the Holy Spirit is leading me. I hold back because there is always tomorrow. Tomorrow prevents me from living today.

Jesus made it clear he wants us to focus on today and not worry about tomorrow.

> "Give your entire attention to what God is doing right now, and don't get worked up about what may or may not happen tomorrow. God will help you deal with whatever hard things come up when the time comes." (Matthew 6:34 MSG)

So what if we live in *today*? What if we live each day to the fullest with no holding back from God and others? What if we wake up every morning and as soon as our feet hit the floor decide to live today as if it were our last 24 hours? How different each day would be if we lived with an eternal perspective.

Live with an Eternal Mindset

Jesus wants his brides to live with an eternal mindset and live each day with purpose and passion. He spoke to his disciples about this.

Read Mark 13:32–37.

Who knows when the second coming of Christ will occur? (Mark 13:32)

What two commands does Jesus give while we are waiting for his return?
(Mark 13:34–37)

Only our Father knows when on his vast kingdom calendar the Bridegroom will return for his bride. While we are waiting for that glorious day, we are to watch, keeping an eternal focus by fixing our eyes on Jesus. We need to focus not on the worries of tomorrow but on the hope of our heavenly home. A mindset alert to his coming will keep us living each day knowing that today could be the last day we have to make an impact. We are also called to seek the Lord and ask for our assigned tasks, take our authority, and pursue our calling with a passion.

Be Ready for His Return

If you were blown away by the events Jesus described in Mark 13, imagine how the disciples felt. What was all this talk about birthing pains and Jesus coming again in the clouds with great power and glory? When he spoke of the fig tree, did Jesus mean Israel? Did the words "the abomination that causes desolation" (v. 14) send them reeling back into the prophetic scrolls of Daniel (Daniel 12:11–12)?

While it can be fascinating to delve into history and God's Word to look for those birthing pains and create calendars predicting when Jesus might return, our Bridegroom commands us to keep our focus elsewhere. The disciples wanted to know "when" but Jesus told them to "watch" and attend to their assigned tasks. Jesus was telling them to keep their focus heavenward and live with purpose. Instead of focusing on when, Jesus wants us to focus on being ready. He wants us to watch and be on our guard. If we truly believe Jesus is coming again, we will watch for him—passionately.

Bible scholars have devoted entire books to the subject of end-time prophecy. It's interesting to read their thoughts and compare different viewpoints. Although not all scholars agree on exactly when Jesus will return or even how all the events in his second coming will happen, all Christians can agree on this fact: one day when we least expect it, the Bridegroom will return for his bride.

The parable of the tenants in the vineyard pictures a loving God who repeatedly warned the nation of Israel through prophets, only to see them killed or beaten. The vineyard represents the nation of Israel and the tenant farmers the Israelites put in place to live and serve the Lord. The servants sent to collect fruit are the Old Testament prophets sent by a loving God. Israel rejected the prophets time after time. Even when the owner sent his son, he was rejected—a picture of the Israelites rejecting God's Son, Jesus. In his New Testament commentary, Jon Courson states this:

This not only speaks volumes concerning the patience of the Father in sending servant after servant and warning after warning, but also concerning the stupidity of man who thinks that because God must be off in some corner of the cosmos, he need not listen to His servants; he need not reverence His Son; he can do whatever he wants. Mankind mistakes the patience of God for impotence.[3]

And so it is with us today—we must take seriously the warning given to the tenants. The owner of the vineyard finally gave the vineyard over to others because the servants did not seize the day! This reflects God offering the gospel to the Gentiles after it was rejected by his chosen people (Romans 10:16–11:36).

Today is the day of salvation. Don't reject him. If you picked up this study to find out more about the Bridegroom but have been reluctant to say yes to his proposal of salvation or surrender to his leading in your life, I urge you to make that decision.

If Today Were My Last Day, I Would …

In New Testament times a Jewish bride knew the day but not the exact time of her bridegroom's return. As she waited, she readied herself and watched with hope for her groom to hold out his hand and lead her to marriage. She waited with breathless expectation for her groom as we eagerly await our King coming in all his glory to rescue us.

As we watch and wait for Jesus, our hearts rest in the promise of heaven, the perfect place he is preparing for his bride. It is this joy set before us that will keep us serving with no holding back.

Living with this eternal perspective will change the way you live. Living for his glory will alter your priorities. Pursuing your calling creates a passion and urgency because our time here is so short. And as you focus on watching for Jesus, your heart will be tied not to the things of this world but to your Bridegroom. Eyes fixed on heaven will bring hope as you battle through this fallen world.

When you hear about end times, you don't have to live in fear. Enjoy the exciting expectation while you wait for your Bridegroom's return. Watch those birthing pains growing in intensity and let them motivate you to live each day to the fullest.

Bride of Christ, what would you do today if you knew it was your last day to live on this earth?

If my Bridegroom were coming tonight, I would live and love today, no holding back. Dressed and ready, with the armor of God, I would stand against injustice. I would take my authority and live out my assigned tasks with purpose and passion. I would not bury my talent in fear but with faith I would move forward with the dreams God has placed in my heart. I would stop procrastinating and start pursuing the pathway he has placed before me. I would believe ALL things are possible through Christ and start to live that way—no holding back. I would not worry about what I lack; I would trust him for everything. I would not wait to change the world or get overwhelmed; I would take the first steps to make this world a better place.

After my relationship with God, relationships with my family and then others would be my top priority. I would be a giver of my all to others. I would take the time to pause and play with the people in my life. I would call friends and family members and share from my heart how much I love them—and I would not hold back. I would give lots of hugs and encouragement to those who come across my path. I would build up instead of tear down.

If today were my last day, I would walk confidently in the authority and ability God has given me to use in my sphere of influence. I would not hesitate to follow the promptings of the Holy Spirit. I would make time to share the gospel with that one God has laid on my heart.

If my Bridegroom were coming tonight, I would not waste one minute in mindless thinking. No more worry, condemnation, or negative self-talk! I would stop trying to figure things out and trust. I would let go of hurts and forgive. I would find ways to love my enemies and pray for them. I would not worry about getting even—I would let go and trust God.

If today were my last day I would take more risks and laugh at my mistakes. I would challenge myself to make new paths and do radical things for Jesus instead of going the same old way. I would not worry about what I lack in time, money, or talent. I would stop hiding and dare to share myself with others.

Live Each Day as If It Were the Last

Bride of Christ, we only have one life to live. Each day is a gift. Let's live it to the fullest. Jesus didn't reveal exact times because that information was hidden even from him. We need to love God and others with all our heart—with no holding back. Living with this eternal perspective will change our focus and the way we live.

You stand still and silent before the treasury with the rest of your life in your hands. Will you give it all to him? Your Bridegroom is watching and waiting for his bride. Allow the truth of his second coming to awaken your soul and make your heart thump. Find yourself as you lose yourself in him by giving your all.

VIDEO SESSION NOTES

Session 10

NO HOLDING BACK

Mark 12:38–44

Videos located online at www.nourishbiblestudyseries.com

Chapter 11
QUIET STRENGTH

DAY 1

Nourish Scripture: Mark 14

 PRAY.

Begin your time with God in prayer.

 MEDITATE ON GOD'S WORD.

Using your Anchor of Truth Card* from last week's Nourish Notes, renew your mind on that truth. Quiet and focus your thoughts. Pray the truth. Say the truth. Meditate on God's truth.

TAKE THE *REVEAL* STEP OF THE NOURISH™ BIBLE STUDY METHOD.

Connect with Jesus by studying the Weekly Nourish Scripture and allowing the Holy Spirit to reveal truth in those verses. Prayerfully read over and reflect on the passage. Mark any phrases, verses, or words that catch your attention. Journal and learn as the Lord leads you.

*Anchor of Truth Cards are available at www.TreasuredMinistries.com/shop

DAY 2
Nourish Scripture: Mark 14

1 PRAY.
Begin your time with God in prayer.

2 MEDITATE ON GOD'S WORD.
Using your Anchor of Truth Card* from last week's Nourish Notes, renew your mind on that truth. Quiet and focus your thoughts. Pray the truth. Say the truth. Meditate on God's truth.

3 TAKE THE *RESPOND* STEP OF THE NOURISH™ BIBLE STUDY METHOD.
Respond to activate truth in your life. The acronym **IMPACT**™ provides questions to help you apply the truth from your weekly Nourish Scripture. **Sometimes you may not have answers for all six questions.**

IMAGE OF GOD TO TRUST? An attribute of God, Jesus, or the Holy Spirit to trust.

MESSAGE TO SHARE? A word of encouragement, truth, or prayer to share.

PROMISE TO TREASURE? A promise in the Bible to believe.

ACTION TO TAKE? A specific step God is calling you to take.

CORE IDENTITY IN CHRIST TO AFFIRM? A truth about how God sees you to affirm.

TRANSGRESSION TO CONFESS? A sin to acknowledge for help, healing, and restoration through Christ.

*Anchor of Truth Cards are available at www.TreasuredMinistries.com/shop

DAY 3

Nourish Scripture: Mark 14

1 PRAY.

Begin your time with God in prayer.

2 MEDITATE ON GOD'S WORD.

Using your Anchor of Truth Card* from last week's Nourish Notes, renew your mind on that truth. Quiet and focus your thoughts. Pray the truth. Say the truth. Meditate on God's truth.

3 TAKE THE *RENEW* STEP OF THE NOURISH™ BIBLE STUDY METHOD.

Like an anchor that secures its vessel, biblical meditation secures truth to transform your life. Take five minutes to *renew* your mind by focusing on one word, verse, or truth that the Holy Spirit revealed through the Bible during your week of study. Record your truth below and on your Anchor of Truth card.* Quiet your thoughts. Focus on the truth. Read the truth. Pray the truth.

4 UTILIZE YOUR *ANCHOR OF TRUTH* CARD AS A BOOKMARK TO CULTIVATE A DAILY PRACTICE OF BIBLICAL MEDITATION.

Place your Anchor of Truth Card* in your Bible study workbook to bookmark tomorrow's day of study. Let your Anchor of Truth bookmark remind you to pause and renew your mind on God's Word. Repeat this process daily, continuing to reflect on your Anchor of Truth to start your quiet time until the next week, when God reveals another truth to you.

*Anchor of Truth Cards are available at www.TreasuredMinistries.com/shop

DAY 4

"In quietness and trust is your strength." —*Isaiah 30:15*

Rosa Parks grew up on a humble farm in rural Alabama just outside Montgomery with her mother and grandparents. Rosa was raised in a world that treated African-Americans like second-class citizens. But she learned from the Bible to be courageous in the face of injustice and hatred.

Rosa may have grown up in humble means, but she had the luxury of learning about her Savior, Jesus. Her grandparents gave her the greatest legacy we can give to the next generation—a firm foundation of faith and trust in God. In *Quiet Strength*, Rosa Parks talks about the foundation of her faith.

> "Every day before supper and before we went to services on Sundays," Parks says, "my grandmother would read the Bible to me, and my grandfather would pray. We even had devotions before going to pick cotton in the fields. Prayer and the Bible," she recalls, "became a part of my everyday thoughts and beliefs. [...]I learned to put my trust in God and to seek Him as my strength."[1]

Everything Rosa did flowed out of her faith. "I'd like for [readers] to know that I had a very spiritual background and that I believe in church and my faith and that has helped to give me the strength and courage to live as I did."[2]

Christianity that requires courage instead of Christianity that demands comfort calls us to stand in the strength that only God can provide.

Strength always comes from a source. Quiet strength comes only from God himself. To plug into God's power, we must pause and pull into his presence daily.

Quiet strength, God's all-surpassing power, is different from worldly power. Worldly power is outward control, dependent on other people and things, and it focuses on self. Quiet strength is the inner strength of a woman led confidently by God to walk in love and live for his glory no matter what circumstances she faces. Love is the most powerful force, and that is what God's power is all about.

It was that quiet strength that would carry Rosa bravely through the events that took place on December 1, 1955. It began as an ordinary day—but God was getting ready to do the extraordinary through her life.

After a long day at work, Rosa boarded the bus that would carry her home. Buses were segregated at that time, so Rosa made her way to the front row of the "colored" section in the back of the bus. At the next stop, Rosa and three African-American men were asked to give up their seats to a white man because no seats were available in their section in the front of the bus. The men got up, but Rosa refused to vacate her seat.

Rosa had grown weary from the injustices shown toward people because of the color of their skin. Although she had not planned to resist the law that day, her decision to remain in her seat led to her arrest—and would change the destiny of our nation.

Sometimes quiet strength means saying no to others so you can say yes to God.

Rosa's refusal to give up her seat set in motion a series of events that would transform the laws regulating racial justice. A 381-day bus boycott in Montgomery led to a ruling in 1956 by the Supreme Court declaring that racial segregation on buses was unconstitutional. Rosa had submitted to arrest, giving up her freedom so others could be free, but she had not been afraid. "Since I have always been a strong believer in God," she says, "I knew that He was with me, and only He could get me through the next step."[3]

I just love that, don't you?

Jesus Is the Source of Quiet Strength

When a woman rests her confidence in her Bridegroom, she can be secure in the most insecure circumstances. She can trust God to use her trials to make a difference for the kingdom. A beautiful freedom is birthed when a woman looks for her identity and security in Christ alone. She becomes strong in Christ—"Christ strong." Quiet strength, like that of Rosa Parks, is Christ strength. And nothing can rob you of that strength because nothing can separate a bride from the love of Christ (Romans 8:35–39).

Read Mark 14:3–9. It took quiet strength and confidence in Jesus, like that of Rosa Parks, for Mary of Bethany to anoint her Bridegroom with the fragrant perfume in her alabaster jar. How did Jesus defend Mary?

_____

_____

_____

Did you ever have someone rebuke you for doing something costly for Jesus? How did you respond?

_____

_____

_____

Can you remember a time when you stood still and Jesus fought your battle for you? Describe what happened.

_____

_____

_____

_____

Mary was rebuked for her elaborate display of affection toward Jesus. She did not speak up and defend herself, because her Bridegroom was quick to silence her accusers with three words: "Leave her alone." Jesus not only silenced her accusers, but he also affirmed her actions and then promised she would leave a legacy.

Let those words from your Bridegroom resonate in your mind. Your Bridegroom takes attacks on his bride very seriously. We can gain quiet strength knowing that Jesus is our defender and will never leave us nor forsake us.

The Gospel of John gives us a bit more detail about this vital moment on the kingdom calendar. Read John 12:1–8. What details does John add to Mark's version of this passage?

_____

_____

_____

_____

_____

Don't underestimate the magnitude of this moment. It speaks to the freedom the Bridegroom brought to women. For a woman to approach a man in this manner was unheard of during this period of history and in that culture. If a rabbi saw his wife out in public, he would not even acknowledge her. A Jewish woman letting her hair down in public was downright radical. This bride not only boldly walked across the room to her rabbi, but she also let down her hair and fell at his feet. Jesus, the Great Rabbi, not only acknowledged her—he defended her. He affirmed her actions and proclaimed that they would be remembered. Mary would leave a legacy.

The disciples rebuked Mary, and Judas judged her, but their words did not stop her. She was not looking for their acceptance and approval. She already had the acceptance and approval of Jesus.

Your Bridegroom Never Sees You as Inferior

Jesus never treated women as inferior. In fact, the way Jesus treated women throughout the Gospels is revolutionary. His promises belong to all God's children.

> "All of you who were baptized into Christ have clothed yourselves with Christ. There is neither Jew nor Gentile, neither slave nor free, nor is there male and female, for you are all one in Christ Jesus." (Galatians 3:27–28 NIV 2011)

> Has anyone ever tried to make you feel inferior because you are a woman—or for any other reason?

_____

_____

_____

History records many stories of the demeaning treatment of women. Because of humankind's fall in the garden of Eden, these stories are still real today. But that attitude does not reflect the heart of our God. In the Old Testament we see God calling women to play significant roles in Hebrew history. The more I pore over the Gospels, the more I see that Jesus treated women with great love and respect.

No one can make you feel inferior unless you give them that power. Take back your security by drawing your value from Christ alone, regardless of the words or attitudes of anyone else. This brings freedom, because you are resting in the One who will never leave or forsake you.

Jesus never intended women to be victims of their circumstances or of other people. He intends us to live for his glory and to love others by walking in the strength only he can provide.

> In Jesus' day, women were expected to serve and were not taught by rabbis. Judging from Luke 10:38–42, why do you think Jesus went against the cultural norms of the day and validated Mary's decision to sit at his feet?

_____

_____

_____

Jesus wanted Mary to sit in his presence because he knew that was the most important thing for her to do (Luke 10: 42; Matthew 6:33).

Quiet strength is not something we take; it's something we receive as we pull away from life's pressures to plug into the presence of Jesus. As it was with Rosa Parks, the key to quiet strength is making a lifestyle of spending time in God's presence.

As my good friend likes to say, "Wise women prepare for a life that glorifies God by gearing up with God's Word."

An expert archer keeps his arrows in his quiver, close to him, so he can sharpen and polish them, releasing them again and again with power, purpose, and precision. Like the expert archer, God is calling not just Mary or Rosa but all his daughters to retreat into his presence to prepare and position their hearts to be released for his glory.

Wherever you are in your walk with God, you are never too far along to retreat inside his quiver and share sacred times close to him. It is in his quiver, concealed and sharpened, that we plug into his quiet strength.

The world is a battlefield where brave hearts make a difference. *Live on purpose by pausing from life's pressures to plug into the limitless power that flows from the presence of Jesus.*

God Had a Greater Purpose for Mary's Actions

Mary's anointing of her Bridegroom revealed her extravagant devotion and love for Jesus. It was also a critical step in fulfilling God's plan. Jesus is not just the Lamb of God. He is also our Great High Priest forever (Hebrews 6:19–20; 7:27).

Mary's movements were intertwined with God's perfect plan. In the Old Testament, kings and priests were anointed before they served. Jesus is our Great High Priest.

Jesus is also the King of Kings, setting up a heavenly kingdom (Matthew 21:5; Mark 14:25; Revelation 19:6). The pouring of Mary's perfume over him fulfilled a purpose (Hebrews 8:5). This "good work" was not just an extravagant display of affection. Whether or not she knew it, her actions also prepared Jesus for the offices he held: Great High Priest and King of Kings.

I wonder if Jesus felt a ray of sunshine piercing through the dark clouds as he looked ahead to the cross. Judas would betray him. Disciples would abandon him. The chosen people would yell, "Crucify him!" When his soul was overwhelmed with sorrow to the point of death in the garden of Gethsemane, perhaps remembering the scent of Mary's perfume and the love it expressed gave him some comfort.

Mary may not have understood the significance of her actions, much like Rosa Parks did not comprehend that refusing to give up her seat would impact our nation. But both women had the courage and conviction to follow Christ and do what they felt in their hearts was right.

Bride of Christ, God will use you to influence others for him when you draw your strength from your Bridegroom and boldly follow him. This quiet confidence carries influence. Much as Mary's perfume filled the room when she anointed Jesus' feet, a woman who is confident in Christ will fill the air with the fragrance of hope. Like Rosa Parks and Mary, you too can bring the light of Christ to the darkest situations, exerting influence that will last through the generations in ways you can't begin to imagine.

DAY 5

"Let us run with perseverance the race marked out for us, fixing our eyes on Jesus, the pioneer and perfecter of faith. For the joy set before him he endured the cross, scorning its shame, and sat down at the right hand of the throne of God. Consider him who endured such opposition from sinners, so that you will not grow weary and lose heart." —*Hebrews 12:1–3 NIV 2011*

Much like shed tears that land on a freshly painted watercolor canvas can distort the masterpiece, our sorrows and disappointments can dilute and distort our faith in God and our image of him. Fixing our faith on an image of God distorted by our circumstances instead of on the truth in his Word can result in misguided actions. Our bold prayer life fades. Fear begins to eclipse our faith. We take the reins of our life again. Giving our whole heart to God seems risky, so while we might play the part by attending church, our hearts are far away from God.

I have been there. How about you?

Regret over the past may cause us to shut down. Anger, blaming, bitterness, and unforgiveness don't improve anything and blind us from seeing the ways God is taking care of us. Regret ties us to yesterday rather than helping us forge ahead into our God-given future.

Sometimes when our *why* isn't fully answered, we can become bitter toward our Bridegroom. Life doesn't match the lessons we were taught in Sunday school. How could a loving God allow this to happen? We want life to make sense, and when our perceptions and thoughts are distorted by negative emotion, it may seem best to take God out of the equation.

But disappointments don't mean God doesn't love you. God *is* love. It is impossible for him to act otherwise. Demonstrating that love, he gave his one and only Son for you. You are not forgotten.

"You keep track of all my sorrows. You have collected all my tears in your bottle. You have recorded each one in your book" (Psalm 56:8 NLT).

Jesus Experienced Deep Sorrow

From Mark 14:32–41, how would you describe how Jesus was feeling? What were some actions he took in the garden of Gethsemane? How can you apply these actions to your own life?

_____

_____

_____

Jesus was crushed with grief to the point of death in the garden of Gethsemane, but ultimately he surrendered to God's plan because he wanted God's will to be done (Mark 14:38).

He prayed. He asked his friends to pray with him. He cried out to the Father. But ultimately he sought God's will and his glory when faced with the cross.

Jesus could have called down an army of angels to rescue him from death, but he chose not to. Jesus was never a doormat. He was not a victim. He _chose_ to lay down his life for his bride because of his great love—no one took his life from him against his will (John 10:17–18).

As you read over the last hours of Jesus' life, you may think that he was a victim of Judas's terrible betrayal (Mark 14:43). On the contrary, Jesus chose to lay down his life. There is a huge difference between weakness and meekness. Jesus was never weak. But for our sake he became meek, and God raised him from the grave. Christ's humility gave us freedom to have a relationship with God.

Jesus kept his eyes on eternity, and because of the joy of the resurrection, our salvation, and God's glory, he endured the cross (Hebrews 12:1–2)

Trusting God When You Don't Understand

God is always painting a masterpiece for his glory. We can't always see the big picture, but we can find hope in any storm by changing the direction of our perception as we, like Jesus, focus on resurrection hope.

Quiet strength is part of our inheritance. Like a holy thread connecting us to heaven, the presence and power of Jesus within us is a confident hope we can hold on to (Ephesians 1:14).

Read John 11:1–44. How do you think the experience described in this passage influenced Mary's insight into the death and resurrection of Jesus? How do you think it encouraged her to believe and have hope even when she could not see? How has a painful experience paved the way for others to see God's glory?

After the death of their brother Lazarus, Martha and Mary were upset that Jesus hadn't come to Bethany in time to heal him. When Jesus first arrived at Bethany after Lazarus's death, Martha came out to see him—but Mary, consumed with despair, stayed home. Martha, filled with resurrection hope after she had spoken to Jesus ("Your brother will rise again," Jesus told her in verse 23), went back and found her sister. "The Teacher is here," Martha told Mary, "and is asking for you" (v. 28). Wise Martha pointed Mary to Jesus.

When Mary came out to meet Jesus, she fell at his feet in grief. "Lord, if you had been here, my brother would not have died" (v. 32). Jesus' response? He wept by the side of his brokenhearted bride.

For every pain you bear, know that your Bridegroom cries with you! One day he will wipe away all of those tears in glory, but for now he asks us to hold on to hope and trust him when we don't understand (John 14:1–4; Revelation 7:17).

When We Have Jesus, Nothing Is Hopeless

In this world we will have trouble we may never understand, but we can still have hope because of the resurrection. Why? Because "the one who is in you is greater than the one who is in the world" (1 John 4:4).

When Mary saw Jesus raise her brother Lazarus from the dead, that experience must certainly have filled her with hope. This new hope, along with her gratitude, may have been what motivated her to take the bold step of anointing Jesus with her precious perfume. I believe her brother's death prepared her for what was yet to come.

Nothing is beyond Jesus' resurrection power. Brides, Jesus brings hope to any hopeless situation. This is our Bridegroom's specialty. We can always live with hope when we turn our hurts over to him, regardless of how dire our circumstances might be. If we believe, we will see the glory of God (John 11:40).

Our quiet strength comes from knowing that whatever happens in this fallen world, we can trust God for life and hope. Faith and hope go hand in hand (Hebrews 11:1).

Sometimes seeing the glory of the resurrection means walking through a valley. But during that time, know that God has not left you. You are not forgotten. He is holding your hand every step of the way.

Beauty Between Two Bookends

You are God's child. As his daughter, you can walk in the assurance that he can help you today with whatever you face—no matter what it is. And he wants to do just that.

You and I are living between the two bookends of God's great story. Genesis tells us about our world's beginnings. The picture of God creating the world reflects his heart for mankind. Adam and Eve lived in fellowship with God and each other. Provision and purposeful work flowed from a perfect environment. But sin interrupted this perfect design, and the world became broken.

The last part of Revelation offers us a glimpse of our glorious ending. Heaven is God's home and will be the eternal home of his children. In heaven, our prepared place, every tear will be wiped away. There will be no more sickness or sin. We will eternally worship our Creator, as this is what he created us to do.

But today you and I are living between these two perfect bookends, where problems exist. Between the beginning and the end, the world is broken. Life happens and we face challenges. *Never let what happened to you define God's heart toward you.*

The One who holds the world in *his* hands promises to hold *ours*. We are never alone. Jesus is the bridge that assures us nothing can separate us from God's love (Romans 8:18–38).

God is there with you in deep waters. When he calls you out into waters too deep for you to touch bottom, he is with you. Watch the Holy Spirit sweep you off your feet and, with his strength, lift you, enabling you to begin walking on the very water that once engulfed you. In Christ's strength, you will find that what seemed impossible to you is possible with him. *In deep waters, he becomes your quiet strength.*

God is there with you in the desert. When life has dried up, when love has dried up, when the provision that sustained you is no more—in the middle of no man's land where only loneliness holds your hand—you can find incredible intimacy with God through prayer. He is enough. He becomes your everything. And just when you think you cannot take another step in the endless stretch of sand, the Living Water will bring a stream in the desert to sustain you. *In the desert, he becomes your supply to uphold you in your journey.*

He is there with you in the darkness. When the way to walk no longer seems clear, when insecurity and confusion steal your confidence and seem to put a blindfold over your eyes, you may be afraid to move anywhere, and night seems to last forever. But in the darkness, you can learn to walk a new way—to walk by faith in God's Word and not by the sight of your eyes. Darkness is no longer dark. Much like sparkling diamonds cast upon black velvet, every word from God becomes a treasure lighting the way. In the darkness, you will find that his Word truly is a lamp to your feet and a light for your path. *In the darkness, his Word shines to light the way.*

You are his daughter. You are never alone. Seek him in deep waters, in the desert, and in the darkness. You will find him in greater measure than you have ever known.

As a child of God, you never have to fear any evil that comes against you. Being his child is a place of quiet strength. Rosa Parks knew this truth, and her broken road changed our nation. You may get bruised in battle, but know that God will always use your difficult times for the greater good for you and for others.

Seek Jesus and find quiet strength as you journey between the two bookends.

DAY 6

"Do this in remembrance of me." —Luke 22:19

My beautiful bride, do this in remembrance of me. This bread is my body, this wine the blood of the covenant poured out for you. One day you and I will be in heaven and there will be no more tears, but for now I need you to remember that I love you and will never leave you nor forsake you. Beautiful bride, do this in remembrance of me so that when you face trials of many kinds, you will remember that I can redeem anything. Remember your provision and protection through the new covenant and the blood of Christ. I am your hiding place. You can find rest under my wings in the darkest of storms. I need you to know this because it will give you courage and quiet strength for the battles you will win for my glory. Others are hurting. I need you to be brave, to send my fragrance into the world, and to influence others to follow me.

"Do this in remembrance of me," Jesus said to us (1 Corinthians 11:24). Now we call this Communion. Sharing Communion with the body of Christ was not merely a suggestion. It was a command of great importance.

Sometimes it's difficult, during the battles we face in life, to believe and hope. Communion is a celebration to help us remember the freedom from sin, the protection, and the provision made available to us through the new covenant by the blood of Jesus Christ.

In our Nourish Scripture this week, we saw that just before Jesus' crucifixion, the disciples came together with Jesus in a room in Jerusalem to celebrate Passover (Mark 14:12–26). The purpose of the Passover Feast was to celebrate and remember God's faithfulness to protect the Israelites and deliver them from slavery in Egypt.

Whether or not the disciples knew it, as they gathered around the table to take part in Passover, their meal symbolically portrayed what Christ would accomplish on the cross in a matter of hours. Jesus paused on his pathway to the cross long enough to prepare his disciples for the hours that would follow. The events of the next days would test their faith.

What is testing your faith today? Find quiet strength, bride of Christ, as we delve deeper into Passover to bring more meaning to Communion and the provisions of the new covenant.

God Works Through Covenants

God uses covenants to establish relationships with his people, and there have been a series of covenants dating back through history. The new covenant we have with God began with Abraham, and it is established through faith in Christ. Its success doesn't depend on us because it is kept by God himself.

Understand, then, that those who believe are children of Abraham. The Scripture foresaw that God would justify the Gentiles by faith, and announced the gospel in advance to Abraham: "All nations will be blessed through you." So those who have faith are blessed along with Abraham, the man of faith. (Galatians 3:7–9)

The covenant God made with Abraham promised to multiply his descendants and give them victory over their enemies (Genesis 22:17). For 430 years, Abraham's descendents, the Israelites, were enslaved by the Egyptians. God raised up Moses to bring them out of captivity and told him to go to Pharaoh, the Egyptian ruler, with this message: Let my people go so they can worship me (Exodus 7:16). Yet even after many miraculous signs and mighty judgments (we call them the ten plagues), Pharaoh wouldn't hear of letting God's people go.

But God had a plan to save his people. Read Exodus 12:1-28 and respond to the following:

When did the Passover occur? (vv. 1–3)

Describe the lamb that had to be selected. (v. 5)

What were the Israelites to do with the blood from the slaughtered lamb and why? (vv. 7, 13, 21–23)

What were they to do with the lamb that night? (v. 8)

What instructions for the future did God give the Israelites regarding Passover? (vv. 24–28)

Let's soak in these scriptures a bit to remember the significance of Passover as it relates to Communion and the protection of the blood of Jesus Christ.

Jesus Christ Our Passover Lamb

It is significant that Christ was crucified on Passover. The Israelites in Egypt provided their own Passover lambs to save their households, as God had instructed. But Christ himself became the Passover Lamb for the whole world—without defect because he was without sin (1 Corinthians 5:7). The Bible says we have been redeemed with the precious blood of Christ, as a Lamb without blemish or sin (1 Peter 1:19). Isaiah 53 describes Christ as our Lamb who would bear our griefs, carry our sorrows, and be wounded for our transgressions and bruised for our iniquities. His stripes would bring healing; his chastisement would bring peace. And his soul would be made an offering for sin. When we come into the new covenant, we can rest in Christ!

God rescued the Israelites from slavery when they put the lamb's blood on the door. Jesus rescues us when we put our faith in his shed blood.

When we accept Jesus as our Savior, we apply the blood of Jesus Christ over the door of our hearts by putting our faith in his finished work on the cross. The shed blood of Christ rescues us from the penalty of sin, the power of sin, and the dominion of darkness (Colossians 2:8–15).

When we celebrate Communion, we celebrate the provision for us in the blood of the Lamb and the broken body of Christ. Communion is a celebration—a celebration of Christ as our hope of glory. We celebrate the blood of Jesus Christ that continuously cleanses us of our sins.

Read the following out loud:

> *Jesus took all my sin and gave me a right standing with God. Jesus took all my sorrows and gave me his joy. He took all my anxiety and gave me his peace. Jesus took all my shame and allowed me to hold my head high. He took all my weakness and gave me his mighty strength through the power of his Spirit. He gave me the armor of God for protection against the enemy's attacks (Ephesians 6:10–18). He took all my sickness and depression and healed me body, soul, and spirit (Matthew 8:17; Isaiah 53). He crucified my flesh and gave me the fruit of the Spirit (Galatians 5:22–23). Everything Jesus has, all that his name means, all that his life represents, is mine. He lives inside me. Because of him, God has invited me to eat from his table and share in his Son's inheritance.*

> *Spiritually, Jesus broke the power of sin in my life. He took my religion and gave me a relationship instead. He took my fear and gave me love (1 John 4:18). He bound up my broken heart (Isaiah 61:1) and proclaimed my freedom. Jesus took my filthy rags and adorned me with a robe of righteousness and a garment of praise (Isaiah 61:3). The curse of the law is broken (Galatians 3:13). And now I am free to have the power of his Spirit (Acts 1:8) and choose to walk into a new way of life.*

Jesus the Author and Perfecter of Our Faith

Bride of Christ, the next time you celebrate Communion, remember the perfection and glory of Jesus. Jesus wants us to celebrate Communion in remembrance of him. What in particular shall we remember about him as we take Communion? Let's remember his per-fection—because doing so helps us remember that perfection is something we will never achieve. Perfectionism is a cancer that has seeped into the mindset of many women. It's a load no one can carry, nor should they. It is a terrible master that drives women to exhaus-tion, eating disorders, depression, and devastating feelings of worthlessness. Instead, let Communion remind you to rest not in your own perfection but in the perfection of your blameless Lamb.

Passover was to be celebrated in the first month, symbolizing our new beginning in Christ. "Get rid of the old yeast that you may be a new batch without yeast—as you really are. For Christ, our Passover lamb, has been sacrificed" (1 Corinthians 5:7). Our Bridegroom is all about new beginnings! When we are in Christ, the old has gone and the new has come (2 Corinthians 5:17).

When you celebrate Communion, use it as an opportunity to forgive yourself and others. When you don't forgive yourself for your past, you remain chained to what you cannot change. When you don't love yourself as God loves you, it is challenging to love others. When you don't give grace to yourself, it becomes difficult to offer that gift to those around you.

An essential step to forgiving yourself is renewing your mind to correspond to your new-covenant position in Christ. Communion can be a part of this process when you see it as an opportunity to pause and remember Jesus.

Refusing to forgive yourself for your faults is the same as saying the blood of Jesus is not enough. When you take Communion, receive with great gratitude what Christ has done, let go of old mistakes, and declare that today is a new day.

Jesus Our Shepherd

In the Old Testament, a covenant between two parties, such as the one between Jonathan and David in 1 Samuel 20:16–17, included an agreement to protect each other, even if doing so meant death. Family members and their descendants were also included in the covenant.

Bride of Christ, how amazing does it feel to know that, when others attack you, God is on your side? An attack on his bride is an attack on God himself. Are you facing an injustice? Because you are in covenant with God, your attackers are essentially attacking God, and he will defend you (Psalm 5:10–12).

Passover was not only a meal of redemption—it was also a meal that reaffirmed God's protection. God told the Israelites that when he saw the blood, he would pass over them. What saved the Israelites? The death of the lamb? The shedding of the blood? Not just those alone; it was the actual application of the blood to the doorposts that saved the Israelites.

Likewise, we are protected through Christ's blood. Jesus is the sacrificial Lamb for us and for the whole world. His blood applied to our hearts cleanses us, delivers us from judgment, and brings us into God's presence and protection.

When we celebrate Communion, we can remember that the Lord is always on our side and will fight for us and defend us. We do not have to fear evil.

The Lord is *your* Shepherd. His staff is there to guide you, and his rod is there to defend you. When the Israelites ate the Passover meal, they celebrated God's mighty power to deliver them.

Moses told the Israelites,

> "Do not be afraid. Stand firm and you will see the deliverance the LORD will bring you today. The Egyptians you see today you will never see again. The LORD will fight for you; you need only to be still" (Exodus 14:13–14).

God wants us to remember, in the heat of the battle when the enemy is hurling his spears at us, that Jesus is our defender and protector. Before he went to the cross, Jesus prayed,

> "Holy Father, protect them by the power of your name—the name you gave me—so that they may be one as we are one. While I was with them, I protected them and kept them safe by that name you gave me" (John 17:11–12).

Having Jesus as our protector does not mean we will not face battles. The blessing is not in the elimination of battles; the blessing is in knowing that God will never leave us and will carry us through every trial.

Living in self-protective mode to avoid adversity, rather than seeking God's plan, robbed me for years of God's best for my life. Live courageously, knowing that you are a child of God.

"Do This in Remembrance of Me"

Jesus wants us to celebrate Communion often. It reminds us of his unconditional love for us and the enormous sacrifice he made because of that love. It reminds us that Christ's death is our gain and encourages us to live the abundant life Christ died to give us.

"And he took bread, gave thanks and broke it, and gave it to them, saying, 'This is my body given for you; do this in remembrance of me.' In the same way, after the supper he took the cup, saying, 'This cup is the new covenant in my blood, which is poured out for you'" (Luke 22:19–20).

Celebrate Communion at your church, around the dinner table with your family, and in those quiet moments when you are alone with your Bridegroom. Every time you do, take time to remember the blessings from the new covenant.

Our Bridegroom wants us to remember the power of his blood to heal, restore, and redeem. It is in his power that you and I can rest in quiet strength.

Jesus said, "I tell you the truth, I will not drink again of the fruit of the vine until that day when I drink it anew in the kingdom of God" (Mark 14:25). Bride, as you finish Communion, lift your head in hope—because God has prepared a better place for you and me. Allow this meal to awaken in you hope and quiet strength.

Key Treasure

Christianity that requires courage instead of Christianity that demands comfort calls us to stand in the strength that only God can provide.

VIDEO SESSION NOTES

Session 11
QUIET STRENGTH
Mark 14:32-42

Chapter 12
HIS PASSION

DAY 1

Nourish Scripture: Mark 15–16

1 PRAY.

Begin your time with God in prayer.

2 MEDITATE ON GOD'S WORD.

Using your Anchor of Truth Card* from last week's Nourish Notes, renew your mind on that truth. Quiet and focus your thoughts. Pray the truth. Say the truth. Meditate on God's truth.

3 TAKE THE *REVEAL* STEP OF THE NOURISH™ BIBLE STUDY METHOD.

Connect with Jesus by studying the Weekly Nourish Scripture and allowing the Holy Spirit to reveal truth in those verses. Prayerfully read over and reflect on the passage. Mark any phrases, verses, or words that catch your attention. Journal and learn as the Lord leads you.

*Anchor of Truth Cards are available at www.TreasuredMinistries.com/shop

DAY 2
Nourish Scripture: Mark 15–16

 PRAY.
Begin your time with God in prayer.

MEDITATE ON GOD'S WORD.
Using your Anchor of Truth Card* from last week's Nourish Notes, renew your mind on that truth. Quiet and focus your thoughts. Pray the truth. Say the truth. Meditate on God's truth.

TAKE THE *RESPOND* STEP OF THE NOURISH™ BIBLE STUDY METHOD.
Respond to activate truth in your life. The acronym **IMPACT**™ provides questions to help you apply the truth from your weekly Nourish Scripture. **Sometimes you may not have answers for all six questions.**

IMAGE OF GOD TO TRUST? An attribute of God, Jesus, or the Holy Spirit to trust.

MESSAGE TO SHARE? A word of encouragement, truth, or prayer to share.

PROMISE TO TREASURE? A promise in the Bible to believe.

ACTION TO TAKE? A specific step God is calling you to take.

CORE IDENTITY IN CHRIST TO AFFIRM? A truth about how God sees you to affirm.

TRANSGRESSION TO CONFESS? A sin to acknowledge for help, healing, and restoration through Christ.

*Anchor of Truth Cards are available at www.TreasuredMinistries.com/shop

DAY 3
Nourish Scripture: Mark 15–16

1 PRAY.

Begin your time with God in prayer.

2 MEDITATE ON GOD'S WORD.

Using your Anchor of Truth Card* from last week's Nourish Notes, renew your mind on that truth. Quiet and focus your thoughts. Pray the truth. Say the truth. Meditate on God's truth.

3 TAKE THE *RENEW* STEP OF THE NOURISH™ BIBLE STUDY METHOD.

Like an anchor that secures its vessel, biblical meditation secures truth to transform your life. Take five minutes to *renew* your mind by focusing on one word, verse, or truth that the Holy Spirit revealed through the Bible during your week of study. Record your truth below and on your Anchor of Truth card.* Quiet your thoughts. Focus on the truth. Read the truth. Pray the truth.

4 UTILIZE YOUR *ANCHOR OF TRUTH* CARD AS A BOOKMARK TO CULTIVATE A DAILY PRACTICE OF BIBLICAL MEDITATION.

Place your Anchor of Truth Card* in your Bible study workbook to bookmark tomorrow's day of study. Let your Anchor of Truth bookmark remind you to pause and renew your mind on God's Word. Repeat this process daily, continuing to reflect on your Anchor of Truth to start your quiet time until the next week, when God reveals another truth to you.

*Anchor of Truth Cards are available at www.TreasuredMinistries.com/shop

DAY 4

When I survey the wondrous cross
On which the Prince of glory died,
My richest gain I count but loss,
And pour contempt on all my pride.

See from His head, His hands, His feet,
Sorrow and love flow mingled down!
Did e'er such love and sorrow meet,
Or thorns compose so rich a crown?

Were the whole realm of nature mine,
That were a present far too small;
Love so amazing, so divine,
Demands my soul, my life, my all.
—Isaac Watts

They stood at a distance. Mary Magdalene, Mary, Salome, and others from Jerusalem who had ministered to Jesus stopped and stood at a distance to survey the cross.

The cross … Calvary … the place where love and sorrow kissed and intertwined. Pain and passion intersected.

Jesus—how sweet the name. Jesus. He was their Teacher, their Healer, their Bridegroom. He captured their hearts. They encountered the love of God through Jesus and they were never the same. He exalted them, he liberated them, he restored them, and he loved them. His love was extravagant.

And as the Bridegroom ministered to others, the women ministered to his needs. They moved to the beat of his grace. After caring for the one they loved, how could they leave him now? And so they watched—from a distance.

Many fled before the first lash tore open Jesus' back. The disciples abandoned him. Judas betrayed him. Peter denied him. Where were the thousands he had fed with the five loaves and two fish? Where were those who had been astounded by his miracles and crowded him with such fervor that he had to slip away? Were the people who yelled "Crucify him" the same ones who had received healing from his hands?

Quiet Strength Kept the Women There

The women stayed. Quiet Strength kept them by the cross. Jesus loved them in a way they had never been loved before. And so they lingered, not wanting to let go. But they watched from a distance.

Although the Gospels record the stories of many men who rejected Jesus, it does not mention any women who spurned him. You see, a woman's heart is a special and fragile place that searches for divine love, and we will go to great lengths to find it. Many times in our journey, our hearts break at the hands of fallen humanity. However, we cannot rest until we find the agape love Jesus gives his bride. The bride's heart belongs to the Bridegroom. Her heart for his glory.

When these women found Jesus, their hearts found rest, and they simply could not let go of the love and security they found with their Savior. They too had known rejection, and they sympathized with Jesus. His love kept them lingering.

Their thoughts must have been focused on him: *He sees me. He accepts me. He doesn't ask me to be somebody I am not. He empowers me. He defends me. He liberates me. He loves me. He changes me. He takes care of me. Dear Jesus, where on earth would I be without you?*

Confusion Put Distance Between the Brides and Their Bridegroom

Imagine how the women felt as they looked on and yet were powerless to stop the insanity before them. Unable to stop the torturous treatment of their Savior, they stood helpless and perhaps a bit confused. Their Bridegroom had delivered them from demons, saved them, and healed their sickness, and yet he was not stopping his own death (Luke 8:1–3).

I feel certain the women were silent, stunned, and scared as they witnessed the suffering their Savior was enduring. The one who had captured their hearts was dying. Did they have to hold each other up or hold each other back from trying to stop the madness? Eyes wide and brimming with tears, throats thick and heavy with sorrow, they could not leave their Savior. Were there perhaps a few like Mary of Bethany who understood that he had to leave to liberate them? Did some know he was not a victim but was choosing to lay down his life? Did they refuse to accept the truth? What fig leaves kept them at a distance? Confusion? Fear? Denial?

The women heard his anguish and suffering. It must have been unbearable to behold, but they refused to leave. Women brought together, standing together in quiet strength because they loved Jesus and wanted to serve him. They knew they belonged to the Bridegroom.

Our Fig Leaves Can Distance Us from Jesus

I have the incredible privilege of serving with women who love Jesus. I close my eyes and tears fall as I think of my sisters who have seen appalling suffering in their lives: sexual abuse, divorce, abusive husbands, betrayal, cancer, rejection, adultery, alcoholic fathers, and more. Like the women who surveyed the cross, they could have turned away from their faith. Instead, they follow Jesus and serve him faithfully by taking care of one of Jesus' needs: empowering women through the Word and the Holy Spirit and the love of Christ.

As I speak to women in all ages and stages of life, each has her story to tell. All brides have experienced bruises from the battles of a fallen world, but if they have the Savior, they have been redeemed. They know they belong with their Bridegroom. And so they follow him …

I follow the Bridegroom too. But sometimes, like those women at Calvary, I stand at a distance. The devastating effects of sin cause me to put up my own wall of defense. Some fig leaves keep me from following too closely. It is a distance I choose, but the distance keeps me from the abundant life Jesus died to give me. Following the Great Shepherd in the fallen world takes courage, trust, and faith. Even though his hand is always right there, sometimes I grab the hand of idols that offer only mere illusions of security, significance, and acceptance and have no real lasting value.

Are your fig leaves keeping you from the closeness Jesus wants you to share with him? I pray that you will find your answer today as we focus on the cross.

Survey the Cross

Come survey the cross with me. I want to share my heart and I invite you to do the same. I can't begin to describe God's love as revealed at the cross. God's love is so great that it's beyond our human thinking. So pray before we begin for the Holy Spirit to give you fresh revelation of Christ's passion on the cross.

Before we begin to survey, let's search some Old Testament scriptures. Prophecies in the Old Testament prove the cross was God's plan all along. His plan to make us his bride.

> Read Isaiah 53. What scriptures can you find that prophesy about the cross?
> Write your findings.

Jesus Suffered More than We Can Imagine

The torture Jesus suffered was excruciating mentally and physically. The Romans were notorious for cruelty to criminals. Even before Jesus was nailed to the cross, he was beaten beyond recognition (Isaiah 53:5). During that time Romans would whip their criminals with instruments that contained metal spikes on the leather straps. As our Bridegroom held to the whipping post, each blow that struck his back ripped his flesh (John 19:1). I believe that between the lashings, Jesus was thinking of you and me.

By his stripes, I am healed. Because he was bound, I am free.

It was a miracle Jesus lived beyond the beating to be bound to the cross. His beating had a purpose—Isaiah 53:5 tells us it is by his stripes that we were healed.[1] But his death on the cross as a sacrificial Lamb also had to take place to fulfill God's plan and redeem us from sin.

Jesus went through all this for you and me. He was despised, and a man familiar with sorrows (Isaiah 53:3). He was rejected so we could be accepted (Ephesians 1:3–4). Jesus was bound and broken so he could bind up the brokenhearted (Isaiah 61:1).

A crown of thorns was carefully created and thrust on his head. The guards mocked him and made him wear a purple robe: "Hail, king of the Jews!" (Matthew 27:29). Jesus did not resist the crown. Christ redeemed us from the curse of the law by becoming a curse for us, for it is written:

> " 'Cursed is everyone who is hung on a tree.' He redeemed us in order that the blessing given to Abraham might come to the Gentiles through Christ Jesus, so that by faith we might receive the promise of the Spirit." (Galatians 3:13–14)

Freedom from the law to follow the Holy Spirit into God's spectacular plan for my life.

When they heaped the heavy, rugged wooden cross on his back, Jesus didn't have enough strength left to carry it up the hill to Calvary. After facing six different trials and being mocked and beaten, he was exhausted. A man named Simon of Cyrene was summoned to carry the cross to its final destination. Did Simon recognize what a privilege it was to carry the cross of Jesus? Do we?

Choose Christ—Not Religion

Part of God's plan was for the cross to be placed outside Jerusalem. Levitical law includes guilt and sin offerings. A person bringing a lamb to the priest would confess his sins and place his hands on the head of the lamb. Symbolically, the sin passed from the person to the lamb. Because the lamb was now defiled, it was taken outside the camp and burned

(Leviticus 16:27–28). In addition, on the Day of Atonement a goat was chosen to represent the sins of the entire nation for a year. This scapegoat was sent out into the desert away from the camp to symbolize carrying away the sins of Israel (Leviticus 16:10).

When Jesus, the perfect Lamb, left Jerusalem walking to Golgotha, he carried our sins with him. He took them "outside the camp." Bride of Christ, you are free from guilt! Jesus has carried all your sins—past, present, and future—outside the camp.

My Bridegroom carried my sins away. I can stop trying to carry my sins outside through my religion, my hiding, and denying. Jesus has cast them out! Jesus died for me to have relationship, not religion.

One of the biggest and most dangerous fig leaves a bride can wear is religion. Religion is whatever we do to get God to love us and accept us. It's dangerous because on the outside it looks like faith, but it keeps us from having a true relationship with God. Christ on the cross took away the need for religion and opened the door for us to have a personal relationship with God. God created us because he wanted someone to love.

Religion breeds fear because we will always be afraid we are not good enough for God. Fear should not define our world. We can never be good enough or do enough to earn our way to a right relationship with God—and so he has offered that relationship as a gift.

That's why Jesus made such an incomprehensible sacrifice for us. He took our sin outside the camp and left us clothed with his righteousness.

That game of plastic smile is exhausting. When we walk in religion instead of relationship, we provide the enemy with a powerful tool for condemning us. We become confused and defeated. It's impossible to feel good enough to be in God's presence and so we shrink away from him. We keep our distance.

God took Jesus outside to bring you inside. This frees you to have a relationship with God that doesn't depend on how religious you are. He frees you just because he loves you. Drop the pretense with God. Drop the religious formulas when you pray. Begin to dance with your Bridegroom, to the beat of the Holy Spirit.

Because of the Joy Ahead, He Endured the Cross

While Jesus traveled outside the camp of Jerusalem like a common criminal, his heart must have warmed knowing he was providing a way for his bride to enter the inner circle and enjoy an intimate relationship with God. The Bible says he focused on the joy set before him as he endured the cross (Hebrews 12:2). I can't imagine it, but he did all this for you and for me.

Jesus' Death on the Cross Brings Healing to Us

On Golgotha, Simon of Cyrene released the cross to the Romans. Amid laughter and jeers, they laid Jesus on the top of the cross. They drove the thick nails into his wrists, spiking through his nervous system and sending pain throughout his body. Then they pulled his feet together and pounded in a final large spike to secure them to the base of the cross.

Contrary to what most observers thought, Jesus' death on the cross was not just a result of political laws and jealous hatred. It fulfilled Scripture. It was God's plan. Many times the Jews had come close to stoning Jesus, but he always escaped (John 8:59; 10:31, 39). His time had not yet come.

Jesus also survived the beatings so his death would take place on the cross, as God had ordained. "Just as Moses lifted up the snake in the desert, so the Son of Man must be lifted up, that everyone who believes in him may have eternal life" (John 3:14–15). When the wandering Israelites were dying from the bites of poisonous snakes of judgment, God instructed Moses to lift up a snake on a pole so all Israelites who looked on it would be healed (Numbers 21:8). The serpent represents evil in the Bible. Jesus became our sin on the cross so we could look to him and be healed, forgiven for our sin. On the cross there was a divine exchange. Jesus bore our hurts to bring us healing.

Because Jesus died on the cross, I can be healed body, soul, and spirit. He took the nails for me. I am purchased and pardoned from the sickness of sin. And as I keep my eyes on my Bridegroom, he will lead me from glory into glory.

It Is Finished

As Jesus hung on the rugged tree, he would push on the nail in his feet to lift his body enough to gain a breath for his collapsed lungs.[2] I believe that with every painful breath he inhaled, he was thinking of his love for you and me.

Some Bible scholars have concluded that the horrible physical pain Jesus knew he would endure on the cross was not what he dreaded the most. Knowing he would bear the burden of humanity's sin caused him to sweat blood in the garden of Gethsemane. He knew sin would separate him from his Father. In that moment on Calvary when Jesus took on all our sin, he cried out, "My God, my God, why have you forsaken me?" Being separated from his Father's presence is what caused his greatest grief.

The Roman soldiers gambled at the foot of the cross for his clothes. They shoved a sponge of wine vinegar to his lips to drink, but Jesus refused. And again they taunted him: "Let's see if Elijah comes to take him down" (Mark 15:36). But Elijah did not need to take him down because the Father was getting ready to take him up. Jesus cried with a loud voice and gave up his spirit.

The earth quaked violently while the thick curtain that hung inside the temple to separate God and man was torn from top to bottom. The power of death and sin was broken. The curse of the law satisfied. There was no more distance. No more guilt and shame. Jesus, our Passover Lamb, had been sacrificed. God's wrath against all the sin we have ever committed and will ever commit was satisfied on that cross. Our relationship with him was restored.

His Passion

And so we have surveyed the cross. Politically, historically, biblically, and relationally, Jesus had to be nailed to a cross. Levitical law revealed our need for a savior. Jesus fulfilled the law by becoming the final and perfect sacrifice for sin. God is legal in all his doings and cannot lie or violate his will. Jesus had to be beaten and crucified and endure the suffering. The cross took the curse to bring us abundant life.

As I began to meditate on the scripture for our last chapter, I was struck anew at the unimaginable suffering our Bridegroom had to bear. I began to pray and ask God, *Why the cross? Why the suffering? The anguish, the agony, and the torment. The mocking and the misery. Why, Lord? I understand that Jesus had to die for my sins, but why did he have to go through such agony?* I could see the historical and biblical reasons, but I felt the Lord wanting to take me deeper this time. God was getting ready to sweep this bride off her feet with a piece of knowledge that had been information but this particular morning would become revelation.

God's answer crashed over my heart with waves of emotion. Suddenly I caught my breath. At first I whispered my answer and then wrote it in the margin of my paper: *You must love me.*

Tears welled up in my eyes to overflowing and blurred the words on the page. Again I whispered, "You must love me." Not just with a fatherly love—although he does—but with a love like a bridegroom has for his bride. *You must love me. If you went through all that suffering, you must love me. You must love me, Jesus, not because I am good but just because you simply love me.*

One More Step: Receive Your Bridegroom's Love

Many times during this study I have talked about the glory of heaven. While heaven will be glorious, can we have abundant life here? There is yet another step to the cross that must happen for us to experience a life of blessing beyond the cross.

It's a step everyone must take.

Love is the last step beyond the cross. What Jesus did for us on the cross was astounding—it was downright extravagant! Your inheritance in Christ is yours, but if you don't believe God loves you, you cannot receive his love. This is one of the hardest things to do because we have been taught in this cold and distant world that we must deserve love. We can never deserve God's love, but he offers us his love as a gift—all made possible by Christ on the cross.

Religion keeps us at a distance from God because religion tells us we have to earn his love. And so we find it difficult to receive the extravagant love of Christ because we don't feel worthy. With that mindset, we will simply survey the cross instead of experiencing it.

The cross was Christ's passion (Acts 1:3 KJV). The cross is our proof that God loves us with a deep, intimate love.

If God will forsake his Son for you, bride of Christ, there is nothing he won't do for you! And he'll continue to pursue you until you stop running.

God does not put a microchip in us to make us robots to choose him. That would not be love. Our free will is one of the greatest gifts God has given us. And so the last step is up to us. We must believe that God loves us unconditionally. We must reach out and receive his gift of love and trust him to guide us into the abundant life he died to give us. Close the distance by looking back at the cross. When he was on the cross, beaten beyond recognition and blood spilling down his face, he was thinking of his love for his bride.

Perhaps you have already received Christ as your Savior. You are born again. But you are running away from the abundant life of freedom God has for you because you are afraid to trust.

As I look to the cross and remember what Jesus did, I say again, "You must love me, Jesus my Bridegroom. I have been running so long. I am going to stop running to receive. Only then can I live the abundant life you are offering me."

Don't Wait—Receive His Love Now

Don't wait until your last days on this earth to experience the abundant life Jesus died to give you. You belong to the Bridegroom, and the cross proves his love for you. This love will bring a trust that bridges the distance. Receive God's extravagant love.

It was love that carried Jesus through the cross. It was passion he felt for you when he took the nails and the blows. It was a love so deep and intimate, he gave his life for you.

He's jealous for you. He's passionate for you. His love knows no bounds. He is pursuing you and will not stop until you give in.

It's time to trust this extravagant love and enjoy all that Jesus died to give you. Open your fragile heart. You belong to the Bridegroom. Don't just stand at a distance. Come closer to the One who is passionate about you.

Your heart will find rest only in Jesus. He is the only one who can love you in the completeness you were created for. The most important fig leaves to shed are the ones that keep you at a distance from your Bridegroom.

Run to Jesus, your Bridegroom. That is where you belong. Jesus Christ is passionate about you. All you have to do is look at the cross to know that's true.

Key Treasure

Your heart will find rest only in Jesus. He is the only one who can love you in the completeness you were created for. The most important fig leaves to shed are the ones that keep you at a distance from your Bridegroom.

DAY 5

"Jesus said, 'Do not hold on to me, for I have not yet ascended to the Father. Go instead to my brothers and tell them, 'I am ascending to my Father and your Father, to my God and your God.'" Mary Magdalene went to the disciples with the news: 'I have seen the Lord!' And she told them that he had said these things to her." —*John 20:17–18 NIV 2011*

You are a beautiful bride of Christ with hope of a heavenly home. As you travel through your life in this fallen world, you can take heart knowing this earth is not your final resting place. While this hope is a precious treasure each bride can carry in her heart, there are other brides bruised from battling in the fallen world who need to know they belong to the Bridegroom. God wants you, like so many women in the Bible, to share this news with others so the revelation of security in Christ can continue. He has risen!

We have spent this special season together. Although it would be good to hold on to our time together, God is calling his brides to bear witness to the Bridegroom. To tell others they can find rest and security in his arms.

To conclude our study, let's travel back to our first chapter together. We began this study with the story in the Gospel of John about the woman at Samaria. She had a love encounter with Jesus and was never the same. Dropping her water jug, she ran out and told the Samaritans about the Bridegroom. Jesus used a woman to be the first to share the gospel with the Samaritans. I just love that about Jesus, don't you?

Jesus also used a woman, Mary Magdalene, to be the first to share the news of his resurrection. The Gospel of John records their meeting in detail. Read Luke 8:1–3 and John 20:10–18.

From Luke 8:1–3, how did Jesus change Mary's Life?

Read John 20:13. What did Mary think about Jesus?

Was this the truth?

_____

_____

_____

What could Mary see in the natural realm that would lead her to think Jesus was dead and someone had stolen his body?

_____

_____

_____

When Mary saw Jesus, the truth was revealed to her. What was the truth?

_____

_____

_____

How did the truth she heard from Jesus change her actions and her attitude?

_____

_____

_____

The Truth Sets Us Free

Jesus chose a woman to be the first to share the resurrection message: "I have seen the Lord!" (John 20:18). The Gospel of John records that precious moment when Mary could not bring herself to leave the empty tomb. She remained sobbing at the gravesite because she thought someone had taken her Lord away.

But what she feared was not true—Jesus was alive!

When Mary realized the truth—that her Savior was standing before her—she ran into his arms. Jesus sent her away to do the amazing: "Go and tell the disciples I have risen." Her countenance changed and off she went to accomplish her task.

What a difference knowing the truth made in the way she lived. What a difference it makes in all our lives.

Regardless of how you feel or what you see, always remember you are not alone. Jesus is with you and wants to anoint you to do the amazing.

The passion of Christ, his love for us, is something we need to remember. Through every circumstance. Through every struggle. What we see in the world will cause us to doubt, but if we allow ourselves to receive the all-consuming love of our Bridegroom, his love—not our problems—will consume us. God's truth is found in the Word. Our circumstances do not dictate truth—God's Word dictates truth. As we continue to believe in his all-consuming love, we can live the abundant life God wants to give us.

Our lack of belief in his passionate love for us holds us back. Clinging to the truth is essential as sorrow swirls about us in this world. Here is truth: Jesus is passionate about his bride. It's easy to believe he is passionate about us when our lives are calm. It's when the storms come that we have to look beyond the clouds, as Mary Magdalene did, to find our faith.

We Are Like Sea Glass

When we believe the Bridegroom is passionate about us, we will stay in his arms regardless of what we see in the world around us. As we rest in his arms, he can take what is broken in our lives and make it beautiful—like sea glass.

Brenda belongs to her Bridegroom. Her story is his story of faithfulness through trials. She shares her heart through a beautiful narrative about sea glass.

> When asked to share my story, I thought, *Oh, my. Lord?* I prayed about it and thought about it and asked God to show me how to share the road I had traveled. I was saved when I was ten years old at a revival in my hometown, and I had a real relationship with God very early on. For seven years of my teen years, I sang in a Christian band, Daystar, that kept me very grounded and connected to God. I grew up in a very loving home, and my life started out perfect.

> And as I thought about my story, I thought I could tell you how at the age of eighteen, I decided to defy my parents for the first time in my life and marry a man I barely knew. And I could tell you scary stories of my secret life of abuse, fear, and danger from someone that is bipolar ... but that's not my story. You see, while I knew I had made a horrible mistake, I prayed and asked God to protect me and help me ... and He did.

> And I could tell you how at twenty-four, I thought if we could just have a baby, then that would fix my broken marriage, and how when I was seven or eight months pregnant, my husband came and told me he was in love with another woman. She was seventeen. I could tell you about the shame I felt being left and being a single mother ... but that's not my story. You see, as God has worked in my heart, I can stand here today and tell you that I love her, and I have shared Jesus with her, and I have forgiven her, and I have forgiven my ex-husband.

And I could tell you at twenty-seven I married a second time to my current husband and how he only knew about God and didn't have a relationship with God. And as I ran away from everything I had known in the past, we lived our selfish fake life, climbing the social ladder to success, never going to church … but that's not my story … because, you see, soon I began to hear the sweet, sweet Spirit of God calling me back, and I cried out to God to change my husband's heart, and He did.

And I could tell you about my husband and me trying to have our own child, and how it felt to lose that first baby. And I could tell you about going to the doctor for a checkup, and him telling me the baby's heart had stopped and I would need to check in the hospital so they could remove the baby … and I could tell you how it felt to lose the third … but that's not my story. Because you see, I cried out to God and said, "We can't do this, Lord!" And at age thirty-five, I gave birth to my sweet baby boy who just celebrated his twentieth birthday.

And I could tell you about my sweet daddy, how I'm a daddy's girl, a princess, loved and adored by my father. And I could tell you how he suffered for ten years from a disease called Alzheimer's and how that disease robbed him of all memory of me, my mom, and my sisters. And I could tell you how he died not even knowing my name … but that's not my story. You see, my Abba Father knows my name. And though my heart grieves for my daddy, I believe in the Bible where it says there is a time to be born and a time to die.

You see, my story is one of restoration, forgiveness, and hope.

One of the hobbies that my husband and I enjoy down at the beach is collecting sea glass. At our home at the coast, I have a tray of the different pieces of sea glass I have found over the years, and I have a book that I like to study about where sea glass comes from in different beaches around the world. And one day, while walking on the beach, God told me that my life was like that piece of sea glass. You see, a piece of glass first gets broken, and it's rough around the edges, often times shattered, or split, and it's thin and jagged, and it gets tossed in the sea of life, just like us, and we get hurt. And we hit some rocks, and there is pain, and we slam against coral and we are bruised, and we get tossed and turned into confusion and unforgiveness, and depression, doubt, fear, and hopelessness. But if we turn our eyes back to Jesus, if we run to the one that can save us, and we cry Abba Father … Please help me!!! … He will.

And we will come out of life's storms like a new piece of sea glass. No longer rough and jagged, broken and thin, but smooth and soft, after being held in the hands of our God. And as He puts us back together, as only He can do, we will be thick, just like that glass, thick with the power of the Holy Spirit and the Word of God.

In life, God gives us our free will, and we make mistakes, and He gives others free will and they make mistakes against us, and this side of heaven we are told there will be suffering, sickness, and death. But as I look at my life, I see God's hand of mercy, and I am reminded of Lamentations 3:22–23 ... Because of the Lord's great love, we are not consumed, for His compassions never fail! We don't have to stay in our failures; we don't have to be consumed in our pain. And verse 23—they are new every morning; great is Your faithfulness ... and that's my story. God is faithful!

I believe this bride has captured the essence of this study with her captivating story of sea glass. Much as Jesus painted pictures of his kingdom principles through parables, Brenda has given us a picture of how our lives can be when our hearts belong to the Bridegroom. I am certain this summer as I walk along the shores, I will never look at sea glass the same again.

When we believe the Bridegroom is passionate about us, we will stay in his arms regardless of what we see in the world around us. As we rest in his arms, he can take what is broken in our lives and make it beautiful—like sea glass.

His Love Brings Security

Women who believe in God's love take on a new attitude of faith: *I believe God loves me. I believe that through the Word and the Spirit, God can take anything in my life and make it beautiful like sea glass. I believe he can use all my experiences to help me influence others in a remarkable way.* Their trials do not consume them. Instead, they provide a fertile ground to cultivate a harvest.

DAY 6

"To the LORD I cry aloud, and he answers me from his holy hill. Selah."
—*Psalm 3:4*

You did it! Twelve weeks of study in the Gospel of Mark—now that's something to celebrate!

Today I want us collectively to review what we've learned in this study. Don't neglect this last step! It is vital to rest, reflect, and remember. We need to remember the milestones so that as we walk forward with our Bridegroom, the whispers in our heart will remain.

Spend time today with your Bridegroom. Ask him to help you remember those important milestones he does not want you to forget. And as you forge forward with your security in Christ to take on new challenges, may you always remember that you, bride of Christ, belong to the Bridegroom.

Out of all the attributes of Jesus you found during your study of the Gospel of Mark, which one is most dear to you and why?

_____

_____

_____

_____

From the twelve chapters of this study, look back over your Nourish Notes pages from Days 1, 2, and 3. What was the most significant message the Holy Spirit whispered to your heart? How did this make an impact in your life?

_____

_____

_____

_____

_____

_____

_____

Reflect over the commentary material from *You Belong to the Bridegroom*. What new insight into what it means to belong to the Bridegroom did you gain from the commentary in Days 4, 5, and 6?

_____

_____

_____

_____

As you think back over the entire study, what will you remember the most?

_____

_____

_____

Conclude your study by celebrating with your Bridegroom! Spend some time in prayer praising him for what the Holy Spirit has revealed to you through the Gospel of Mark. Write any thoughts below.

_____

_____

_____

_____

When I was in the baby stages of writing this study, I was praying on my screened-in porch. I remember the Lord impressing this on my heart: *You are getting ready to meet your heavenly husband*. And so this study became a search to find my relationship with God on a whole new intimate level. But what I learned is that Jesus found me—his bride. His love for me is intimate. It is this love that brings me security as I live in this fallen world.

Only when we trust Jesus completely with our hearts can we find the abundant life he died to give us. Trust is born out of love. It was seeing the passionate love Jesus had for me on the cross that gave me a new confidence in my Creator and security that freed me to soar.

I pray you have been blessed through *You Belong to the Bridegroom*. I would love to hear about your journey--you can write me at aliene@treasuredministries.com.

You belong to the Bridegroom. Find freedom from fear and security through perfect love.

ONWARD!

VIDEO SESSION NOTES

Session 12

HIS PASSION

Mark 16

SOURCE NOTES

Chapter 1: HE SPEAKS

1. Richard Chartres, The Diocese of London, "The Wedding of Prince William and Catherine Middleton," The Diocese of London: www.london.anglican.org/SermonShow_14544, (April, 2011).

2. Jon Courson, *Jon Courson's Application Commentary New Testament* (Nashville, TN: Thomas Nelson, Inc., 2003), 712.

Chapter 2: THE PROPOSAL

1. Dictionary and word search for *echō* (Strong's G2192). *Blue Letter Bible.* www.blueletterbible .org/lang/lexicon/lexicon.cfm?Strongs=G2192&t+KJV (accessed May 2012).

Chapter 3: IN HIS PRESENCE

1. R. A. Torrey, Christian Prayer Quotes. www.christian-prayer-quotes.christian-attorney.net (August 2010).

2. Corrie Ten Boom, Christian Prayer Quotes. www.christian-prayer-quotes.christian-attorney .net (August 2010).

3. Andy Stanley, *Next Generation Leader* (Colorado Springs, Colo.: Multnomah Books, 2003), 17–45. Stanley, *Next Generation Leader*, 17–45.

4. Andy Stanley, *Next Generation Leader*, 17–45.

5. Charlie White, *Blog: Ecuador 2010.* www.333technologies.com (August 2010).

Chapter 4: FREEDOM

1. Loren Cunningham and David Joel Hamilton, *Why Not Women* (Seattle: YWAM Publishing, 2000), 26–27.

Chapter 5: SEEDS OF SECURITY

1. Dictionary and word search for *kardia* (Strong's G2588). *Blue Letter Bible.* www. blueletterbible.org/lang/lexicon/lexicon.cfm?Strongs=G2588&t=NKJV (September 26, 2010).

2. Dictionary and word search for *hodos* (Strong's G3598). *Blue Letter Bible.* www. blueletterbible.org/lang/lexicon/lexicon.cfm?Strongs=G3598&t=KJV (September 30, 2010).

3. Neil T. Anderson, *Restored: Experience Life with Jesus* (Franklin, TN: e3 Resources, 2008) p. 63.

4. George H. Van Allen, *Wing Haven: A Gift to a City* (Charlotte, NC: The Wing Haven Foundation, GVA Productions, 1981).

5. Dictionary and word search for *hypomoné* (Strong's G5281). *Blue Letter Bible.* www. blueletterbible.org/lang/lexicon/lexicon.cfm? Strongs=G5281&t=KJV (October 2010).

Chapter 6: ROCK OF AGES

1. *Be Transformed: Discovering Biblical Solutions to Life's Problems* (Scope Ministries International, 2005), 4.31.

2. Nancy Alcorn, Celebrate Mercy Women's Conference, Nashville, TN, April 2008.

3. Nancy Alcorn, Celebrate Mercy Women's Conference, Nashville, TN, April 2008.

Chapter 7: THE DANCE

1. Andy Stanley, "I Owe You," message given at North Point Community Church, November 28, 2010.

2. Warren Wiersbe, *The Bible Exposition Commentary, New Testament*, volume 1 (Colorado Springs: Cook Communication Ministries, 2001), 143.

3. Warren Wiersbe, *The Bible Exposition Commentary*, 143.

4. Beth Moore, *When Godly People Do Ungodly Things: Arming Yourself in the Age of Seduction* (Nashville, Tennessee, Broadman & Holman Publishers, 2002), 161.

5. Beth Moore, *When Godly People Do Ungodly Things*, 173.

Chapter 8: HER HEART

1. John Eldredge and Stasi Eldredge, *Captivating: Unveiling the Mystery of a Woman's Soul* (Nashville: Thomas Nelson, 2005), 97–98.

2. Dictionary and Word Search for *diakoneō* (Strong's G1247). *Blue Letter Bible*. www.blueletter bible.org/lang/lexicon/lexicon.cfm?Strongs=G1247&t=KJV (accessed June 2012).

3. Dictionary and Word Search for *ginōskō* (Strong's G1097). *Blue Letter Bible*. www.blueletter bible.org/lang/lexicon/lexicon.cfm?Strongs=G1097&t=KJV (accessed June 2012).

4. Dictionary and Word Search for `ezer (Strong's H5828). *Blue Letter Bible*. www. blueletterbible.org/lang/lexicon/lexicon.cfm?Strongs=H5828&t=KJV (accessed June 2012).

5. April Cassidy, *The Peaceful Wife: Living in Submission to Christ as Lord* (Grand Rapids: Kregel, 2016), 99.

Chapter 9: MY FATHER'S HOUSE

1. Jim Cymbala with Dean Merrill, *Fresh Wind, Fresh Fire*, (Grand Rapids, Mich.: Zondervan, 1997), 96.

2. Charlotte Scalon Gambill, Wave Church Women's Conference, Virginia Beach, VA, February 2010.

3. Neil Anderson, *The Steps to Freedom in Christ*, (Ventura, Calif.: Gospel Light).

Chapter 10: NO HOLDING BACK

1. Christine Caine, Certain Uncertainty, Gerber Ministries.

2. Warren Wiersbe, *The Bible Exposition Commentary, New Testament*, volume 1 (Colorado Springs: Cook Communication Ministries, 2001), 152.

3. Jon Courson, *Jon Courson's Application Commentary: New Testament* (Nashville: Thomas Nelson, 2004), 273.

Chapter 11: QUIET STRENGTH

1. Charles Colson, "The Woman on the Bus: The Faith of Rosa Parks," *BreakPoint Commentary* #90625, June 25, 1999. *Leadership U:* www.leaderu.com/critical/colson-parks.html (February 2011). Quotes from Rosa Parks, *Quiet Strength: The Faith, The Hope, and the Heart of a Woman Who Changed a Nation* (Grand Rapids: Zondervan, 2000), 54 and 16–17.

2. Kira Albin, "Rosa Parks, The Woman Who Changed a Nation," 1996. *Grandtimes.com:* www.grandtimes.com/rosa.html (February 2011).

3. Parks, *Quiet Strength*, 23.

Chapter 12: HIS PASSION

1. T.D. Jakes, *From the Cross to Pentecost* (New York, NY: Howard Books, 2010), 55.

2. T.D. Jakes, *From the Cross to Pentecost*, 56.

PRAYER REQUESTS

PRAYER REQUESTS

Made in United States
Orlando, FL
19 April 2022

16956217R00148